DREAMING OF THEE

Tere Davies

Cover Photo & Design: Jan Kaluza (jankaluza.info)

Co-Published by: WordWyze Publishing (WordWyze.nz)

Printed in New Zealand by YourBooks.co.nz

A catalogue record for this book is available from the National Library of New Zealand

Printed Soft-cover edition: ISBN 978-0-473-51755-7

Epub Edition: ISBN 978-0-473-51756-4

Dedicated to all those who made
sacrifices during WW2

ACKNOWLEDGEMENTS

Thanks go firstly to my Uncle Terry for writing so eloquently home to his Mum and the boys.

Secondly, I have got to offer a very big and grateful thanks to my father Dem, for seeing to it (after all the dramas and stress of his moves and big life changes at his time of life), that he himself handed this treasure trove of stories into my hands, and in doing so, seeing that it was studied and used for the "POWER OF GOODNESS" - This is something both my father and mother strongly believed would shine through, colouring and improving their lives and mine for future generations.

This sharing of our story written in very personal form, from the voice of the feminine essence of my heritage, speaks out for people to share stories and memories. They are not, it would seem, as easy to measure as monetary wealth of possessions, but they allow us to listen and give us the opportunity to understand just why the people in these pages lived and died as they did.

I wish also to thank my many long suffering friends who over the past 3 years heard me mention "The book" so often, and still remained interested in its progress - also my Children who seemed keen for me to reach some sort of completion.

And last, but not least, I would like to offer a very special thanks to my new-found friend and publisher, Colleen Kaluza of WordWyze Publishing. This woman has given so much of herself over to the process of nurturing me through a very emotional journey. I often could not get my head around the new technology and would go back to my old portable typewriter - a similar typewriter my Gran had used during the war. I found I almost needed to be upskilled or retrained to transfer my mindset from an old typewriter to the computer keyboard. She patiently encouraged and nursed me along with such humility, making sure always to remind me just why I had started this project in the very first place. I became very excited when, during our Writer-Editor communication, it was apparent that she was truly becoming engaged with the family members within the pages - We were able to both share special stories and I am much richer for having had her in particular guide me through this process.

Contents

INTRODUCTION

On my Gran's mantelpiece, was a framed photograph of a young man, so handsome, so revered – surrounded by beautiful art-deco pieces of flying memorabilia such as a cast aluminium, shiny silver, miniature aeroplane – (never allowed to be a toy); book ends with aeroplanes in relief on them in the green and black colours Gran favoured; a lamp and cigarette stand all with stainless steel aeroplanes; and also a terracotta little brown Kiwi.

Growing up, I wanted to know who this mysterious person was, and why I had been named after him. I felt it unfair that I have, what I considered, a boy's name. Why was I named after this now-deceased person? Why Me? Where was he? Who was he?

When I was about 6 or 7, my father took me to the Dawn Parade on a cold and wet April 25th, travelling on a metal road for an hour, catching a ferry over the Auckland harbour (this was way before the Auckland Harbour Bridge was built) and showed me this man's name, Terence Dixon, on a huge marble wall of names inside the Auckland War Memorial Museum. It did not look very special to me, and told me nothing about him.

It told me that he was someone who could bring my Gran to tears and my father to go white and pass out at the last Dawn Parade he ever took me to -

the man I saw as a strong protector, weakened by 2 names in gold on the Hall of Remembrance. It was probably the last Dawn Parade he ever attended, too. All of this was still a mystery to me till 2018, when my father, then aged 91, and with failing mental competency, gave me a little old make-up case that had belonged to my Gran – inside were the many letters her dear eldest son, Terry Dixon, had written to her while he was off overseas *"Doing His Bit"* for the war effort (or as my father was told, *"keeping his land, this Turangawaiwai, secure, safe and free"* for him and future generations to enjoy).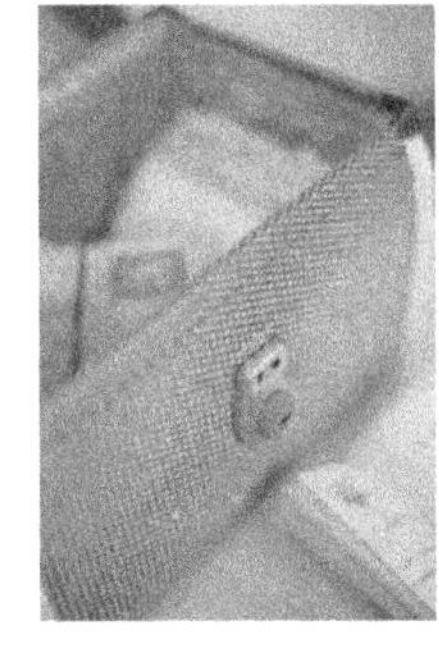

The little old make-up case had in it, Terry's story in diary form: an epistolary of his time serving in the R.N.Z.A.F., during World War 2 (WW2).

CHAPTER ONE – DO YOUR BIT

At the start of 1939, war clouds were gathering over Europe. On 1 September of that same year, Germany invaded Poland, and as allies of Poland, Great Britain and France declared war on Germany. This was the start of World War Two.

New Zealand, being a British colony, was one of the first to send trained airmen to aid in the war effort. So many young men went to fight for King and Country, and everybody, the soldiers as well as those back home, were expected to *Do Their Bit*.

My Gran's younger brother Duncan had already applied to be trained for the R.A.F. before the war broke out. Inspired by this, Terry, Gran's eldest son, and only two years younger than his uncle, signed up a year later, when the war broke out, this time with the Royal New Zealand Air Force (R.N.Z.A.F.). My father, Terry's younger brother, Dem, had been sent to a boarding school, and later, Gran signed up with the Women's Auxiliary Air Force (WAAF).

At the time, my father didn't understand why he was being sent away, as he was still quite young, and this was a place of abuse and trauma in itself. Whenever he felt hurt or upset, he was told that everyone had to *Do Their Bit*. Hence, boarding school, while his mother *Did Her Bit* in the WAAF, and his father *Doing His Bit* as a farmer, and who ran the small town Home Guard.

Gran seemed to me a very hard woman, but now, having read those letters from her son, I've come to understand a different side of her, and indeed, have come to respect her for her strength and tenacity. It could not have been easy sending one son off to war, another son off to boarding school, and then joining the Air Force herself, so she could be in close contact with her eldest son, and also her little brother, Duncan, who had gone to war a year earlier.

War tears families apart, and this one affected my family in many ways that still has repercussions. I hope that by putting this sad and moving story to paper it will, in some small way, have some healing effect on all of us who are still moved by the lives of these two young men, filled with love and spunk, and a generous spirit of responsibility and duty to King and Country.

CHAPTER TWO –
WHO WERE THEY?

Before I get to the letters home from Terry to his mother, I feel I ought to give you a little more background information, and introduce you to the various members of my family, who make up the story behind the letters.

SIDNEY (also known as Deirdre/ Gaga)

To start, we need to go back to my Great Grandmother, **Sidney Elvira Herdson**, known to most of us as Gaga. I knew of her only as a proud New Zealand Lady from Upper class heritage, who had come from British stock. She was first married to *Francis McArthur*, from Scottish descendants, who was a Gent of some means and the local Town Dental Surgeon. They had 3 children, Roma (my Gran), Mavis, and much later, Duncan. Roma was about 13 when her mother gave birth to Duncan Harold McArthur at age 36.

Gaga had grown and been raised, as she did her daughter Roma (my Gran) in the time when Elizabeth Bowes Lyon was being raised up. All through my Gran's life she referred to The Queen first and then the Queen Mother - these women of the Dominions drank up every bit of news of their royals and did their upmost to uphold the values they had come with to this new land.

They developed a very powerful set of values based on their social status and Christian beliefs.

Around the time of Duncan's birth, his father ran off with his dental nurse assistant, who was also pregnant with his child. This left Sidney to raise her three children on her own. The affair seemed to have caused quite a local stir and there was consequently a lot of gossip. No doubt, the breakdown of this family caused the children, Roma, Mavis, and Duncan a lot of distress and perhaps was the result of their reactions and relationships thereafter.

I was told by my father that he knew very little of his Grandfather McArthur. Gran's comments to my father when he asked, were often, "That you did not say anything if you could not find something nice to say about someone." However, she did seem to express that he was a very heavy drinker and had a very powerfully strong and perhaps what we would now call a chauvinistic personality. But what was a fact, was that he had had an affair with his dental nurse and both he and this nurse had conceived a child and my Gaga was devastated. They went off to another part of the country and married after his divorce to Gaga. They went on to have a second child, but sadly, my father found out later that both the children, while quite young, had passed away.

Not long after Duncan's birth, his eldest sister Roma, now 14, fell pregnant and was forced to marry the young man responsible. This did not work out, and they parted ways. Roma gave birth to her son, Terence Albert Dixon at the tender age of 15.

Duncan and Terence (also known as Terry or Tegs), grew up together as almost brothers, with a mere 22 months age difference.

In those days, boys were raised with a sense of responsibility and duty to support their mothers in the absence of fathers, and so both these boys had very close bonds with their mothers, as will be seen in Terry's letters, and later, in the communications of Gaga and the authorities, but more on that later.

Duncan's father, Francis died relatively young (early 50s), apparently from a *bad liver*, possibly from drinking too much, although he may have carried the family genetic fault of hemochromatosis.

After her marriage to Francis failed, Gaga went to work as a housekeeper and a farm worker for a 'gentleman' farmer.

Gaga remarried some years later, to a Mr. J. H. Wall, who owned a farm, and had himself been a Pilot Officer in the United Kingdom during the First World War. Mr. Wall became a real inspiration to Duncan to reach for the skies, knuckle down and work hard to become a pilot, despite the hardship of working on the farm to help support his mother, and she him.

Gaga must have been a strong woman and a fiercely dynamic Mother. There were choices she had to make that would have been very uncomfortable, and she was left in the small Northland district to pick up the pieces of a broken family during the Depression, once Francis had left with his nurse. The shame, particularly with such a prominent family in this small town, must have been terrible, so I do not wonder why in some of the forms for these boys to go and *DO THEIR BIT*, that both my Gaga and Gran wrote "Widow" in their forms — to help these boys not be smeared with these men's choices and disregard for the offspring they left to carry on.

The reason I mention all this, is to help the readers to understand how both my Gaga and Gran pressed on during the War and indeed the Depression.

DUNCAN

Duncan Harold McArthur (known to us as Cully) was born on 15th July 1920 in Warkworth, as the third child and only son born to Sidney and Francis McArthur. He was a 6'2" talented, handsome and very young boy – blue-eyed, fair-haired and very Ambitious Kiwi Male. He was educated at Parua Bay School, and later Whangarei Boys High School. Later, Duncan studied at Gilbeys Commercial College. He played Rugby, being a member of his school's 1st XV and also cricket and tennis. He was a keen athlete and took part in swimming. His smile, especially his nose, mouth and teeth are so like my father's face.

I understand that Duncan was a boy full of mischief – Happy, Jolly and a very Dynamic young man who influenced both his nephew Terry and his sister, Roma (my Gran) to always do their best and above all *DO THEIR BIT* for their King and Country. This family was very loyal to their motherland, Old England, and were very proud to serve. Duncan was considered very intelligent and very generous of spirit, who felt he should always do the honourable thing, no matter what.

His dream was to become a Pilot, like his stepfather, and he worked hard to fulfill that dream.

In 1938, this dream was fulfilled when he was accepted to be trained at Wigram, and then flown out to Britain as one of the first pilots to take part in the war in the R.A.F., in 1939.

There is more detailed information on Duncan in Chapter 11, but for now, we will move on to my Gran, his eldest sister Roma, and her son, Terry, whose letters home from the war, form the bulk of this book.

ROMA (My Gran)

Roma Elizabeth Lascelles MᶜArthur (The second name influenced by her mother's fondness for the Royal Family of British Empire), was the eldest daughter of Sidney and Francis McArthur, and also the eldest sister of Duncan McArthur, my great uncle mentioned earlier. As mentioned before, she become a mother at 15, to Terry.

It is said that her younger sister, Mavis, was very beautiful as a child, and that she got all the father's attention, which seemed then quite sad, and Gran often seemed very sad. Then came the apple of Gaga's eye, Duncan, her little brother, and Gaga's only son, and so Roma felt that she was pushed aside.

In Gran's War service records, I learnt a little more of this woman who had always scared me a little. I knew she loved the Royals and English traditions; she enjoyed an attitude of, what I thought was, snobbery, but really, she felt she had achieved much as a single mother. I now know a little of why she held elitist attitudes.

She had had it hard, but she had been treated very generously by the families who she came into contact with after Terry was born. I now understand why she worked so hard in the forces and why she worked so hard to keep her standards, and her head held high. She felt shame for her father running off with his nurse. She felt guilty for getting pregnant so very young, and she knew there was a better way. She did not want to end up working as hard as her mother had, once her husband had left.

Duncan, Gran's younger brother, was only born 22 months before her own son Terry, so for Gran there was an awful lot going on, and her feelings of abandonment from her father's betrayal, would either sink or swim a young influential mind.

Gran chose to rise above it, but it certainly caused her temperament to be somewhat either angry or sad (maybe in today's time, she would be diagnosed as bipolar or maybe just diagnosed with layers of post-traumatic stress disorder). One thing is for sure, she had an ability to terrify me and fascinate me as well.

Roma married Cyril Dixon, Terry's father, but shortly after his birth, they were divorced.

As a young 15 year old, single mother, Roma and her new-born son, Terry were taken in by a widow, Blessit, whose daughter, Cookie, was Roma's best friend. It was here she was shown love and acceptance, taught mothering and housekeeping skills. It is also here, that Roma met and later married my Grandfather, **Edward Kawenata (Kawe) Simons**, and together they had another two sons, **Desmond** (Dem – my father) and **Peter** (Pete), less than 2 years apart. But again, this marriage didn't last long, and they, too, divorced.

Gran's first Employer from 1930 – 1935 was Colmore Williams from Colmore-Williams Auctioneers and Valuers in Dargaville, whom she'd met at a church function. She left this employment to go into business with Blessit. By then she was already heavily influenced by this much older man, Colmore, her first employer (Or Colly, as Terry refers to him in his letters). Colly became Gran's lover for many years, but he was a married man.

This business with Blessit was in Newmarket, Auckland city (to Gran the big lights where all the action in life was). From 1935-1938, Gran and Blessit worked so hard that they achieved considerable amassed wealth from their bakery. After the business was sold, Gran had enough to put a large deposit on their new family home in Audrey Road, before Terry left to do his service – something of

an achievement for a single parent, and woman. Certainly, more than 3 years on a farm would have achieved.

In February 1941, Gran chose to join up with the Woman's Auxiliary Air Force (WAAF), once Terry had been sent off to Canada to continue his Air Force Training.

Gran and Gaga, over the previous 3 years from about

1938, were both supporting and being supported by their eldest boys – both these boys worked and studied to improve their lot and the lot of their mothers. How did single mothers or sole mothers and women manage without welfare? Well, often it was expected that the Eldest boys would work to support their mothers and families, and Terry and Duncan were no exception to this, and indeed wanted to do so. The forces asked my Gran why she was joining up and what she had been doing for the last 3 years, and in her words she states: *"For the past 3 years I have been running my own home – my son who was helping in the upkeep of the home is now with the R.N.Z.A.F., hence I find it necessary to seek employment."*

One of her referees was indeed Colemore Williams; the other was C. H. Herdson of Mission Bay, a retired Dentist and one of Gaga's family, possibly her Grandfather, or Uncle. The third referee was a solicitor, also one of the family connections, Mr. Blampied – she also inserted that her eldest son was in boarding school.

Despite the child she bore at age 15, and the year or two off school, Gran received her High School Proficiency. Cookie, Blessit's daughter, and she studied together. My Gran had put on the application that she was a widow. Well, maybe this was for Terry and Dem and Pete's sake, but it could have been because of the shame of having left two husbands, but neither of these men were indeed dead at the time, when she actually was just a very independent woman who knew what she wanted.

Roma with her three boys. Terry is standing, Pete is on the left, and Dem is sitting on the right, kicking his feet out in front.

One thing is very evident and has been throughout my life, is that my Gran loved her boys very fiercely. She did not think much of my mother, though. My mother felt it was a class thing. In the earlier years, this tense relationship did cause issues.

I can remember hearing my parents exchange insults of one another's parents, and it hurt me DEEPLY. However, over the years, my mother and Gran became quite fond of each other. I feel Gran was very grateful for my Mum's kindness as she became old and frail, and depended on my father's support more and more. It showed me a lesson, when thereafter, Mum displayed to Gran that it is always better to be on good terms with all people, without surrendering your values. I think as a result, it did make life a lot easier for all of us.

My grandfather Simons was sadly misunderstood because he never did speak up for himself, but as you will see later, he remained honourable to my Gran, continuing to pay for the boys' upkeep, and keeping in contact with her.

Gran was medically discharged on 23 December 1943 at the age of 38. She was a very committed and hard-working woman, but she insisted in trying to improve herself and work her way up the ranks despite her personal losses and her health issues. Generally, at the time here in New Zealand, a career with the Air Force was considered a man's job, and women were employed to replace the men's administrative work. So, sadly, it seems as though they took advantage of Gran not having a husband to back her, and even used her sons in News Paper promotion without remuneration. From some communications in her war records it is apparent that she tried to advance in the ranks, but this became a bit of a nuisance to her superiors, and it seems they used her illness as a way to get rid of her. Peter was 13, Dem was 14 and Terry 18, when Terry left to be trained in the Air Force, and also when Roma joined the WAAF.

I am now proud of my Gran's ambition and her tenacity. I see from her health issues that she suffered from similar issues as I did. The genetic test to understand and treat my condition only became available in New Zealand in the 80's, so I am fortunate, but my Gran was not, and most of her health was simply put down to "women's problems" and never taken seriously. Yet her health never stopped her from being creative, competitive and ambitious for her two younger boys. Once she lost her eldest son Terry, she put her heart and soul into the lives of her remaining sons and their families - she truly wanted the best for them all. Sadly, she did not have much faith in my parents' parenting skills. She feared her second-born granddaughter, MYSELF would end up having a life like hers. It was distressing when the things that she had been through seemed to also be similar to my life's journey. To sum up, she was an extraordinary woman, mother, and grandmother who managed much in a very difficult time in our history.

My Gaga and my Gran loved to read about the British Royals, and their very actions, from fashions to fancies were all powerfully influenced by Britain. No wonder they gave so very much…

My Gran, to me, represented a woman who was her own person, and she seemed to want to be more a woman of substance rather than seen as a wife and mother. She became very proud and I though very bitter, but in reading these letters, I am beginning to see just what a trap becoming a mother so very young, must have been.

TERRY

Terence Albert Dixon was born at Whangarei on the 30th May 1922 to

Roma Dixon, later Roma Simons. He received his secondary education at the Auckland Grammar school, passing the University Entrance examination. He afterwards studied bookkeeping and commercial art by night classes at the Seddon Memorial Technical College. He was 5'8", had brown hair and grey eyes.

The following comes from Terry's file sent to me, which I requested from the New Zealand Defence Forces Records Department, after I'd read through his letters. They were very helpful, but this is information not given to Gran.

When applying for the enlistment in aircrew on the 22nd January 1940, Terence was employed by Ross and Glendenning Ltd., at Auckland Pilot Officer Dixon was enlisted at the Initial Training Wing, Levin, on the 24th November 1940, and embarked for Canada on the 30th January 1941, for training under the Empire Air Training Scheme.

Shortly after arrival there, he was posted on the 16th February, to No. 4 Air Observer School, London, Ontario, and then on the 11th May, to No. 1 Bombing and Gunnery School, Jarvis, Ontario. Here, on the 23rd June, he was awarded the Air Observer Badge and promoted to the rank of Sergeant.

While in the Middle East, he was commissioned in the rank of Pilot Officer, on the 27th May 1942. Meantime, on the 23rd June 1941, he had been posted to No. 1 Air Navigator School, Rivers, Manitoba, for a short course, before proceeding, on the 17th September, to No. 1 "Y" Depot, Halifax, Nova Scotia, for embarkation to the United Kingdom.

Pilot Officer Dixon arrived at No. 3 Personnel Reception Centre, Bournemouth, on the 22nd of the month, and was posted on the 30th of the same month to No. 11 Operational Training Unit, Bassingbourn, Hertfordshire. Here, he crewed up and completed his training as Navigator of Wellington bomber aircraft before being posted to Harwell, Berkshire, on the 21st December for embarkation by air to the Middle East, arriving there late the same month. On the 23rd January 1942, he joined No. 37 Squadron in the Western Desert, and completed a tour of operations as Navigator of Wellington bomber aircraft.

Pilot Officer Dixon was a passenger in the Flying Boat "Clare", proceeding from the Middle East to the United Kingdom on the 14th September 1942, and which failed to arrive at its destination; all the passengers and crew being classified as missing. In due course, his death was officially presumed to have occurred at sea without trace on the 14th September 1942.

Terry had joined the R.N.Z.A.F. on the 24th November 1939 at the age of 18 and a half, after serving in the Dargaville Air Cadets for 3.5 years. He was warm and loving, and really close to his then only 32-year-old mother

When Terry went off to war, my Gran found it necessary, as many women, who had lost their main income support had to, to find other work. (Terry had become a huge financial and emotional support to my gran by this time).

It was said, in a speech by Winston Churchill, "Never in the field of human conflict was so much owed by so many to so few."

This story, the letters home to my Gran from her son, my Uncle Terry are documented in the following chapters, and still do not cover the whole war-time stories.

Gran's Clerk's G.O. Training class group photograph taken in Levin; she is the third female in the bottom row from the Left. On the back are all the signed names – opposite.

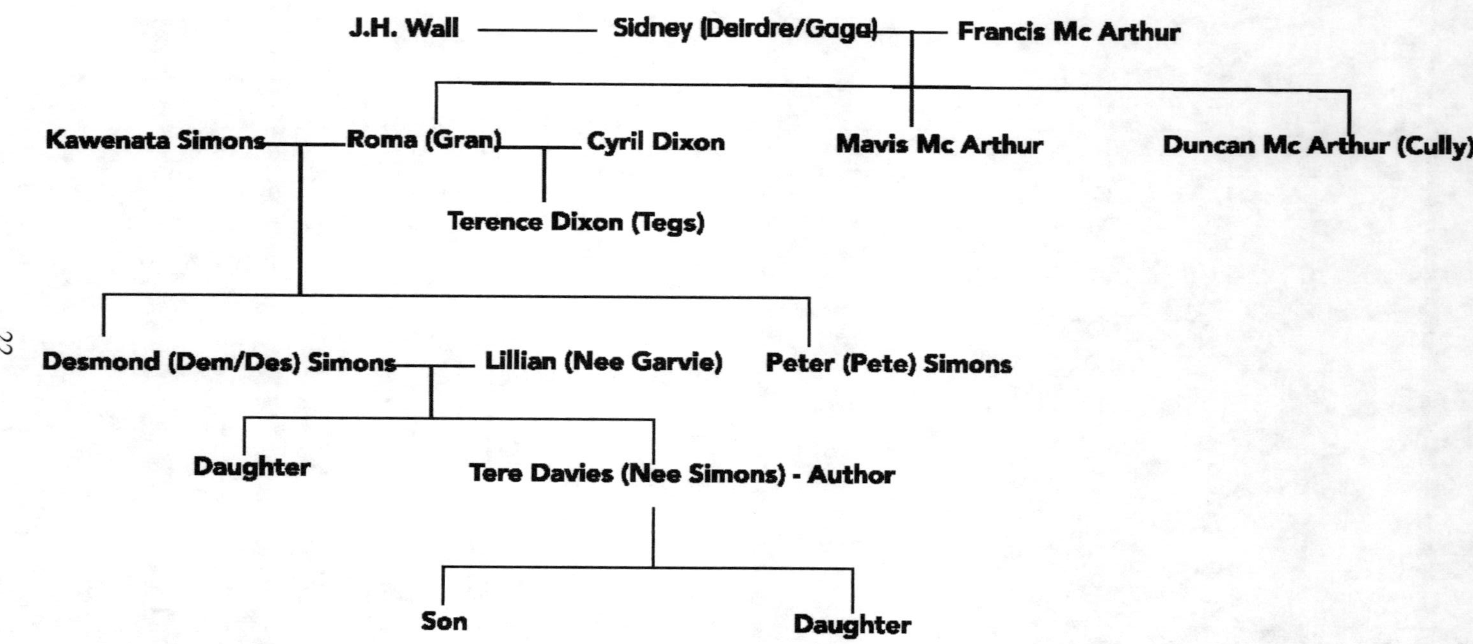

J.H. Wall
Sidney (Deirdre/Gaga)
Francis Mc Arthur
Kawenata Simons
Roma (Gran)
Cyril Dixon
Mavis Mc Arthur
Duncan Mc Arthur (Cully)
Terence Dixon (Tegs)
Desmond (Dem/Des) Simons
Lillian (Nee Garvie)
Peter (Pete) Simons
Daughter
Tere Davies (Nee Simons) - Author
Son
Daughter

CHAPTER THREE –
LETTERS HOME FROM LEVIN

In this, and chapters 5 to 8, you will read Terry's letters as I've transcribed them. The only changes that have been made were to add some punctuation for easier reading, and changing the spelling of photoes to photos. I did also change certain wording that he used which would not be acceptable in today's time. Other than that, these letters are as he sent them. Some of his last letters were received in a different order to which he wrote them. We have rearranged them to read more chronologically, as he wrote them.

DREAMING OF THEE

Letter One:-

Sent on RNZAF paper from - in the first instance

Grand Training School

R.N.Z.A.F. Levin

(Later amended on page 2 of this letter):

L.A.C. Dixon T.A.
Class 2
No.1 Flight
No.2 Squadron
R.N.Z.A.F. Private Bag,
Levin

Dated 25/11/40

Dear Mum,

Awfully sorry I didn't write last night but believe me, baby, you hardly get time to go to the ablution block in this joint.

Before I go any further – will you please send down my hippies – I think they're in my drawer.

I will begin at the beginning and give you a chronicle of events.

To start with, I sat where my luggage was in the train, and everything was alright. Some of the boys (who had reserved seats) had to stand till about Mercer! (train travel from Auckland) At about…, (I was interrupted by a lecture there, Mum) and by this time I change my address to the second one on this page as above.

It is lengthy – I can't remember this myself yet, so I don't know how you are going to get it either.

Another thing from this most recent lecture is our training here might be one month – it might be two. It will depend on Ballot or some other means as to whether I go at the end of the month or stay. I have very little time for much more because we have to be by our bed at 9:30pm and our tent has no light – time now is 9:15pm. Lights out at 10:15pm.

The trip down to Levin took 19 hours because we had to make a detour, but I quite enjoyed it. We haven't been doing much the last two days but get our uniforms (quite a good fit) and do fatigues and drill.

There are two things I don't quite appreciate – Boots and Glengarries. But bed good, grub good – miles of hot water – good tent mate – commanding NCO like Captain Blight etc. etc. etc.

Can't write any more. Must have good old cup of tea before retiring.

I am writing this letter in Y.M.C.A. hall (also very nice).

Will write again soon, a nice letter. By the way, not a bit homesick.

> Love to all
> Terry
> (signed again L.A.C. Dixon T. A.)

₭⇳₭⇳

Letter Two – *written just 2 days later on*   27/11/1940

> Dixon T.A.
> Air Observer
> Class 2
> No.1 Flight
> No.2 Squadron
> R.N.Z.A.F. Private Bag,
> Levin

Dear Ma,

So sorry, Old Bean, my first letter was so hurried and messy, but I wanted to tell you everything I could and to be quite honest, at the time I did not know whether I was on my head or my heels.

There is really nothing much to tell you this time, except that, My Love, I have settled down now and quite honestly enjoying life. Tonight, I had a haircut and believe me, Baby, it's SHORT. You'll like it! I DON'T!!

Just in passing, would it be too much trouble for you to send me red or black cotton, a needle and jink of that white tape you've got at home there.

I hope that the move isn't proving too strenuous and to wish in a way I was there to help you. Are you having marvellous weather! Ours is absolutely superb – hot as blazes. In fact, I'm now a lobster-faced b—d like Colly.

I have parted my hair on the other side now – so the top edge of the cap sits along the parting, and it looks much better. Actually, looks as if I have a part. The only damned trouble is that where my hair used to fall over my brow is now bare and it's gone like roast pork does on top.

As Dan said, the beer here is like no other liquid on God's earth – It is terrible. The only consolation is the stout isn't bad. Don't go thinking I get drunk every night – I've only had two shots.

By the way, the pay is £3.2.6 per week nett – Not bad eh!! I'm not growling anyway. Yesterday we had physical training. It was nowhere near as tough as I thought it would be, but it was bad enough – we haven't had to run 6 miles yet – I suppose they are saving that up.

Next Sunday we have leave, and for the small sum of 5/- shillings return we can go to Wellington – So I am going. I am a bit hazy about other weekends, etc., but I will let you know in due course. That's about all for now. Give my love to Colly and the kids and keep the home fires burning, Love. Chin up and don't work too hard.

Lots of love

Terry

ഏരുഉരു

Letter Three.   **28/11/1940**

(At the top of this letter were the words: "When you have finished reading, turn to the back of this letter; I had some more to say)

Dixon T.A.
Air Observer
Class 2
No.1 Flight
No.2 Squadron
R.N.Z.A.F. Private Bag,
Levin

Dear Zooz,

Thanks very much for the poem, but it is mush, and I told you to cut out that mush – The damn thing nearly made me ball. Thanks also for the assignment, but I purposely left the blasted thing behind because I've got two of that number. So pleased to hear the kids have been good to you, give them my love and tell them to keep it up. Also, I would appreciate letters from them. As regards Aunty Norma I'm rather sorry things got so frigid, but I think they'll thaw out because I wrote to them.

About Leave – I know nothing more about it now than I did before, except that we have leave tonight, tomorrow night and all Sunday after church parade.

If and when I get weekend leave, it only consists of from Saturday afternoon to Sunday night. The boys that stay here two months don't, as a rule, get leave between months.

You seem to be a bit worried about my boots. Well, I might as well tell you that they just feel like slippers now. Incidentally, we don't do any tramping and we still haven't had to run 6 miles yet.

The most trying times of the day are squadron parade at 8am and drill some time during the day. At Squadron Parade, we are inspected and have to stand about half an hour either at attention or stand-at-ease (not stand easy) and as for drill, it's just half an hour of being yelled at and moving like a scolded cat. I've never moved so fast in my life as I do here sometimes. Just by the way, I have cut down smoking quite a bit lately. Also, just by the way, I am sending you a surprise as soon as I can find some brown paper to wrap it in. (That's got you puzzled)

The last couple of days, I've had lectures on anti-gas. It's great fun. We wear gas masks and mess about having a lot of fun. I believe that in the next couple of lectures we have to go through a gas chamber.

Tomorrow and Sunday I have to wait on tables in the Officer's Mess.

I'll tell you about it later.

You know how I said I had to cut down on smoking, well another funny thing's happening. I've hardly thought about women all week – laugh if you want to – it might be just the life – but I'm quite convinced they dope the tucker. This morning there were two little blue grains like condes (only a different colour) in the bottom of my cup after a drink of milk.

Speaking of milk – I hardly drink anything else – and the butter I have about half an inch thick on my bread.

Did you know that this place was once a boy's reformatory school? It was built in about 1917 and cost £66,000. You would be surprised at the extent of it – the buildings and grounds cover about 10 acres or more – that is just a guess – and of course, there is no Aerodrome.

I suppose I told you I slept in a tent – a PWD one. It's absolutely corker. Marvellous bed – better than mine at home, and My Lady, Roslyn blankets!!

I got 4/- shilling today – Lucky boy aren't I – When we arrived here, they asked us what expenses we had on the train – I only had dinner at Frankton costing 2/- shillings – anyway I too said I had the allowable two meals – don't tell anyone. I'm going over to the Y.M.C.A. now for supper. The YM organization must be marvellous. Even down here they run the post office and have a large recreation hall where you can read, write, listen to the wireless or play one of the many games they have there.

DREAMING OF THEE

You can buy supper there from 7.30pm to 9.30pm – they have tea or coffee, cakes and pies – the price of tea or coffee 1d *(1 penny)* a cup – returns are free – cakes asre 1d each also and pies 3d.

It is a bit cooler tonight, and the wind is making the tent flap and the boys (the majority of them) are in town, so this place is very quiet. Down the tent line, a chap is playing the accordion which he plays beautifully. He plays a lot of lovely old songs as well as swing. We have him, a guitarist and a banjoist and me - aren't we lucky?

Don't expect another letter like this one, I don't know how I've done it. Well, Adios. I'm going over for my pie and tea.

Love to everybody and you, you little devil, cut out too much work – make Colly do it – Ha Ha!

> Yours
>
> Terry

P.S.

I won't write for a while now, old girl, after this spontaneous outburst because there are few other people to write to and also, I will have to do some Swot.

There's a hell of a lot to learn in a month.

P.S.S.

Please send me Gaga's address.

P.S.S.S.

Excuse the tightness over the use of the paper, but remember… "There is a war on."

ഇരുബ്രുരു

Another letter from the same date

Letter 3B

28/11/40
R.N.Z.A.F.
LEVIN

Dear Mum

You'll excuse me for writing so many letters, but it's like having a chat with you now and then – only I do all the talking!

What I mainly wanted to tell you is that tonight I had my medical. It was the old one all over again, just about. I didn't do so well on some things. For instance, on holding the mercury at a certain level. I only managed to keep it up for 45 seconds. The boys were very nice at the hospital. They gave me a cup of coffee when I had finished. I was, of course, last.

You or somebody who reads this might ask just what we study here:- We have:- Navigation, Mathematics, Law and Discipline, anti-gas Signals (Lamp and Buzzer), General Ammunition and Hygiene. We have to get 80% to pass. We're always having to pass something. Well Bonsoir, it's lights out in about 10 minutes.

Love and kisses, Love to the kids.

Your First Born

Terry.

P.S. Just by the way I forgot to mention, I'm pretty sure that I have passed the medical test.

ഌരാഌരാ

Letter Four

3/12/1940

L.A.C. Dixon Air Observer
Class 2
Flight No.1
Squadron No.2
R.N.Z.A.F.
LEVIN

Dear Mummy and Pete,

I swore I'd cut out this letter-writing business, as I could do more Swot – but I love getting letters – I've had one every day lately, and I can't expect to get one every day if I don't write some.

I'm pleased to hear you got good marks, Pete old bean, but if you don't laugh at my old woman's wisecracks, I'll knock your block off.

You asked me if things were tough… You've no conception. We did not drill well enough today – so tonight we have to clean out the dykes for half an hour. Re the swot, there isn't really time to swot, and I go to sleep in lectures, so it is very likely I'll be here the two months. Didn't I tell you the pay, it's £3.2.6d. nett per week.

The trip to Wellington was a big success. I went to the address Frank Harold told me, and he was there on holiday himself.

The people were very nice, a gorgeous daughter and plenty of money. The only catch is that the girl is Frank's girlfriend, although she is only about 19 years old. Mrs Woodward (the lady of the house) fussed around me as if I was a long lost son – she sewed my L.A.C. badge on for me and was charming in every way. In the afternoon, we went to hear the Air Force Band at the Basin Reserve. After that, we went for a swim at Evans Bay, and it was good – I'll say after tea, Lois and I saw Frank off on the Limited. Our corporal saw us on the station, and he told me this morning he did not know whether he felt like seducing the joker or the girl – (Frank does look like a bit of a pansy).

Later I went to the Minister's Club and had a dance – Corker place, everything available for us. By the way, we can go anywhere we like on the Wellington Trams for 2pence.

I think you had better squash the idea of coming to Wellington for my weekend leave. I'll only get about 24 hours' notice, and that won't be much use to you. Whatever happens, I'll be going to Wellington (it might be this weekend!!)

I think I'll toddle off to bed now, old Loves. I only get 7 hours' sleep and believe me; I NEED all of it.

Love to all of you – if anybody complains that I haven't written, tell them I'll write if they write to me first.

I have met two corker chaps here, Mum. Real good fellows. We are just like the three musketeers. One aged 22 and the other is 25. So, you see, I am being well looked after.

(Am sending the surprise – I'll probably want to burn it when I get home).
YOURS, Tegs
NB P.S.

Have just applied for a weekend – have this weekend Friday is the soonest I can let you know the answer – will WIRE YOU THEN.

ൠൠൠൠ

Letter Five   11th December 1940
                                                        R.N.Z.A.F.
                                                        LEVIN

Dear Mum,

Just a little note to tell you how things are going. This correspondence business is getting me down, - two days running I've had three letters a day. I haven't got an earthly of answering all of them. Dear old Tom wrote to me the other day, and I haven't answered that yet. The point is the exams are starting this week, and I MUST do a bit of Swot. I don't think I have an earthly of GOING this month. It has come from quite a reliable source that only 42 out of 150 Observers are indeed going because they can't get enough boats. Another thing, Christmas leave is highly improbable. Before I forget, will you please send me the following, which were last seen in my kit bag: a set square, a protractor, compass - ... *(there seems to be a page missing here)*

At the time it nearly killed me – and but actually, I only did it so I could skite to you – but on the whole, I think it did me quite a bit of good.

Today we had a lecture on our rates of pay. In N.Z. we receive £150 per annum.

On the boat we receive N.Z pay and 2/6 a day allowance.

In Canada, we receive [1]£15 per month plus 75c per day for flying.

On the day of Embarkation, from Canada onwards, we become Acting Sergeants and receive 9/- a day and 3/11 a day deferred pay. After 6 months' service, we become Sergeants and receive 12/6 a day and 2/- a day deferred pay.

This deferred pay rate isn't a mistake as you might think – as your pay goes up deferred pay goes down.

An airman's wife allowance (NOT APPLICABLE) is 3/- per day and an allotment which the airman (or the serviceman's wife) decides for himself.

That is all for now. I suppose Boey (*Pete*) reads these as it is really superfluous writing to him as well, but tell him I do appreciate his lovely little letters very much and to keep them up even if he hasn't the advantage of a personal reply. Tell Dem I'll write to him as soon as I get a chance.

Love to you all and a big kick in the pants to Colly where his bum ought to be:- xxxxxx MUM – X Pete *(picture of a boot)* Colly

Yours Terry.

இஐஇஐ

---

[1] Terry used the £ sign, but probably meant $ for the Canadian currency.

Letter Six   3rd January 1941

<u>LEVIN</u>

Dear Ma,

How did your New Year go!? Mine was corker – Ray and I went into Levin in the afternoon. We went to the baths and were slipped up by the two plumbs we were going to meet, but Ray soon remedied that by meeting up with someone else. The whole trouble was, there was only one – and we both fell for her – terribly nice girl too – She came out to the dance on New Year's Night and Ray could not do any dancing because of his back, so I had my share, then some.

He is having his share tonight – He's taken her to the pictures.

Gosh it was marvellous dance the other night – the band comprising of six instruments was better than anything I've heard in Auckland, and the women – Blimey Bert there was thousands of them. The darned affair didn't finish till about 2 o'clock, and I've been half asleep ever since. However, I will catch up with it all on Sunday. Your cake was absolutely jolly marvellous, Sweetheart. My appetite wasn't too good at all when I came back to camp, but it is improving considerably now. Tonight, I cleaned up a pile of fish, spuds and swedes and another pile of rice pudding.

We did not touch the cake until New Year's Eve and that night, Ray and I decided to miss tea and have some – well we ate half of it that night.

I got a letter from Audrey today, and she seemed pleased about you asking them over during final.

I am not sure if I told you the marks that I got last course – but here they are:- Navigation 50% Maths 77% Brenning Gun 85% Law and Discipline 64% General 85% Anti-gas 91% and actual average 75.3%.

Placement 48th out of 100 – If I had to have got about 15% more in Navigation, I probably would have gone.

That is all for now – Love to ALL.

Your loving Airman

Terry

⁖℟⁗ℝ ⁖℟⁗ℝ

Letter Seven:-   8th January 1941
                                                              L.A.C. Dixon A/Obs
                                                  No. 1A Flight (Senior Observer)
                                                                No. 3 Squadron
                                                                     R.N.Z.A.F.
                                                                        LEVIN

Dearest Mother,

It was nice to get a typewritten letter from you. It's not that I don't like your writing, but type seems so much more compact. It seems as if we all had a pretty good New Year, but my wire seemed to be your only bright spot on the New Year's Eve. Ray and I have proved that 3 is not a crowd. We both took Joan to the pictures on Saturday night, and things went swimmingly.

On Sunday, we went to Joan's grand-parents' place after lunch, but we found that she had gone to the beach. We went to the beach – but it was the wrong one. It was only 15 miles, and there were no buses or anything. How did we get there? Hitch-hike - we had rides in a Chev coupe – a Chrysler and were finally picked up by a Vauxhall with three girls and their mother in it. When we got to the beach, they said they were returning to Levin about 4pm and would we like to come too? I'll say we would! It was a beautiful dull day – sounds funny doesn't it, but you savvy. We walked along the beach about a mile and had a look at the wreck of the old Hyderabad. The Hyderabad was one of the first steel vessels built and was wrecked there about 70 years ago. The hull is still all there but cracked in a couple of places. The name of the beach, by the way, is Waitarere. We went into the local shop there and had a drink and asked the shopman if we could hire some togs. He did not have any, but somebody overheard us and lent us one pair. Ray went first and then I went in. We both had to borrow somebody else's towels but things like that were beginning to become mere nothings. The water was simply marvellous.

The beach at Waitarere is similar to the coast at Dargaville but the sandhills aren't so high and the breakers are nowhere near as high and there is no under-tow at any tide. About six o'clock we went back to Joan's place and she still wasn't there, so they asked us to stay. We were there about three hours and we are both now damn near members of the family. It's a great family – the old people are very old and have about six offspring. One son went to the last war and went all through Egypt and France and the youngest (about 30 years) is in Trentham now. One daughter is Joan's mother and is married to some big shot in Palmerston North and has been all over the world – that's only four but I think there are a couple more kicking around somewhere.

DREAMING OF THEE

Joan had gone to the beach with their youngest son and his wife, and they turned up about 8pm, with a big bag of Toheroas, but no Joan.

They had left her at some other aunt's. Anyway, they took us in their car to look for her. A big Morris this time. We missed her at the Aunt's and finally tracked her down after she had been to town again and was on her way home. We took her home and the triangle worked beautifully again.

You probably don't understand, Old Bean, but the threesome was great – we were just like two brothers and a sister, and she smells almost as nice as you. Somebody I told about her, said she sounded like a scalp hunter, but such ideas never occurred to anyone's head less than it has occurred to her beautiful one – That person is going to get a good telling off! Another thing - she has got sparkling brown eyes and when the starlight sparkles in them, it makes you think of moonlit lagoons and palm trees.

As always, one has to pay for one's pleasure and for a couple of days I was worn out, and for the first time since I have been here, I had to report sick with a stye like a volcano. Everything is wonderful now though and today I've been like a love-singing canary.

Well, I hope you are enjoying all that twoddle about angels and hitchhikes because it will be the last till after exams – they start tomorrow – Wish me luck??!!

Yours with tons of love

Teg

P.S. Just because I am stopping writing letters don't you stop. I appreciate letters more than ever now, and I get very dam few of late!

P.S.S. I've just read part of this to Alf, and he says it's hypocritically unpractical and Irish! What do you think?!

ᎦᏬᏓᎦᏬᏓ

Letter Eight:-   15th January 1941

Dear Mum,

We've finished exams and what a marvellous feeling it is – To say it wasn't a relief, wouldn't be powerful enough. To make life more thrilling just about now I can be just about sure of 85% in Navigation and 95% in Mathematics of facts, but it is what I feel I have done.

I am so thrilled that letter-writing is rather difficult. I'll give the programme for the next couple of days.

Today we get paid – this afternoon and get drunk tonight. Tomorrow we go before the selection committee and find out whether we are to go to Canada or not.

On Friday, we leave by 3 o'clock train if we are coming. I'll wire and let you know anyway. This is only one page, but I must get this in the one o'clock mail.

Au Revoir

Tegs

CHAPTER FOUR –
A LITTLE INTERJECTION

Now, at this point, I feel I need to remind the reader that these letters are now very old and frail, as is my father who is now in his 94th year. He told me he sadly sat on these letters, having secreted them away after his mother, my Gran passed – he had been appointed executor of her estate and being the ever-respectful son, he had asked her what he should do with the little old make-up case of letters (she being then very old, going blind, and in a lot of pain from an arthritic condition said, "They don't mean much to anyone now, so I guess throw them or burn them… I have outlived every one of them now") My father was still, himself, very much affected by the effects of the wartime and wanted to sit down and read his brother's letters…

This was the start of a growing and healing (albeit a little late) for my father – who every year since then, around a week or two before April 25th (when New Zealand honours the fallen from both WW1 and WW2 – ANZAC DAY), would squirrel himself into his office and pore over these letters written so very long ago.

The reason is very clear to me now. The very act of writing down one's thoughts in a communicable fashion is similar to thinking aloud… one can actually hear the writer talking to one – especially when one has had such a close and loving relationship with the writer, each letter is like a tiny recording of their voice in one's head. My father had pulled some letters and then relented and put them back in order.

He told me recently that he had felt, growing up into a man, that he had thought the relationship his mother had had with her eldest son, my Uncle Terry, was perhaps a little too close and they shared too much in a personal manner. But when I told him that is the relationship I have with, not only my son, but with my daughter and that it was a perfectly healthy, loving relationship, he was a little more relaxed – You see, my father came to understand that the years he'd spent almost excommunicated from normal family life because he was sent to

Dilworth, had severely hampered his ability to relate to the fairer sex throughout his life. The sexual abuse that my father suffered in this boarding school, he felt was his shame and his fault and it was to be kept secret (this is the ultimate way these powerful abusers of power perpetrate and carry forth their evil). My father is such a passive and forgiving man – he tried for many years - as is evident now from how he read and reread these letters, making notes and keeping them in folders, carefully copied - to share this powerful family story, but felt in his usual humble way he was raised, that *these personal matters* mattered little to anyone else. How wrong we all now understand this thinking to be. As we all understand now, sharing our own stories of this, our human condition, is *important* and holds important messages and lessons – our past is who and how we are, warts and all – and for the most part we do the best with what we have at our time to improve, share and grow.

My Gran, as I have mentioned, was to me a fearsome woman, but she was to be respected, and now I feel much admiration for how she managed as a single mother of 3 boys, to own her own home, run a business with a very dear Help, and indeed a loving group of friends and family, with whom she always felt it very important to stay in contact, and show her interest in all their lives – she left my father with a very strong moral code and sense of strength – despite the fact he often, especially around ANZAC time, went into a funk and was visited by the 'big black dog' or a case of the blues. He never stopped praising his mother for how she had endured such huge grief (for to me, losing my eldest first-born would be something I could not endure).

Gran often said I was going to be like her and that I was a lot like Terry also; she knew I loved to draw and loved animals as did Terry. She had also lived to see 5 living generations of her family sharing the same time - she thought this was amazing effort, post-WW2. I understand now how right she was. It is important that we keep connected and share with one another. The human spirit desires to be connected and to have a purpose and a worth – more and more we see our elders being filed away in retirement homes, often left alone and only valued or measured in a financial manner – BUT the family stories these old people still remember and want to share, are what has given us the life we have today.

I was not just "Terry's Namesake", I was determined – even after hearing the nonsense that adults sometimes spoke of, that *she will end up being just like her Gran*, has led me now to find out just who my Gran was, and why she chose the pathways she did, and indeed how I can come to understand just what it must have been like to be a woman and a mother in those times.

<h1 style="text-align:center">A LITTLE INTERJECTION</h1>

We need to understand the ups and the downs – the whens and the whys to grow into a wholesome and helpful honourable nation because only by being so worthy will we receive worthwhile existence.

My Gran's mother and father weren't very well known to my father, he tells me, because although they were considered Upper-class in the small country town in Northland in which my Gran grew up, the shame of her father running off with his nurse, and then she herself made to feel great shame for becoming pregnant at the very young age of 14 and giving birth at 15, was a source for huge speculation and gossip. So, his mother, Roma, was taken in by Blessit and her family, and then later Dem being sent off to Dilworth, he didn't have much to do with his maternal grandparents.

Yet, these two women, Sidney (Gaga) and Roma (Gran) still became united in their similar experiences of raising young intelligent boys who both wanted to learn to fly the very new modern technology of the day - aeroplanes. The boys came to inspire one another and became great friends, acting more like brothers during their training and their time overseas, representing New Zealand and *doing their bit* for their mother country during WW2.

Both their mothers back home in New Zealand were forging strong friendships and family ties, also doing more than *their bits* for the country they loved. I am weaving these little stories into this chronicle in order to inform the reader a little more of how life was then – and how the events in the letters related to all our lives now.

My father's father, Grandad Kawenata Simons was indeed alive and my Gran's 2nd husband on paper, but really the only man who wanted to take in both herself and her eldest son, Terry – and who fathered my dad and my Uncle Pete, loved my Gran very very much and never remarried, was indeed in the picture all the way through this time, but he and my Gran had become estranged.

It is said my Gran was given to temper fits and would just up and leave, and then return later. At first, she had left the two little boys born only 11 or 13 months apart (my dad, Dem, and Pete). We know now, the farm Grandad would not give up on, was very tired as was the farm home cottage. They had just all been living from hand to mouth during the Great Depression, and Grandad had had to drag them all down to Auckland where the living was very hard, and where he walked door to door selling brushes all over Auckland. A very soul-destroying time. Grandad and Gran fought over the farm and the hard times, and she finally left with the children. This was when Gran settled into a business with Blessit. The reason Blessit went to Auckland to open a home cookery with my Gran was manifold, but she had recently become a widow and needed to make a living to continue sustaining her mortgage which her daughter and son-in-law took over later. Blessit was a wonderful cook. Gran was a wonderful people-person who loved to do all the bookwork and handle the monies – the early Auckland-Newmarket home cookery grew very successful very fast, and there were some big money and big ego issues to come. I am told by my Gran's old School friend, Cookie, and indeed the daughter of Blessit, that they had a falling out and the home cookery had to be sold. The sale helped my grandmother become a home-owner, by enabling her to realise a larger-than-normal deposit for the North Shore home at Audrey Road, Milford – the home Terry was helping her maintain when he enlisted and went off to fight for King and Country.

The story goes that Gran had unthinkingly and tactlessly said to Blessit, "You are old and not attractive. You need to stay out the back and do the cooking. I should manage the shop and do the serving."

My father, who often remembers also helping serve pies to crowds of service personnel, who were swarming the Newmarket area during the first efforts of enlisting towards the war, tells me he also used to help the luncheon rush times in the shop and poor old Blessit was slaving long hours in the kitchen – Blessit thought it was to be a partnership and being very wounded at my Gran's tactless nature, insisted the business come to a close. It was around this time that the Airforce records show my Gran being interviewed and subsequently also enlisting in the Airforce as a New Zealand WAAF. Blessit, when returning to the Northland town, was taken on as a housekeeper on my Grandad's farm. The farm that was now Responsible as an Essential Services to the war effort and needed workers – both she and her daughter, Cookie, felt sorry for my Grandad and the whole situation, but becoming members of a large helpful extended family, particularly during the wartime, meant they could share the space and spoils of the farm-fresh milk and cream; eggs from the organic and bio-dynamic mixed unit; and bacon from the pigs. He became a top dairy, pig and sheep farmer ending with the acquisition of 5 farms into one.

I am telling you a little of these characters now, to point out just what dynamic and strong women I had growing up, to inspire and indeed encourage me when I felt the task ahead of me as a single parent, was far too great. When I asked them questions, they all had different answers, but not one of them would dare to be negative of the others, which I have to say now, showed me how valuable it was to follow their example of: "If you can't say something nice about someone, you should not say anything at all."

Terry, just before he left for Canada with Pete on the left, and Dem on the right.

CHAPTER FIVE –
LETTERS ABOARD THE SHIP

Following is a hand-written poem that moved Terry enough that he should, in December, copy it from a magazine and share this with his mother, December 1940.

HEROINES ALL

A Sonnet to My Mother

– written by Gerald Rawson

Dear Mother, this is to you I long have owed,
This humble verse of praise and gratitude;
Your love and sacrifice so oft bestowed,
Seemed heeded not, yet, fearing to intrude
My shy response (oh had you only known)
I've feared to say what deeply I have felt.
Now, far from home, where oft in dreams I have flown,
I still record your fondness when I knelt
in childhood at your knees to say my prayers.
Now once again in pity let me kneel
in heartfelt thanks – Forget you? No! and Ne'er
My debt to you will verse reveal.
This, mother, through the years I've longed to show,
Your love and sacrifice full well I know.

DREAMING OF THEE

EN ROUTE TO CANADA

Written on Royal New Zealand Air Force Stationary

Letter 1:- Ship

dated 1/2/1941

Somewhere at sea

Dear Mum, How's the world treating you, Love?

Things are going absolutely spiffing with me.

We used to get a great thrill out of a bit of rough weather on the harbour, but although we've had no rough weather, the old barge pitches or rolls all the time. The waves are just more or less a swell, and it is surprising to see how small they are and yet they can move such a big thing around so much. I have never before seen so many different colours of the sea. It was a light green in the harbour and when we got out into the gulf, it was a beautiful dark green. Similar to the colour of Colly's car. Later on, it was a very dark blue.

Yesterday, which was a perfect day, it was one of the most beautiful colours of blue I have ever seen; a sort of royal and as the wash breaks into foam, the water underneath turns a lovely light greenish-blue.

It was a very funny feeling moving down the gulf and picking out all the North Shore Beaches. I could even pick out quite clearly No 13 Audrey Road, Takapuna – further up the coast I picked out Takatu, Leigh and Goat Island.

Going up the coast, there were porpoises all around the boat. They are beautiful things. For a while, there were two diving in and out of the water right close to the bow. A little later, I saw a couple of flying fish. On Thursday, we did not do much at all. Yesterday, we played games, sunbathed and slept. We put on our tropical kit yesterday, and with about two hours in the sun, I have a very pink face and neck. Last night, we had pictures: Laurel & Hardy in the "Flying Deuces." Quite a good show it was too. Today we started the real Air Force routine with physical training at 7:30am then from 9am till 12, we had lectures.

The tucker (I should say the cuisine) on the boat is wonderful. Never have I seen such a variety of food, nor have I ever eaten so much. If I get a chance, I will send you one of the menus. I find it very hard to write letters lately. It's not because there are other things to do either – I am lying on my bunk now and the porthole which is open all day is right next to my head. I can lie here for hours and watch the sea. I think I went out with too many women those last few days, because I dream of you for a couple of hours, then it is time to eat.

After eating, I came back here and dream again, my Darling, Love of thee – "Dreaming of Thee". You might think I am crazy, but I love it!

The sea and the flying fish go well with dreaming.

I felt a bit squeamish the first day. I think it was all the beer. I might mention I haven't had a drink onboard yet. Only about two of the boys have been really sick. They have beautiful chimes to call you to meals – and there they go… and so, to go to afternoon tea. So toodle-oo till next time.

Love to all – chin up

Terry

"Dreaming of Thee"

ഇൻ   ഇൻ

Letter 2:-   5th February 1941

(Still somewhere at sea.)

Dear MUM,

Thank goodness I didn't join the navy; I am bored still and long for the sight of trees and grass and live things and for the society of people other than airmen (aboard ship). They are a swell bunch, but it would be great to meet someone different.

The boys are very funny, sometimes – If you shut a bull up in a paddock for a while, he's pretty well roaring to go – the boys haven't been on the boat a very long time, but a bull locked up in a paddock is nothing to it. Any decent party would have at least one woman to a man, but this party was a woman (one) to a hundred and fifty men. Strangely enough, there is one thing I am not sick of yet, and everyone else is moaning about – that is the heat. Day and night, it is about six times hotter than the hottest, muggiest day of an Auckland summer. I have never seen such perspiration in my life. I've estimated that if all the perspiration sweated out, by everyone on this trip so far, was collected, you would get about 2000 gallons and that is no exaggeration. I have got my shirt off as much as possible, and I bought a pair of real Japanese sandals which keep my feet quite cool. We have only had about three sunny days on the trip; for the most part, it has been overcast. The sea has been the same all the time; just so delightful; swell at night. At night it becomes absolutely smooth like curved glass. One night Alf and I were right up in the bow. The wind was blowing fairly hard and striking the side of the ship it shot up the side like a terrible gale; the sky was covered with heavy black clouds and it looked as if we were in for a storm. We had been there about a quarter of an hour when the enormity of everything seemed to strike me. It was just plain eerie. Alf said he had the same feeling, too. We were just like a couple of little boys, scared of the dark really, but actually, there was more in it than that. The other night, I had deck patrol which consists of wearing a red band around your arm and trying to look important getting all the rest you can, and now and again gazing steadfastly at the sea and sky – you can guess what for. The first shift was from 9-11pm. The second (I will never forget it) was from 3am to 5am – your little Teggy was one hell of a wreck the next day. I don't know whether I told you last time, but we have baths on board, and I spend quite a bit of time in them. They are about 12 foot 10 by six foot, and there is saltwater running through them all the time. Another thing I have found on board, which will interest D&P *(Dem & Pete)* – the loves, is a Gymnasium with a rowing machine, punch ball, parallel bars and two stationary bicycles. I just about ruined myself on the rowing machine and one of the bikes the other day.

Speaking of the devilish younger sons (don't read this to them). The way they helped you and their demonstrations of love and devotion to me those last few days before departure, were to me a great delight and I appreciated them much more than I showed. You will probably think that I didn't appreciate anything much, Darling, the last few days, but I did, very much and am still appreciative of it in my dreams. You were an angel, Colly was a devil/angel and a few other people were pretty marvellous too. I haven't seen a hell of a lot of Don on board, but I think he has been pretty happy – otherwise now he is a bit bored just like everybody else.

We are going to have a concert in about a week, and Alf and I and another chap have formed a Harmony trio. I will let you know how things went with the concert. Growing a moustache is quite the vogue thing on board, so I of course, have to be in it. My two days' growth is showing up quite well. Alf is being in the vogue too. Lately, we have been issued with Barley Sugar, chewing gum and cigarettes. I think they came from the National Patriotic Fund Board. It was a very nice thought but definitely a waste of the country's money.

I see flying fish just about every day, some of them fly for about 100 yards. The boys saw a whale yesterday, and again this morning we saw a school of porpoises.

You must think that by these titbits that I am struggling for news. I am struggling for ship news but here comes the tasty bit of the whole outfit. I am going to tell you all about Suva.

A lot of the boys were disappointed – they said they had expected a Paradise – they could not close their eyes to the rain, the heat and some of the stinking filth – perhaps they have not got my young romantic mind, but I did find a paradise – I found something new that was much above expectations. At every turn, I had a new thrill – before telling you about my experiences of the Island, I will quote to you the following from the Ship's diary. Newspaper – Incidentally, it is exactly what I came in contact with, except for a few minor exceptions.

"Probably in no other country in the world is such a happy and contented native population to be found." (wrote a contributor to FIJI)

I might put in here myself, that they are the happiest people I have ever seen. That is the Fijians themselves. The Indians of which there are nearly as many, are just the usual double-dipped dealing lot of bb's

To continue the Ship's diary article:

"A genial climate enables him/the Fijian to wear merely sufficient clothing to cover his body, and even on the outskirts of the capital, fat brown children can be seen playing on the grounds – unclothed, unembarrassed and completely happy."

Just a word now about their clothing. Nearly all the men here wear skirts and no shirt and none of them, not even the police, wear shoes or stockings or socks. Speaking of the police, they are some of the finest specimens of manhood I have ever seen. They are tall and straight and beautifully made; they wear white skirts with a long pointed zig-zag cut and a navy flannel sort of shirt/blouse piped with red – they wear no hat or shoes but carry a proper man-killing affair of a truncheon. There we go again….

"In Fiji's luxuriant climate, native vegetables and fruit grow here abundantly, and many varieties of fish and shellfish are readily obtained in the bays and rivers. A simple diet, but that it contains all the requirements mankind could ever hope for, to grow and maintain the physique of the Fijians."

When I spoke of the magnificent physique of the native police, I forgot to mention that nearly all the Fijians are like that. None of them have handsome faces, but when they smile, it pleases you to the core. Happiness and merriment absolutely sparkle in their smiles which is more infectious than a cold or the flu.

"In their villages, the natives live under their own happy communal system. As far as possible, their own social laws have been preserved, probably one of the reasons for the great success that has attended the British rule following the cession of Fiji to Great Britain by the ruling chiefs on 10th October 1874. Thanks largely to the preservation of the Fijian social life and customs, the visitors to Fiji today can still witness many of the elaborate ceremonies of the past in which the Fijian above all the other races of the South Pacific was acknowledged. War dances in all their barbaric splendour, the more graceful movements of the women dancers – the thrilling spectacle of the fire walkers of Benga – all these are available for the visitor to Fiji whether these journeys take him/her to the villages along the Palm-fringed shores of the coast or the mountain festivities of some inland tribe, the visitors will receive nothing but courtesy and hospitality from these charming and interesting people."

I'm rather afraid that is all I can copy out of the paper – so now I will give you a few of my ideas and doings.

We arrived in the Fiji group early on Sunday morning and passed numerous Islands before we finally steamed into Suva Harbour. We struck it a bit unlucky because it was raining on the island. I say we were unlucky, but the rain enhanced the charm of the island. It hung like a mist through the hills and valleys and looked simply marvellous. The wharf was covered with numerous natives all smiling and acting the goat and willing to do anything they could to bring the ship in. I forgot to mention before, but I did not think it was possible in this modern, civilised, artificial world to find such perfect teeth as the Fijian have. They are so perfect and white; it makes you feel you want to steal them from them and shut them in a glass case.

After we had had some money changed, we went ashore, and an Indian taxi driver invited to take us around the island for the reduced charge of 35/- with eight of us – it was a big car at 5/- each this gave him 5/- for himself which he accepted in the usual taciturn manner of an Indian. He was a very nice chap though and condescended to take eight which was one too many and against the law of the land. He also answered questions very patiently throughout the whole journey. These questions were fired at him one after another like machine-gun bullets. During the talk, he echoed the time-worn native philosophy: "If man be good to me, I be good to him."

Suva, the town itself, is lovely even if it has got some very disgusting parts. Where all the shops are, it is flat and faces the sea. All up behind the shops, right up to the tops of the hills, are the residential suburbs. The streets are wide and clean, and palms and vegetation of all sorts grow in every bit of spare ground. The whole town is about the same size as Dargaville. The native word for "good day" or "Howdy" is "Boola" pronounced Bull-uh! Everyone we met we said this to, and gee did we get Cheery replies!?

After leaving town, we climbed up into the hills, and it was like driving around Waiwera except that we were not in so close to the water. The view was superb and all around us, was dense vegetation, very little in the way of large trees, but there were Palm trees, Banana trees, ferns and masses and masses of tangled undergrowth – every here and there were plantations of taro (similar to kumeras) and tapioca trees. After a few miles of the hills, we came down into a river valley most of which was dairy farming, and owned by Indians. If you could imagine the palms weren't there, you would imagine yourself on the Dargaville flats. Out on this road, was a nice little Pub. We stopped and had a look around but couldn't be bothered waiting for a drink. Further on, we stopped at a sort of reserve of native bush and to our great satisfaction, saw a sign directing us to a swimming pool. Luckily a couple of us had our togs. Well, that swimming pool was the most beautiful little bit of heaven I have ever seen; it was right in the middle of the bush and was part of a fairly big stream. The pool itself, was about as big as the Parnell Baths, except for one end it was about 10' deep all over. There was a diving board in one place and at one end, there was a fallen tree, right across the stream. Seemingly to give greater effect, there was a native sitting high up in the bows of the tree. On the whole, it was a marvellous swim and one I won't forget in a hurry.

I nearly forgot to tell you one of the most interesting parts of our little tour which happened before we got to the swimming pool. It was our visit to the Native Village. Believe you me, their little grass huts stink a bit, but the people themselves are very clean. As I said before, the kids run around nuddy and ghee – you should see some of those navels! Anyway, we approached rather wearily, shouting lustily, "Boolah! Boolah!" We met a couple of old village Mommas who insisted in shaking hands all around meanwhile gabbling away in their delightful language. They didn't know much English, but they knew enough to ask us if we had any cigarettes. Between us, we managed to scrape up about 20 for which they were very grateful. Before we parted out, they were smoking bits of rolled-up newspaper. They ran their hands all over us and did a bit more gabbling. We learnt later that they had put a good luck charm on us. We asked them if they had any bananas, pineapples or coconuts – they didn't have any of the first two, but they pointed up at the palms and managed to tell us that we could have some coconuts if we could get them. They wouldn't even be bribed to climb for us because it was Sunday and they were evidently under the influence of a Methodist Mission. I climbed up one tree and came down faster than I went up, nearly breaking my ruddy neck. However, we found an easier one to climb and between another chap and I, we managed to get four or five coconuts. We in New Zealand don't know what coconut tastes like. The milk has a peculiar flavour, but it is very cool and refreshing, the flesh is delicious; it is soft and juicy and white, and you can tear it off the shell with your hands. It is impossible to describe the taste of it. The coconut itself is encased in fibrous stuff which is white, and the outside of the whole thing is green as the greenest apple. After many goodbyes ("Samothi" in Fijian), we hopped aboard the taxi and returned to Suva. When we got there, we met a couple of old men carrying a whole head of bananas on a pole. We bought a couple of bunches for a bob each, which we discovered later was about 8 pence a bunch too much, to get to the point. However, those bananas were just like Angel's food. You know my usual attitude towards bananas. Now I have been craving them ever since we left Fiji, those things you get in New Zealand aren't bananas, they're just belch-provokers. I gobbled the Fijian ones and didn't belch once. They were much smaller and yellower and softer and juicier.

It seems strange to be using up such a lot of paper to tell you about bananas, but I can't get over how marvellous they were. We visited souvenir shops then. The Souvenirs were all either trash or too expensive. So, we went and visited the pubs. Just about everything was open for our benefit, and for the most part that it was Sunday, didn't matter. One Pub we went into was corker. The lounge was a big room that ended up in a verandah that was like a beer garden. All the waiters were great big bare-footed Fijians in white shirts, half the darned ship was in the lounge, and the hilarity was humming. Somebody was playing the piano and if you could manage to get hold of one of the half dozen women that were there, you could have a dance.

Waitemata *(Beer)* is 2/- a quart bottle – but Gin is 9pence a glass. They give you a glass with a much bigger capacity than the Auckland ones, and they half fill it with Gin, then you can fill the other half with whatever you like. I had about three of these and was as happy as blazes.

Before we went back to the ship, I had a bit of Fijian money left, so I bought a little native boy an ice cream and gave him sixpence. I think he is my friend for life. A whole lot of other little boys joined us too, and you would have laughed if you could have seen me walking along the main street of Suva with a whole lot of little black boys trailing behind us.

Down by the Wharf, or should I say, in front of the Wharf, is a Park and here, half the population had turned out to Farewell us. Also, there were Souvenir sellers who were getting desperate and selling things for next to nothing. A big fellow shoved a bow and 3 arrows into my hand and said 2/-. I just couldn't resist it because they were beautifully made and a real Souvenir. Now I am cursing myself because I don't know what to do with them.

Do you remember me saying at the beginning of the letter something about a concert? Well, it has come and gone. I was cut out of the harmony trio because my voice wasn't suitable. Instead, I sang with Alf in an act called the "Decameron Nights" – it consisted of a Sultan with all his wives dancing around him to the tune of Alf and I dressed as Sheikhs singing, "Persian Market". The singing wasn't bad except Alf said "hole" instead of "soul" and I started to giggle – the gist of the act was that a tourist was chasing a young lady across the scene every now and then and it finally ends up with him carrying her skirt and she, his pants. The Aussies had a concert a few nights before and the jokes in it were too smutty. So, we were determined to put on a good show and keep it clean. I am afraid though we did not stick to our good intentions. The boys got a bit pickled and the jokes were smuttier than the Aussies'. For all that, I think ours was the better concert.

I said a while back that I was growing a mo. One night about eight of the boys grabbed Alf and I, and after a terrific struggle left us with half a Mo each. It was too bad Alf and I were beginning to respectively look like Ronald Colman and Clark Gable.

As you can imagine, things are getting frigging frigid now, and last night, Alf and I had Look-out duty from 9-10, 1-2, 5-6. Remember the one about the brass Monkey? Well, it was something like that.

I am sending you a pair of Moccasins as I said I would. I hope they fit, but if they don't, keep them as a souvenir. Just in case you are interested, they only cost 14/6 on the ship. I am also sending you a couple of quid, which is for yourself and I insist on you spending it. It is no good to me now and will be less use to anybody stuck in the bank. If anybody bemoans the fact that I haven't written to them, give them the same line of argument as you used about Duncan because it is definitely a fact. I am going to write fairly decent letters to you which I will consider pages of my diary. My real diary I can not be bothered keeping.

Well, that is about all now. The next letter will probably be from London, Ontario.

Love to all and tons for yourself.

Your loving airman,

Terry xxxxx

CHAPTER SIX – CANADA

Letter 3:-

> L.A.C. Dixon T.A.
> NZ404678
> C/o R.C.A.F.
> HQ's Jackson Buildings
> Ottawa
> Canada
>
> 26 February 1941

Dear Mum,

I've certainly got a lot to tell you this time, but I'll have to condense it up quite a bit because I really can't afford more than one night at it.

It is hardly chronological starting to tell you about things that happened today, but while it is fresh in my memory, I must tell you about my first flight. We had breakfast about half an hour earlier than usual and then after a short lecture we went over to the hangars and put on our parachute harness and flying suits. We fly in Avro Hudson bombers which are simply marvellous planes. Some of the ones we have here participated in the evacuation of Dunkirk and have actually been shot down. We took off at about 8.40am and crisscrossed all over Ontario for about 400 miles or I should say, for about 3½ hours. There were 3 of us excluding the pilot in our plane. All we had to do was keep a log showing the different towns we passed over and the times we passed over them. The countryside is very drab, it is all covered in snow of course, little lakes are completely frozen over and the big lakes - you know the really big ones – are frozen for about two miles out from the shore. We had a real wag of a pilot in our plane and another one had a mock dogfight – boy was it fun. After you had finished messing about you felt as if you wanted to grab your tummy and put it back in its right place. You would think our flying boots would keep anything warm, but I've never had such cold feet in my life. I had been walking around for about half an hour before the circulation came back to them properly. My hands were so frozen too, that I could hardly write towards the end. All the boys were the same – I suppose we will get used to it just like we have got used to Canadian weather.

That's all there is to say about the trip so I must turn back the pages of my memoirs to our arrival and trip through Canada.

We arrived in Victoria just as the sun was setting and what a beautiful sunset it was. Victoria Harbour is just like a fjord and all one side are snow-capped peaks and the other side are beautiful forests. We landed at Victoria for an official welcome, but we were not allowed to look at the town. We went to bed about 10 o'clock and the next morning, we were in Vancouver. We docked after breakfast and we had to march straight from the boat to the train. That will give you some idea how much we saw of Vancouver and I would have loved to have had a look at it. The little bit we did see was marvellous – big skyscrapers and all sorts of things.

After our marvellous accommodation on the boat, the train was a heart-breaking come-down. We had the worst old carriages the C.P.R. have in their possession. There were double seats facing each other with a collapsible table between. Above these, in the place where our luggage racks are at home, there were sort of wooden beds that came down like bunks. Alf and I slept on one of these, and to me it was just like sleeping on concrete. For the first half of the journey we had to dish out our own meals on blasted tin plates and it was much worse than Levin.

The first night and day, we travelled through the Rockies. There were beautiful little towns in the foothills of the Rockies and all round there is the most beautiful part of Canada although the Londoners are quite positive Ontario is. We passed through the highest part of the Rockies at night, but Alf and I were fortunate enough to be woken by one of the boys, and it was bright moonlight, so we saw the beautiful peaks and crevasses and things quite close up. After leaving the Rockies, we came out on the Prairies and that I think is the worst part of Canada. Can you imagine the Dargaville Flats with about 1 hundredth of the houses on it and any land that wasn't covered in snow just dirty brown dead grass and all this in every direction as far as the eye can see? This part of Canada makes her the world's largest wheat producer. The first real city we stopped at, was Calgary, which is about as big as Christchurch. I didn't think much of it. It was here that we came into contact with any "wrong side of the road" traffic. Gosh, it's nuts. It makes you feel as if everything's back-to-front. It's bad enough as a pedestrian (I've nearly been run over a couple of times), but when you are in a car, you'd swear you are going to hit something. You come out of a side road and expect to cross over to the other side, and you get in a mental panic for a moment. All the cars here are BIG American ones and about half of them are 1941 models, and do they travel fast?! The taxi we went into town in, the other day, did 65mph nearly all the way and a car in front of us was doing about 75mph – all on a snowy, slippery road too. The taxi driver said that although the highway speed limit was 50mph, what he was doing was nothing out of the ordinary.

Well, to get back to the prairies – we stopped at numerous small towns but never for more than about 15 minutes. Then we came to Winnipeg – which is a very big place. The temperature there, by the way, was 40 degrees below zero. I don't think you can imagine how cold that actually is. We never got cold in the body because we had too much on, but our faces, ears and feet suffered terribly. Your ears get so cold they burn and feel as if they are going to drop off. It was at Winnipeg that we said goodbye to the gunners, and our carriage was put onto another train, on which we had, thank the Lord, a dining car. The difference was marvellous; it made one feel like a gentleman again. The food isn't very much different here. The most notable things are that they have tomato juice before every meal and they always give you a glass of water (sometimes with lumps of ice in it) with your meal. They also eat a lot of ice-cream right through the winter.

From Winnipeg on, it was just another series of snow-covered "below zero" Canadian towns. Some of these towns were very quaint with the horse-drawn sledges, fur-coated people, and icicles and things but it annoyed me after a while, and I am quite sure I could never bear to live at any of them. Do you know that a terrible lot of that middle part of Canada has snow on the ground for nine months of the year?

The big event of the whole trip (even more thrilling that the concert) was our short stay at the little mining town and railway junction called Sudbury. I shouldn't say "little" really, because it was a 75,000-population town. It was here that we left the main eastern line and turned off on to the line running down to Ontario. Here I said goodbye to Sgt. Jim Butt and Dan. As soon as we got off the train, we were marched up to the YMCA where we had a shower and a nude swim in some marvellous indoor tepid baths. After that, we split up a bit and one bunch of us was escorted through the town and down to the RSA room where we had a few beers. The Canadian beer is marvellous – almost as good as Waitemata. There are no hotels, or should I say, Pubs like ours. Hotels certainly do have parlours though. What I am trying to get at, is that you can get beer from parlours which do not have accommodation behind them. At these parlours you cannot get spirits. If you want spirits, you have to have a license and buy it from a place they called a "liquor store". After we left the RSA, we were escorted to a dance given in our honour by the Woman's Auxiliary. At the dance you could buy all the beer you wanted so everybody proceeded to get Happy. The girls were wonderful, and as they were the first, we had had anything to do with for about three weeks, you can well imagine how things went with a swing. Lovemaking was indulged in openly in the middle of the dance floor by all. I guess you were expecting this. I met a lovely, gorgeous, honey, peach of a girl!! I think if she were living in London, I'd marry her – Conceit now – I don't think she'd need to be asked twice either. About half of the boys did equally as well for themselves and for days, they raved over Sudbury and longed to return. They still rave over that night and none of us have had half as good a time in London, although we can't complain.

Well, I am absolutely tired out, so I 'll turn in now and finish this tomorrow. Bon Soir, my Love – Flying certainly makes you tired.

Well, here we are again. It is now 9-10am, and I have been doing homework since about quarter to six.

Well, now to continue our journey. The next morning, we arrived in Toronto, which is the second-largest city in Canada. It was certainly very impressive, but it was very cold and miserable. It was about 7 o'clock in the morning, but it was still dark. In Toronto, everybody seems to be up and having breakfast at a sort of lunch counter of which there are hundreds. The one we went into was Wonderful – we only had coffee and toast. We had tomato juice and marmalade and about 3 glasses of water each.

When we got back on the train, we just had time to pack and have our breakfast, and we were in London. We were brought out to the station which is about six miles from London – by the pilots who are all civilians by the way.

I have never seen the boys so depressed as when they surveyed their barracks and rooms – and the layout of the station. To make things worse, the boys who came last month, seemed to take great delight in telling us how much work we were going to have to do, and how inferior the girls in London are! There are all New Zealanders at the camp, by the way. The barrack rooms hold about sixty, I should say. The bunks are two-story. The main complaint about these rooms is that there are NO lockers, cupboards for anything. Nearly everything has to be kept in the kit bag. There are plenty of basins and showers etc., but the Loos are just like a lot of cowbails and have NO doors. There are two things I like to do in private and that is one of them. The food here is simply wonderful. You can wander in for it anytime within about an hour and it is served very nicely. All the cooks are mess hands – they wear white coats and caps, and everything is as clean as a whistle.

I don't know whether I should tell you this, but the station is run by civilians. The only Air Force apart from us, are a few N.C.O.s, and of course, the ground instructors and administration officers. The school is actually owned by a private company who lease it to the Air Force, but who do all things on it which do not have to be done by airmen or officers.

We get quite a bit of leave, but it is not much good to us because we have too much work to do.

Every night we can have from 4:30 to 10:30pm, and two nights a week we can have till 1:30am. About four times during the course, we have a 48-hour weekend leave. By the way, the course here is 12 weeks, after that we have 6 weeks at a Bombing and Gunnery School. We get our flying approval after that, but we still have to have a month at Astral navigation. Just by the way, I put the station address on this letter, but we have been instructed to stick to the Ottawa address.

On Saturday night we went to town. (London is about as big as Christchurch). We toured the town and visited the parlour of the "London" Hotel. The parlours stay open here till midnight and open at ten in the morning. I'll continue tomorrow night. I'm fagged again.

After we left the London, we went to a dance at the Y.M.C.A. There were some beautiful girls there, but they are terribly reserved, they can't dance for nuts, and of course they all talk through their noses and talk about *Noo* Zealand. It is not at all my own idea that they are very stand-offish, all the boys said the same thing.

Just as a sort of diversion, I must tell you how the Canadians dress. The men are the biggest lot of pansies you ever saw. I'll give you an idea what the smart young man about town wears. To start off with, all the men wear hats and they are nearly all wide-brimmed felts which scoop up at the back and have a big snap in the front. They wear stiff collars with wide stripes and very colourful ties – their suits are invariably double-breasted, and the trousers are worn half-mast and very narrow with wide cuffs, this shows off their flash socks which are usually bright red tartans. Their shoes are usually very pointed tan ones with fancy punched designs on them. A lot of men wear big fur coats, and do they look a scream?!! A terrible lot of men wear great big flashy rings. I really haven't had much time to study the women's dress, but I think they dress a darn sight quieter and better than the men. Except for their millinery which is terrible. The more extreme they wear their hats, the smarter they are supposed to be. I don't know why it should be, but nearly all Canadian girls (80% at least) have lovely teeth and lovely legs and they wear very nice shoes and stockings.

I was told this at home, and I didn't believe it, but not throughout all the Canada I've seen, have I seen a decently dressed shop window. Not even in Toronto. If you put one of Milne's displays beside the best display in Toronto, the Toronto one would look like the window of a country store.

Talking of shops – a drug store is the funniest looking place you ever saw. In them, you can buy anything from Kotex to a milk-shake. They have marvellous jewellery here at very reasonable prices, and I'm going to see if I can dig up something for you. Anything you want under the value of £5 – I can send you duty-free so just tell me anything because things are very much cheaper here.

Still talking shop – the shop girls here are a much lower class than the ones in New Zealand. They all have to work like blazes, and they're all dead scared of their boss. Also, they have lousy hours – shops are open every day in the week including Saturday from 9am till 6pm – No sorry, on Saturday, they're open till 10pm. I believe Wednesday is a half-day for Barbers, boot shops and grocers and all the shop girls have one half-day a week, but the hours are still lousy. Imagine working till 10 o'clock on a Saturday night?

Canadians think our Labour Government is wonderful and when I see things like the Canadian shop hours, I begin to think it isn't so bad myself.

While I think of it DIXON is a very common name over here, and there are literally thousands of Drews.

On Sunday evening last, we had a really wonderful time. The whole flight was asked out to tea by hostesses in London, Alf and I went together and were called for at 5pm by the people in a big flash Dodge- excuse me for using the word flash so often. I know you don't like it, but it describes an awful lot of things here. They drove us around and showed us all the sights of London and then took us to their home. None of the suburban homes here have any fences around their gardens, and the houses are tall and narrow, and all are two-storeyed. The one we went to, was two and a half storeys. It was the townhouse of the THREE houses these people owned. It was very old-fashioned, but everything was good and artistic. The most notable things about it were that the main resort of the household was the Library on the first floor where their radio is. There is no fireplace in this room, but heat came through an opening from the fire below. The half story on top is the suite of the Help.

On the ground floor, there was the dining room and the lounge. The most remarkable thing about the lounge was the number of lamps in it. I counted 6 standard lamps and one in the middle - All going too - by the way, the reason for the number of lights is that a standard lamp throws a very subdued light which is easier on the eyes and only one lamp wouldn't be enough to light the room. Sometimes the lights are on all day in Canadian homes. I guess it is about time I described the family. The old man was big and fat and prosperous - The owner of an insurance firm. He was very proud of the fact that his family had lived in Ontario for 120 years, but he mentioned that he had always had a desire to see *Noo* Zealand. He said something too, about having an income tax of $2000 a year. The mother was just a nice middle-aged lady – that's about all I can say about her. The son who wasn't there is a second lieutenant in the army, the oldest daughter is a doctor with a big practice in London and the most charming member of the whole family - She has studied in Ireland, England and the continent. When in London she met Sir Truby King, with whom she was very taken. The other daughter is just a lady of leisure, about 24 yrs old, but nevertheless a B.A. Now, to get to the dinner – everything was laid out by the maid and she rang a little bell when everything was ready. The old man said grace and we drank our tomato juice - then oh what a feed we had. Simply marvellous roast fowl (quite a common dish here), spinach, turnip and spuds - I darn near burst, but it was pushed on us - for dessert we had Pumpkin pie (pronounced Punkin) which was corker. They were simply astonished when I said we had never tasted Punkin Pie and when I told them that in New Zealand we roast and boil Pumpkin they couldn't get over it and somebody said what a waste of good "Punkin" - They get plenty of good vegetables here quite cheap - they eat a lot of canned produce and they get a lot from the States. They get Strawberries all the year around and the dearest they ever get is 25 cents a box. The cheapest they get is 10 cents a box - you can hardly imagine it, can you? After dinner we talked a lot about world affairs and New Zealand for a while, then we retired to the Library and listened to some American radio stations and (London/England) as clear as Wellington to us. The American radio puts over the worst lot of bumpkin you ever heard - mostly comments on the War and the glorification of the States.

We also heard a preacher who talked like an auctioneer and Charlie McCarthy in the wood and the Ford Symphony Orchestra. That was just marvellous. The Ford company has an hour on a Detroit station every Sunday night, and they have their own Orchestra conducted by a world-famous musician and their own choir.

The people drove us home about 10 o'clock. It was Monday that we had our first flight about which I have already told you. Nothing much happened yesterday, but today we were up flying again. We flew at 10,000 ft. today and when we came down, I was a bit deaf. One ear is still a bit deaf - I think it is because I have got a cold.

Now to get back to my sending you your money and items you requested - The spare money I wanted you to have to spend on yourself alone. I have had a bit of trouble over this - It has to be sent through the bank — I very near had to write to the governor to send out of the country. Let me know if you get it anyway. I am sending the money with this and please remember what I said. It is for you to spend in the way you see fit. Anyone would think it is about £100 the way I talk, but I am rather scared of you and your funny ideas.

I am also sending the first film, with which I am very pleased, and some C.P.K. Menus. ('We didn't have these menus, by the way, but they are at least souvenirs). I'm going to write to others soon, but their letters certainly won't be as long as this - it took nearly a week.

That's all now Adios Tons of love to everybody.

Your loving son e'loique'

Terry

P.S:- With the menus: You'll find a nude woman out of "Esquire". She was too beautiful to throw out - Keep her till I come home.

ഇരുഇരു

Letter 4:-   sent March 5th 1941

Training workload high
"Through adversity to the stars"
C/- R.C.A.F. Headquarters Ottawa – Canada

Dear Mum,

I've had three tries to send you the enclosed money - I do hope I am successful this time. After a lot of mucking around, I have been advised to try this way. You're lucky because this way you get an extra letter. I hadn't intended to write for about another week. In the other letter I said a whole lot about the money but seeing you won't get it till later I'd better say it again. The cash is a present for you. I don't need it and anyway, even if I tried, I mightn't be able to get it changed to $ (dollars). By the way, it's only the most important thing that's happened today or should I say since I left New Zealand and for the moment, I forgot all about it. I received my first letter from home today and boy what a thrill to get. I wasn't feeling particularly happy, but Now I am on top of the world. Take note of that last sentence and you won't slip on your letter writing I don't suppose you will anyway. There was never a truer motto than the Air Force one which you see above. "Through adversities to the stars". Adversities are right. Yesterday our working time was 13 hours. This afternoon a lot of us were taken into the Y.M.C.A. in London for games. We had a marvellous time playing rounders and swimming and all sorts of things. It's a bit of a red-letter day today - Tonight we are broadcasting messages to New Zealand. I'm sorry I couldn't say "Hello Mum," but personal messages were not allowed. Well, I haven't got any more news and I have got a hell of a lot of work to do. So long for the present.

Love to you all

Terry XXXX

ഇരുജ്ഞരു

Letter Number 5:-

17th March 1941
C/- R.C.A.F. Headquarters Jackson Buildings
OTTAWA —- CANADA

Dear Mother and Kids,

It must be nearly a fortnight since I wrote you and I suppose you'll be going a bit crook, so here goes. Incidentally, I haven't written to anyone else in the meantime, but I guess you've gathered that. The only mail I have had since your first airmail letter was an airmail letter from Nganae. Have you heard our broadcast yet!? If you haven't don't forget to listen in - even if I was knocking at the knees, I think my little speech was alright- It was all Bullsh.. by the way. You've probably heard this before, but my godfather, the work here is tough. Lately, we've had navigation problems that take 12 hours to do- A whole exercise takes about 3 nights. I haven't been to bed before 10.45pm since I have been here, and when there does happen to be a bit of a break in the homework, you simply have to go out or you'd go properly nuts.

The A flight that was here when we came have passed out now and five of them were put down to gunners, We are now B flight, and in two days' time we are having an intermediate exam in navigation to see if we are worth keeping or not – I'm scared stiff too, but I guess a gunner wouldn't be such a bad life. The new bunch that have just come in are Canuks (Canadians) and when the new A flight go out in 3 weeks, we will be the only New Zealanders here. The weather has been going from bad to worse the last few days, and tonight there is a real blizzard blowing. We are nine hours behind in our flying times owing to the weather. I now have 23 flying hours to my credit, so that is something. The little social life that I've had lately, has been wonderful and I think I have just about got myself a girlfriend, but more on her later. I must be chronological, or I'll forget something and that would never do because, by Jove, I regard your letters as my Diary.

The weekend before last, we had a 36-hour leave. We didn't know about it till 12.30pm on the Saturday, so it wasn't much use going anywhere. Alf and I went into London with a couple of the boys who took a room at the Hotel London, which has got the Waverly, or the Station Hotel in Auckland, licked. The rooms are wonderful- they have everything that opens and shuts including a private bathroom. The floor we were on, or should I say one wing of the floor we were on, is reserved every Saturday night for Air Force. The rate for the rooms, by the way, was $5.20 and meals are separate. They were double rooms - after a few beers and dinner, Alf and I went to a dance; we met a couple of charming young things and took them to supper. We took them home, and they flirted outrageously all the way, but when we got there and were about to move in smartly for a cuddle, they went for their lives and said good-night from the other side of the street. It made me feel like tearing something apart because after all, a man is a man, especially when he hasn't been out with a woman for about a month (nearly anyway). We went back to the hotel and indulged in a few pints. The whole darn place seemed full of Air Force personnel. They were in and out of rooms and all over the place and every room seemed to have a couple of dozen empties in it. About all of the lads were R.A.F. chaps who had come over here to further their knowledge or to be instructors or something. There were Sergeant Observers, Sergeant Pilots and two Flight Lieutenants, one of who was a D.F.C. Alf and I got parted during the evening and he went home about 4am, but I was too tired to follow him, so I crawled in with one of the boys. We slept nearly all day Sunday (when I should have been writing letters), and on Sunday night, we had another dinner invitation. I believe I have mentioned them before, they are arranged by the Active Service Club. They were lovely people. Very nice and homely and they didn't even have a car or a telephone, and when you haven't got those - you're not supposed to be much here, but I had a better time that night than I did at the Big Shots Place.

When we left, we had to go to another chap's place, who was taking us home. He was a broker and I don't think I have seen a more marvellous home in my life. London, by the way, is the wealthiest town in Canada for its size. They invited us into what is called the Playroom. It was a simply wonderful room. The floor was coloured squares, the walls were natural polished wood and the ceiling was beautifully designed white stuff. There was a ping pong table there, and a screen for movies and all-round the walls were coloured photos of the old man's sporting trophies and of their trip through Europe. In one corner was a lounge where we were handed a beer in marvellous red handles. We didn't see much of the rest of the house because we weren't there long, but what we did see was rich and good looking, and antique. We were driven home in a 1941 La Solle. You can't have everything though, these people had a half-soft daughter, their only child.

On Wednesday night we went into town and saw a game of Ice hockey. They were only kids of about 14, but boy do they move? You can hardly follow it; they go so fast.

This Saturday night we had another invitation to dinner. Alf didn't want to come this time, so I went with another chap. I don't think he realizes yet just what he missed. The mother was an English woman - one of the real true blue - something like Colly - is he listening? What a wonderful thing it was to hear unadulterated English again. It acted like a tonic. I used to say I liked Canadian and American speech but now it nearly drives me crackers - Especially the women. The father was a real Highland Scot. It was their son's 20th Birthday and until I told them they thought I was older than he was. The daughter - ah???!!! Now we are getting somewhere. Yes, I thought perhaps one of you who read this might like to hear about her. To start off with, her name was Diana and if there is anything I love, it is a Diana. Secondly, she had a lovely figure and was certainly not hard to look at, with light brown hair, blue eyes and teeth certainly not like pearls, but infinitely better than that. Thirdly, she has a beautiful voice and is at present playing in an amateur operetta. Fourthly, she can dance beautifully in a ballroom, and is a ballet dancer as well - do you think she will qualify - she is 18 and never been kissed - neither have I?!! Derek's (the son) girlfriend was there too. Oh, I nearly forgot, the mainstays of the family - They have two marvellous (I'll have to try and extend my list of adjectives - but everything is marvellous and wonderful) wirehaired foxies - just like Mr. Smith- 'Spunky and Skippy.' During dinner, the talk was witty and breezy, just like home, and we had a long discussion on accent - Mrs. Thompson and I backing proper English speech like she speaks - The kids backing Canadian speech, the old man and Selwyn (my new friend) were neutral - We won - After dinner, we had a real old sing-song around the piano - Marvellous - Later the young-bloods, including us, went off to a dance at the Y.M.C.A. - marvellous again - I danced with Diana the whole night. It was with great regret that I left that happy family,

BUT I'll be back. Last night (Sunday), we, the New Zealanders, gave Items at concert and did those Canadians lap it all up.

Give my love to everyone who wants it, Mum. There's a terribly empty spot in the corner of my heart and visions of old New Zealand always flash through my mind, no matter what. Canadian glitter and glitz tries to black them out. Mail from home is still the greatest event that happens here.

Love and love and love and Tons of it to you all.

Terry

ഇരുഭ്രൂ

LETTER 6 :-

L.A.C. Dixon T. A.
C/- R.C.A.F. Headquarters Jackson Buildings
Ottawa CANADA
Postmark date: 2nd April 1941,

Dear Mother and Kids,

I have lately received up to letter No.4 written by yourself on the 26th February. About a week ago, I received (8) letters in two days: 3 from yourself, three from Rae and 2 from Dem - You have no idea what a thrill it was. I darn near ate them. I still haven't received the Kiwi. Since I received your letters, I have been worrying about answering them, and now at 8.30pm on a Sunday night, I've pinched a bit of time by leaving some of my homework.

Congratulations Dem, for your superb swimming performance. If I could be as good a navigator as you are a swimmer, I might get somewhere, but I guess a gunner's life won't be so bad. Your letters are great.

Diana left school about three months ago, but kept on in the operetta when she left. I'm not just saying this because I know the person, but the dancing definitely stole the show. Diana made up all the dance sequences and trained the girls and led them. The dances ranged from beautiful graceful ballet to the snappiest modern tap imaginable. I really enjoyed the evening and Derek insisted on running me home and picked up some of the other boys as well. They (the Thompson family) can't seem to do enough for me. When I rang Diana about a week later, she asked me to come to a play for which she had two complimentary tickets. The best seats again of course - This time the orchestra stalls. I enjoyed the evening too.

Keep up the good work and letter writing, Dem. I enjoy them (almost as good as Mum's) haha???!!! - Keep them up.

I don't think I mentioned this before - I passed the intermediate exam with 62% and not very far from the bottom of the class - Four of our course were put down to gunners. Alf was warned that he would have to do better or he would be kicked out too. That is just an idea of how tough things are here. Final exams are three weeks away and the Observers wings only 12 weeks away.

Remember me telling you about the Thompsons and Diana? I feel as if I have known them for years now and the hospitality is almost embarrassing, in fact, rather annoying, because there is No Way to repay it. For instance, Diana was in an Operetta which I mentioned more than once - I said I would like to see it - It seemed it was all sold out and had been sold out a week before, but the next time I rang up, Mrs. Thompson had wrangled a couple of seats so Derek and I could go.

It was the Technical Schools Operetta, but some of it you would swear was straight out of Broadway. When we went in, we were referred to as the boys from Noo Zealand, even if Derek was in civvies and definitely a (Canuck). I was introduced to the Headmaster, and we were conducted to two complimentary seats in the front row of the gallery - The best in the Theatre, while others who had waited for hours, had to stand in the aisles. I say Theatre because although it was really their school assembly hall it was about the same but much bigger than the "Gaiety Theatre" back home. About 18,000 day-pupils go to this school and the school runs 24 hours a day, training War workers all night. Everybody else said the acting was punk, but I thought it was great. I suppose it was because I have never seen a play before.

In the Operetta:- there was love and murder and all sorts of things in it and to see it on a stage was quite a change from the Pictures (Cinema). We were driven to the theatre, driven home for coffee and cookies, and then they insisted on driving me home.

I was to go to a Dance with Diane last night, but we are C.C. for a week as a duty watch. It is the second time this has happened. They keep a whole flight here all the time in case of fire or anything. Last weekend we had a 48-hour leave, so we went to Windsor on the American border. We went down on a Greyhound bus - a photo of which I have enclosed. They weren't bad buses at all. The engines are at the back. They seat about 40 people and they hoop along the highway at 65mph. Windsor is not a bad place - I suppose you know it is exactly opposite Detroit - in fact it used to be a suburb of Detroit. The population of Detroit is about 11,2 million and is among the 6 largest cities in America. It is only about a mile across the river from Canada. I am sending you photos of

Detroit later. We were in Windsor on the night of the Joe Louis - Albe Simon fight and would we have loved to have gone over and seen it - BUT alas, it is *impossible* for us to get into the States. Do you remember in "Uncle Toms Cabin," Liza running across the river on the ice floes? Well Detroit is where she did it and her Log Cabin still stands in Windsor.

On Saturday morning, some other New Zealanders from a bombing school and we were taken over the Ford Factory which covers 600 acres and employs 11,000 people. I am led to believe this factory is only a pup compared to the one in the States. We saw the making of a car right from crude iron to a finished job, everything moves along on conveyors, and at the end, they drive the car off. The publicity men took photos of us which will sooner or later appear in the Ford advertisements in New Zealand. After looking over the factory, which took about 3 hours, they gave us a lunch of steak and mushrooms. It was really a marvellous morning.

In the afternoon some of us went to a hotel where you can combine drinking and dancing and eating. We didn't dance much because Canadian girls simply won't dance with you unless you have been introduced. Not even the tough ones. Secondly, we didn't drink much beer because this chemical Canadian beer makes one belch and burp too much; thirdly, we didn't eat because we weren't hungry after such a big Lunch.

On Saturday night, the Y.M.C.A. turned on a dance for us —- and were some of these girls NICE? I got on with a beautiful brunette - quite honestly one of the most beautiful women I've met and a marvellous dancer. Naturally, being one of the nicest bits 'off the ice' there, some of the others did their best to "move in smartly," so poor little Teggy, in not having enough "self assurance," lost this beautiful Snow White - I think the whole trouble was that she found out just how old I was - she was 23yrs. I've tried to get over this age business by growing another mo, but the boys don't like it, so I guess I'll have to cut it off. To continue, the other girls there (younger ones) were terribly concerned at my loss and just about turned the YM inside out trying to find me another girlfriend, but failed, so they insisted that I join a party that was going to a girl's place for supper. After they had got the supper, the Ma and Pa went to bed and left us. We didn't go home till 3am but there was NO Nonsense. If you touch one of these darned Canuck females, they jump about a mile. I haven't had a decent cuddle since I left home, and tell me, Lady Fair, what is life without a bit of affection? Maybe I am Slow, because Alf had a lovely bit of a thing in Windsor, and in the afternoon (Sunday), she and some friends of hers took Alf and I for a drive.

We came home about 10pm, or should I say arrived about 10pm, and that was the first time since I was a very small boy, that I dreaded returning home after a holiday.

This last week has been a real trial- working like fiends from dawn till dark. Thursday, I got in the worst temper I've been in for many moons. We had been for a flight, and the first thing we heard when we got down, was that we had to change our shoulder badges. The only way to describe the new ones is <u>BLOODY AWFUL</u> - They are like this. **

To start off with they are badly made and faded. Secondly, the Eagle is more like a constipated caterpillar than a bird and thirdly, the general public could read New Zealand alright, but they are not going to be able to work out R.N.Z.A.F. so we will probably lose all our fans. To make us more happy that afternoon, they informed us about this duty watch stuff, then refused to give us late leave, so we could have a binge before it got started. We decided to have early leave anyway, but Diana turned me down so that wasn't much good either. We all decided then and there that next War, we would all be conscientious objectors. I know my spelling is getting terrible but, in my favour, I maintain that I can't be a mathematician, navigator and good speller as well.

My photography is improving. My last film taken on superXX is the best bunch of photos I've seen for a long time and I will send them on when I can get them all collected together.

Mum, old bean, would you mind showing my letters to Rae sometimes because you are the only one, I get time to write to, and she writes regularly.

My suggestion for a Birthday Present if you insist, is a letter-writing set and one with plenty of room in it - if they are not too expensive.

About what Dick said about "self-assurance." He's right. I never did have much, and it annoys me entirely. It's the Dixon element that causes it. However, it has improved a lot in the Air Force, and as I get older, I hope it will develop.

I realize every day what a kid I am, but this business ought to turn out something resembling a MAN. Give my love to Colly and tell him I watch for white horses too and Mum. remember that big empty corner I spoke of? I know why Duncan got married so quickly now and might even do it myself yet, but it certainly won't be a Canuck! Love to the Kids and everybody –

Bonsoir mes Che'ries

  Yours,

   Terry

Letter 7:-
London
Ontario, Canada

20-4-1941

Dearest Mum

I won't attempt to make this a newsy letter. It is just to say "Hello" and "I love you". I received your cable yesterday, and I appreciated it more than I can say because I'm going to need all the luck I can get. I was also glad to hear you had the money. I hope you bought yourself something nice. For the moment I thought that cable was going to be the announcement of a birth. I hope you do cable that event – I'm interested in new cousins. Just while I think of it, would you get me Wattie's address. I wrote to him in Levin and received my letter back here a couple of weeks ago!? My correspondence has slipped badly lately. I received a simply marvellous letter from Aroha the other day, and from it I gleaned that I have the happy knack of pleasing her. I bet I can mention a few people who aren't very pleased with me right now. I bet you weren't till you got this. We are the only New Zealanders left here now apart from one Englishman and one Scot, all the rest of the men are Canucks. The English lads are great. I'd rather have 50 Englishmen than one Canadian. I do hope the censor doesn't take offense at that. I've done quite a few things lately. I went to see Ella Shields' "Sunny side up" and Dante - and last Sunday, I went riding (simply wonderful marvellous - super?!)! - By the way that autograph on the Dante book is quite genuine. I wish I could tell you more about Dante and riding and things, but I haven't the time.

Diana is 18 today, so last night ten of us went to a dance. I sent her a dozen of the most beautiful roses imaginable and I think that's done it - She loves me now!!! I'll definitely have to forget such a person exists for the next week though, because exams and Diana's don't mix.

This is short and sweet, but perhaps I'll have more time as an (image)

l hope you like this poem. It came out of the Levin magazine. The other was what we had at church parade this morning .

Love to you all

Terry

Letter 7B:-

14th May 1941
C/O - R.C.A.F. Headquarters
Jackson Buildings Ottawa Canada

Dearest Mother,

I suppose by the time you get this letter I will have received numerous rebukes for not writing. You know the usual Dixon style of leaving things till the last minute? Well, the last three weeks at Crumlin constituted the greatest effort I have ever made. When it was all over I was so pleased I didn't even worry about my marks.

I did find out however, that I came 26th out of a class of 41. A bit different from first certainly but at least I am now a fully qualified Air Navigator and only six weeks away from being a Sergeant - Observer.

I did receive your cable of congratulations today too.

A young heart is a queer thing for the first two months here at Crumlin there was no more homesick boy in camp than Terrance Albert - but towards the end of that last two months and for all of the third month I had a new home and I did not think of little old New Zealand as much as I might have.

Mrs Thompson, whose real name is Muriel, but who I call Kit, took my interests to heart completely. She insisted that I cut out tea and coffee and made me drink milk and always have heaps of green vegetables for my meals there because I complained I didn't get enough. She made me study and would have been as disappointed as any of us had I failed.

She also called me Teg. Diana has become a real pal who I have taught to ride and who has done her best to teach me to Rumba and to play tennis. We have done almost everything together, and I have only kissed her once. Mr. Thompson, the dear old Scot, who is run by his family, has been rather indifferent but likeable. I think he likes me because I remind him of his youth and the days when he was a Sergeant and courted the charming English girl Muriel Secretan (Now Mrs. T).

Derek, the typical Canadian youth, I got on very well with but did not see a great deal of because he was always out with his little university student.

My Darling Mother, I hope I have not made you jealous of this family, but you can have no conception of what they have meant to me. Before I was more or less adopted, I had been slipping badly. Drinking a bit and associating with people much below that breeding of mine which is our pride. The Thompsons influence was such that I cut out all of that and now even mention of it fills me with disgust. Diana even did her best to stop me from smoking. I do not think I have written since Diana's Birthday. That was my last night out before the exams, and believe me it was lovely. Before I went out to the house I had a dozen roses sent. I could not have sent anything more appropriate. The appreciation was overwhelming and those roses lasted much longer in their vase than most do on the bush. We went to a dance that evening and finished up with a really good dance and Sing-along at home.

From that night on and for about two weeks, we were harassed by exams. Then came two wonderful weekends of rest and most uplifting entertainment.

One night, we went to Port Stanley – A dance hall on the Lake. It is a wonderful place and is so big that in one dance – you can only get about quarter of the way around the floor. Another time, we went to a place in London, called Wonderland and whow what a Wonder-land?! It really consisted of an open air dance floor in the middle of bush and beside a river. The dance floor is marble and a better dancing surface, I never met. In the middle of the floor, there is a beautifully lit rockery with little ornamental elves sitting on it. The band, consisting of about 8 instruments, played from a sound shell at one end, as well as the dance floor, there is a swimming pool set in among the trees. There are all sorts of woodland walks as well and I think it is one of the most romantic places I have ever seen.

There was one evening during the last week at London, which broke down all my good resolutions. It was our graduation dinner. We held it at a lovely little country tavern, a few miles from London. Everybody proceeded to get pickled and I could not resist the temptation. The evening went off with a real swing. They had a boy on the Piano accordian and a little dark boy who is definitely the most wonderful drummer I have ever seen or heard. They also had dancing girls and I helped things along by doing a Hula act, which, judging by the applause, couldn't have been too bad – although when I looked at old Alfie, he just said... "Pickled Dixon?"

After Dinner, a few of us went to a place called Springbank, where you can eat, drink, dance or ride on the scenic railway and gosh it was good fun.

We left London on Sunday morning. It made me feel like a ship that had found refuge for a while and was now going out to face a storm again. I was a bit home-sick again for a couple of days but Number One Bombing and Gunnery School, Jarvis Ontario is really a wonderful station. It is the biggest we have been on yet and trains within its precincts are New Zealanders, Aussies, Canadians, Norwegians and R.A.F. men. Work is nowhere near as strenuous and so far, I have only two complaints to make about it. Firstly, the food and the mess hall are not what they might be and secondly, it is 80 miles from London and buses between here and there are not at all convenient.

The Airman's lounge on the Station is better than any lounge I have seen in all New Zealand and the canteen is better appointed and furnished than any cafeteria in Auckland. It also has a huge hall used for dancing, entertainment or pictures and a big games hall too. We fly in Fairey Battle aircraft – as a snappier little plane as you could ever wish to see. That is about all my news now. I will write again soon giving you progress reports on my B & G training. Give my love to 3Ns and tell them I'm writing soon.

Love to All,

Teg. Xxxx

P.S.   In Crumlin, we had the page to the weekly with Duncan and the other D.F.C.s on the wall. I intended to grab it, but it was taken down and destroyed to make way for some carpentering. Shame:- It was a great source of inspiration.

₹₺₹₺

Letter 8:-

22 May 1941

Dearest Mother,

I am sorry I forgot to number the last letter, but so you see it was number 7 - I've just realized how wicked I've been. I must have been away about 15 weeks and this is only the eighth letter. Needless to say, my conscience is pricking me gently, so here we are by Pan American Trans-Pacific - so you'll probably get this letter before number 7.

Today I received 15 letters - 14 from New Zealand and one from London, Ontario. From you 9,10,11,12 and 13 - I will run through them and reply to them - there is nothing much to reply to really except to ask you to tell Colly that instead of putting smart little cracks (very much appreciated) in your letters, to write a letter of his own full of smart little cracks, which would be very much more appreciated. Number 10 ~ I certainly must have moaned a lot about the cold - well it was cold - flying with frozen feet was particularly miserable - but all buildings in Canada where any person is likely to stick their nose, is heated up to about 60°. As for the weather now - It is almost tropical. This morning was like a beautiful New Zealand summer day and almost as hot (I believe it gets a hell of a lot hotter) and then tonight there was the most vivid thunderstorm imaginable. Thunderstorms here have about 6 times the intensity of those at home. I nearly weed myself AT LAUGHING over your joke about the fishing lines - little things like that, that you describe come vividly into my mind as if I was actually there. (Especially Colly's wink) - I was very glad to hear what a champ Don has been, but very sorry to hear he had split from Dick. Tell Don I was hellishly sorry I forgot his Birthday and wish him many happy's from me. Seems funny Boy's voices breaking. So glad you spent my money as requested, too darn bad that that bag I sent wasn't brown.

Number 11 - was the cause of tear-filled eyes and very clenched teeth. First you talk about "Smiling through" and "Loves old Sweet Song," then you go on to speak of the moon coming up behind Rangitoto - I'm afraid it was almost too much for me, but keep on writing things like that, my Darling Mother, because although they make me a little sad, they also make me very very happy. About this fur you want - It's a wonderful idea for a birthday present, but I've got my doubts about what I can get. However, I'll do my best. That fishing you do off the rocks sounds very successful.

Number 12 - Thanks for the photos - very very very much appreciated please could you get me some view of perhaps Pictorial review of Auckland. The Thompsons are terribly interested in anything that even smells like New Zealand, and I haven't much to show them - I'm on a big scavenge in this paragraph could you send me a little silver fern leaf with New Zealand on it like the one Lloyd gave me. I want it for Diana, she almost pleaded for mine - she thought it was marvellous. Another thing I would like is some of Grey's tobacco -(silk cut) - Pete's letter was absolutely super - he must be growing up! Of course I get Dem's lovely letters regularly and hope to be able to write him a little personal note for himself very soon.

Fancy Bo liking Gilbert and Sullivan. I didn't first time, but of course I was hanging on By my toenails up in the Gods - meanwhile young brovs goes with the nobs.

It's nice to know I could be worth £790 but I would rather have you than £70000000000000, thanks. That joke about pulling the chain that wasn't there was quite indecently decent. You talk a devil of a lot about my social activities, as if I was doing my best to pick up a wife. Please realize, my love, that anything I say about marriage is home bull - in that I feel that I will never marry at all. The only person I would marry now, would be Diana and I wouldn't.

Number 13 - sorry dear I have not yet received the Kiwi, but I am doing my best to locate it. If it was registered it is possible to trace it from Auckland. I have received all letters and Farmquest group - Birthday cake should be here tomorrow.

To get onto my favourite subject again. Mrs. Thompson informed me today that she has written to you, and you should receive it soon after this. I don't know but it might be addressed Mrs. Dixon - regarding my true blueness - yes I hate anything Yakeefied!

I nearly blubbed again at the end of number 13 letter - something about a gap that couldn't be filled - still keep it up - I love it. Sometimes I really wonder if you know Little Teggy, Mum - some of your letters make me a man too good to be true - I guess though, there'll be a blast in the next letter from you. Regarding this question of swot - it will definitely stop when the final course is finished but the job will always be pretty tough. The course doesn't finish till about a month after Wings- we have another month of Astro Navigation.

I'm beginning to like this station a bit more now - the leave is the only rotten thing about it: only ½ day every 4 days but work all day Saturday and Sunday. Yesterday we did our first bombing flight - my results are pretty near bottom - but I hope to improve- These aircraft are lousy to fly in compared to the others. We have to wear helmets and goggles and I'm going to try and get a photo of myself in them - Last night we had our first leave from here from 4pm one day, till 12 noon the next day. A friend (Jeffrey Reddell A/Obs) hitchhiked to London (8O miles away); and spent the night with the Thompsons. We went to Wonderland and had a really marvellous time- We hitchhiked back and arrived at 5 minutes to 12- Not bad, seeing we didn't start till 10.

Well, Sweetest, there is nothing more to talk about, so I will toodle along. Give my love to the 3ns to whom I have written and all the others.

Bombs full of Love, Old Bean

Teg   XXXX

ಬಂಬಂ

Letter 9:-   28th May 1941

Jarvis B&G Training Canada

Dearest, Sweetest of Mothers,

I'm doing my best to catch up on my letters here is No9. I am afraid it will have to be short, though, because the "dearest of sons" is Tre's fatique'. We have flown continually for a day and a half, and it certainly takes it out of you. My bombing hasn't improved any of late, but I quite enjoy it now. This morning we had two gunnery flights - The first was one camera gun exercise and if it had been a real gun I would have shot my own flaming tail off! The second exercise was with a real gun flirting at targets in the water that was Tre's Bon. After that exercise we climbed to 15,000ft and did a few stunts and boy did I curse myself for being an Observer! I know I will never make a good Observer but a pilot who knows?

Incidentally, I loved that I received my birthday cake yesterday. It was very nice, but just the weeniest bit dry- I also received a tin from Remuera containing socks, hankies, barley sugar, cake and gum. Of course I haven't had my Birthday yet but I might mention it is on Friday and we have Thursday night and Friday off. Alf and 1 are going to hitchhike to London again.

Last Sunday night, the Thompsons came and picked us up and took us home. We couldn't do much as it was a Sunday. On Monday morning, we did a very successful Hitchhike. Mrs. Thompson drove us to the Highway and we got a ride straight away to St. Thomas (18 miles from London) We only spent about 20 minutes in St. Thomas and we were picked up and driven straight through to Jarvis. We arrived about an hour behind schedule because we travelled at about 65M.P.H all the way. Things certainly move here. The people who picked us up live at North Bay about ten miles from the home of the quints. They invited us up to stay with them and they said they will take us to see the aforementioned quints. Just the same, I do doubt as if we will get a chance Alf and I haven't even seen Niagara falls yet, and as it's only 50 miles from here. It is important that we make time to have a visit.

Did you see the photo of F/O McArthur and his wife in the weekly? She looks lovely, and I hope I'm as lucky as he when I get married (about 20 years hence). I have written and cabled him but as yet have had NO reply. I should see him in about two months - That's all the news here, Beautiful.

Love
    Teggy XXXX

P.S:- I can get very little in furs for $25 or £5 = but Mrs. Thompson is going to help me have a look around. If I sent one of greater value, you would have to pay some ridiculous amount of duty. However I will definitely send you some gloves and please don't offend me by suggesting that you pay for them.

ഇൽ൫ഇൽ

Letter 10:-
Jarvis
1st June 1941

Enclosed please find my latest attempts at photography –
The new Musketeer is Jeff. The old musketeer is Ray Doggett.
He is now out of the AF because his back was so bad.

Dearest,

I haven't much to tell you, but I guess I can give you quality of letters, even if the quantity is poor. Anyway, I am ashamed of the score: this is only number 10 this end - but I am moving up slowly.

I suppose you would like to hear about my Nineteenth - well like my eighteenth before it, it was one of the Happiest days of the year -

On the Thursday night (Friday 30th) - Jeff and I hitchhiked to London. About three of the other lads hitchhiked to London too, and there were about 4 R.A.F. boys from Crumlin at Thompson's. Unluckily Diana and a few of the other girls were in a Theatrical production for the first part of the evening; we had to do without them. We went to a carnival and I took Mrs. Thompson on the whirligigs and things. One we went on was such a whopper that she had to scream all the time, or she would have "sold out." I left Kit for a moment and a couple of others and I, not knowing what the female of the species body was like, had to go and see some striptease acts. It was a bit disgusting, in fact, it made me feel like a bath and something else too (the bath could have been later). Don't worry, Darling, your little Teggy was never safer from women than he was in that tent. They were the hardest looking, Lousy sum of women I've ever seen, but I must admit they did have lovely bodies. After the main show which was pretty hot, they asked the "Gentlemen" to come around to the back and for another 25c they could show us some real spice. They certainly gave us our monies' worth but I would rather see Higher class nudity for rise.

Kit was rightly disgusted when we had told her where we had been —- but I soon got round her. After that, we left the carnival and while the others returned to <u>(965)</u>, Jeff and I picked up Diana and Norma, and we went to Wonderland, where we met others of the Party. When 12 O'clock came round, they danced around me singing, 'Happy Birthday to you'?! Of course, I felt a bit of a twerp, but never the less was tickled pink. After that, I seemed to be forgiven everything and Diana and I danced some lovely waltzes with lovelight in our eyes....Bulsh......! After much messing about, we arrived home about 2am. When we arrived, I was presented with a <u>lovely engraved writing set</u> by Diana and a framed snap of the family by Kit. If you have sent me a writing set too, do not be in the least worried because I never in my life needed two of one thing, as much as I need two writing sets.

DREAMING OF THEE

May 30th is a National holiday in the States being Declaration Day or something and that morning there were more American cars on Ontario highways than Canadians. The shortest way from Detroit to Buffalo and Niagara is through Canada and Yanks get 10c extra for their dollar here, so there are always quite a few around. Gosh, you should see some of the new American cars. I think the new Cadillac is one of the most beautiful man-made things I've ever seen.

However, we got picked up by a couple of Yanks in a Pontiac, which only cost $350 bucks - £70 approx. Petrol in U.S.A. is about 15c a gallon. In Canada it costs 31c a gallon. We were driven through to Jarvis at about 75mph - Of course the reason for these great speeds I am always talking about, is the broad flat and straight highways, which are like the Great South Road between Auckland and Otahuhu. People try to tell us Ontario is hilly, but the average hill here is something like that little dip between Takapuna Post office and Halls Corner.

We arrived back in camp and found we had to fly. That was all right because I really enjoy flying now, every time we go up we do stunts.

After the flight, I found two cables and a card for me. A cable from you and one from Gaga, for which I thank you both. The card was from Diana. Isn't it wonderful that all this way away you can time the cables for the right day? I was thrilled to bits.

About those furs of yours, Gorgeous. They are just as dear here as in New Zealand, and for £5 you can buy just about nil. Canada actually imports New Zealand rabbit skins which incidentally are the best rabbit skins in the world. I am sending you two pairs of gloves and two pairs of stockings for your Birthday. I just have to pray that they all fit. Many happy returns love and by the way - How old are you!?

To get back to gunnery and bombing again, I've been doing well lately. Yesterday, when we were doing gunnery, the pilot had a look at the target and said it was absolutely riddled and in his remarks column, he put "dam good gunner"?! In the afternoon, I was doing low level bombing and got a score of 55.5yds (average distance is six bombs from target) -

It was quite the best score of the day and nearly beat the station record. That was a wonderful flight because after that nice bit of bombing, the pilot did a few dives and stall turns and then took us through a series of slow rolls which were delightful - The ground looks great from an upside-down position. I blacked out (almost) in a dive the other day, but it was nothing and happens to quite a few chaps.

Well Sweetest I wish I could come home with my wing when I get it - but I have just got to have a crack at the Huns. When I get behind a machine gun, I just feel lovely. I am going to try and be a front gunner and bomb aimer (that's still an observer) because I loathe navigation. There is no thrill in it at all.

Well, my One Love (no kidding I'll love No One like I love you or anywhere near it) I must say toodle-oo. Keep your chin up and look after old New Zealand for me. I'll be coming home soon with a wink and wings.

Love to you all
A big Hug and fifty kisses
    Yours
        Teggy.

ഔറയഔറ

Letter 11:-   Jarvis - Canada
                                                 5th June 1941

Hello Sweetest One,

My letter-writing technique is getting down to a fine art - All the other girls are "Sweet one" but you are "Sweetest one" – Ghee, have I had some rumpty cables? One from Dick Lavender congratulating me on my Observers' wing - when I haven't got the darn thing and one from Naenie with the startling news that I have been made Godfather! That is one of the greatest compliments I have had paid to me yet and I am deeply honoured. Ghee, I'll bet he's a beaut. You know I was strangely relieved when I got that cable. Goodness knows why anyone would think I was his father instead of his Godfather. Why the name Michael? Ngarae is getting very complicated mixing up the French and Irish, but I think Michael is lovely as long as they don't make it Mike or Mick. One thing, it will be easy to remember his birthday, as it must be darn near to 30th May. That's something I never thought of before either, he must have been born under the same star sign as myself, so I'm afraid his future isn't going to be too promising.

I don't think I ever told you about the re-institution of my moustache. You remember I had one on the boat which was forcibly removed, Kit (Mrs. T) has a great weakness for moustaches, so she kidded me into growing one. After about a month of careful attention, I have managed to produce quite a Clark Gable which isn't bad but is invisible at anything less than 6 feet away because it is so fair. Kit and Diana think it is just wonderful and periodically Kit trims it for me.

You may wonder at the oft mentioned Jeffrey Reddell in my letters and the minimised mention of Alf. Alf and I are still buddies just as much as ever and we still bunk together and yarn for hours about Operas, poetry and politics etc., - Jeff, as much as I, is in big with Diana and the Thompsons, so of course, we always go there together on leave. Jeff is a nice lad of 19 and as you see from his photo, devilishly good looking. So good looking in fact, that he often beats me for the women, which is good for me because it is helping to get rid of my conceit. He is damn lazy and slow, but is also good-natured, happy, generous and sentimental. You see, Darling, I am half a kid and half a man, so I have a friend for the kid and friend for the man. On the whole, the four of us are one big happy family- Terry (Kid) Terry (man) Alf and Jeff.

About a couple of weeks ago, I sent a huge pile of photos to you. I trust you received them. If I can find them, I will also include a few with this, These ones I did not take but never the less are interesting.

It seems funny in this country - America is definitely the centre of entertainment. Nearly all the radio programmes you hear here are original (not recordings) - last night, I listened to Eddie Cantor and Alf Jolson - tonight it's Bing Crosby and Bob Burns. Other people I've heard direct are Deanna Durban, Grace Moore, Walter Winchell, F.D.R. Lindbergh. Apart from the radio, the original programmes around here are amazing too. Gracie Fields was in Canada just before we came, Grace Moore and Gladys Swarthout both gave programmes in London Ontario. While we were there, Buster Crable was in a water show in Toronto and Louis Armstrong's band plays at a dance hall not ten miles from here. I'm afraid I don't get to see as many of these things as perhaps I should, but home life and something to love makes me sometimes a stick in the mud. So I zoom every leave off, I go to London.

Sometimes I curse my loving nature. It's only about six days since I was at Thompsons, but I'm longing for tomorrow when I'll be scooting off there again. Lately, I've been restless and moody and - I don't know why I should tell you this - but dying for a woman to hold?! I think it is the heat. You probably recently heard our broadcast in which nearly everyone moaned about the cold. That was three months ago, and now it is as hot as blazes. It's a sticky humid heat far worse than Auckland - All the Canucks are wearing summer uniforms.

I've opened up a lot tonight and had a good old yarn just like we used to have. I hope I have not given you anything to worry about - If you should ever worry about me, I ask you to inwardly reflect for a moment and think of your firstborn in this light. "He is getting the best of the deal: He has more money than he has had in his life before. He has a strong wise guiding hand - The Air Force. He is meeting wonderful people and experiencing all that I have missed. He does get homesick sometimes, but it will do him good - He has his little troubles, but he has a lot of common sense and he is doing alright - sometimes he longs to be home but he realizes also that he doesn't want to return yet - he does not want to return to the humdrum existence he left to get away from. Apart from all these things, he goes forward to fight for all the things we hold dear, and he carries my colours and my prayers with him. Also I have two other fine sons to worry about. (You) have two other fine sons there at home - Their futures to map out and their welfares to think of in the tough fight for existence - life ahead of them." All this I ask you to always remember and trust that you will.

As for me, I remember:-

"I said to the man who stood at the gate of the year...'Give me light that I may tread safely into the unknown' and he replied ' Go forth into the darkness and put your hand into the hand of God, that shall be to you better than a light and safer than a known way."

That's all for tonight, little Darling, and by the way - Happy Birthday and many of them.

I'll write again soon, but I doubt if there will be so much Bullsh... in the next one.

Love to my real true loves Dem, Pete, Colly Yourself and Michael.

Love again.

Teggey (nineteen-year-old)

ဢႃႃ

Letter No. 12:-

Note from Terry:
Mum, please keep mailing letters to Ottawa - I will cable you when to change to the following address:-=

R.N.Z.A.F. C/- NZ High Commissioner,
415 Strand, LONDON - ENGLAND

Dear Mum,
On 21st June 1941, I shall be receiving my wing. I also received 14,15,16,17,18 - loveliest batch of letters so far. I kept up the McArthur tradition by being the

smartest man on wing parade, although my knees shook and the long march by myself up to the C.O. was killing.

A photo was taken of Diane and I and should appear in a London Ontario paper (name of that later) - After the ceremony, we (a bunch of us) got pickled with the Thompsons, then we had to enter the train immediately to come out here. Rivers Manitoba right in the middle of the monotonous prairies... The temperature was 94° today, and the sun didn't set till 8.30pm - The last time we were near here, it was 38° below zero. Although we are sergeant observers, the course ahead is tough and our future in the Air Force depends on it. Regarding your question about the photo -

I don't know?! We were stationed at Crumlin airport, London, and the photo will be of our course, but we've had so many photos taken, I just can't remember them all. The only way we can be sure, is if you send the photo to me and I'll send it back. Great flow to hear about Coll's transfer, specially when looked forward to meeting was close but will probably spend my first leave in England with Peggy and my new cousin.

Did you mean "Begin the Beginni'n"?

No:15

I have received all your cables! Thanks for your consideration of Rae - she thinks a lot of me and letters to her are few and far between. Don't worry, My Love, about my not getting someone good enough for myself- You'd say Diane was more than good enough, but just the same - I think I'll still be a bachelor. Kit begs to contradict and maybe you do too, but the bites you've had went right through to me, so I will always be wary. It seems funny now, receiving your answers to my cries of loneliness, because never was a strange person taken so completely into the confidence and affection of a family, than I into the Thompsons. I hope you don't mind - I have let Kit read some of your letters. The last lot brought a lump to her throat. <u>It is no use fooling you, but please don't let even an inkling of what I am going to say creep into any letter that you might write to Kit, because I don't think she knows herself?!</u>

Diana is sweet and lovely and worthy of everything I have said about her, but her mother is the woman. She understands me backwards, and I at least understand her forwards. She is the one I have had in my subconscious thoughts and the one (although I didn't know it) who I have always rushed to see. But for a matter of 15 years in age, you might have had something to worry about, and if there are girls in England like the Muriel Secreton that was, and I met one, you will know your son is well matched. So don't misunderstand me, there has been no embrace beyond a duty peck, neither has there been a misplaced word - only has there been flashing blue eyes wrapping messages with mine.

I received another letter from Dem and one from Pete - both absolutely corker - apart from their newsiness, adorably humorous. People say my letters are funny, but I know two people who have me whacked. Re the 3Ns I should not say this because they have always done so much for me, but compare their attitude to Rae's who compares every other man she meets to me and yet sleeps with my photo - Rae said "A postcard sometimes would be lovely and even perhaps a letter once in a blue moon",

"Isn't it wonderful, Mum?" he treats your letters like something straight from heaven.??!!

How did he know - It's true?! I always pick out your letters and leave them till last, then lap them up. I usually read them twice - then I answer them.

I haven't got Nganie's address so I couldn't congratulate her on Michael, but please do it for me, Mum, and also thank her for the great honour she bestowed upon me. I am sending something to Michael and it is not what you think. Give my love to Lin and kids,

Love to you all and much love to you

Teg

৪৩෮৪৩෮

Letter 13:-

Jarvis
15th June 1941

Well, we're nearly there, we HOPE - yesterday we had both the gunnery and bombing exams. The gunnery exam wasn't bad, but the bombing exam was a proper stinker - I feel I might have to sit a supplementary, but I am hoping. I still have three oral exams to have, but I think I should manage them alright. Everything being well, I should be a sergeant in six days. Kit and Diana will be your representatives at the ceremony, but I do wish you could be there - It will be one of the proudest days of my life. A P/O would be lovely, but a sergeant isn't bad, and I will feel I have at least done something to make you proud of me. The other day a press photographer from the Toronto Star took individual photos of us all to send to the Auckland star. They will definitely be published along with a short note we were also permitted to send home. I believe you have heard our broadcast - I didn't say much did I? But you know what a twerp I am when it comes to saying things - I find 'DREAMING OF THEE!' covers a lot of ground.

DREAMING OF THEE

Once when I was in London (Canada) idly reeling of that particular poem to myself and somebody heard me - I've had to say it in front of every gathering (small) I've been in since. When I have read it, I am sending you a book-length poem by an American Poetess, called White Cliffs (the poem). It is really a story and comes very near to prose in parts and gives all the insights to the feelings between Englishmen and Americans.

In a way, it is a war story, so I wouldn't recommend you to read it, but it expresses such beautiful feelings sometimes, that I just had to buy it for an addition to my small library. Kit is reading it at present and she says it makes her terribly homesick - The White cliffs, of course, being the White Cliffs of Dover. Kit is a true Englishwoman and hates Canada and Canadians although she has lived here for years. She is a bit worried right now because she has not heard from her relations over there. Incidentally, I haven't heard from mine over there either. I wrote to F/O McArthur months ago and also cabled him when I left Crumlin, but I have not heard from him yet.

Last Sunday, the Thompsons came for us after work and took us for a Picnic to Port Dover - A beach town on Lake Erie. The old lake isn't bad, but oh my God, how I long to see the sea again.

The lakes are like seas because you can't see the other side, but there is no salty smell or rollers or anything, and although a Lake might be beautiful in its own way, there is no romance about it like there is the sea. Comparing the sea and the Lake is like comparing Canadians with New Zealanders and the Thompsons. I have nothing against the lake or Canadians, but they just don't click, that's all. The Picnic was lovely, but it was a bit cold to swim, but we hired a motorboat and went for a ride which was great fun.

You won't have to put up with the Thompson family in my letters much longer because after next Saturday, I might never see them again, unless of course, I can manage to get back to London, Canada - We are on the way to old London which should be about six weeks. For the astral navigation course, we will be stationed at Rivers Manitoba - plumb in the centre of Canada. I suppose it will be as hot as blazes.

Talking of weather - we had a rumpty thunderstorm today - At lunchtime it was a beautiful sunny day then at about 1.30pm the Thunder crashed and the rain came down in torrents. I probably have got you completely puzzled over my relations with Diana. I have never consistently stuck with a girl so long before, and never before have I been so attentive or considerate. I don't think for a moment, that only she has held me and knowing myself, I will probably fall just as hard for the next girl I meet, although she will have to be pretty good to come up to my Goddess of the Chase.

What has really held us together is the love between the entire household and Jeff and myself. It is only a week since we saw them, but I'm dying to get back there again. To change the subject a bit, I often wonder how I am ever going to end up over the matrimonial question. My thoughts concentrate on the one of the moment, but all round I never forget the old ones. - I don't love and forget - I love the old girl friends almost as much as when I was going with them. Although I only knew Aroha about 24 hours we will still correspond. I think I must be fickle. Anyway, what I started to tell you about, was Diana and myself. One night I was annoyed with her over something, so I told her all about it - How I didn't like the way she was becoming cool, and flirting too much with Jeff, etc, etc. I believe she was told off by her family about it too — anyway, to show you what a charming sensible girl I think so much of, I will quote you her reply to me. Of course some of her ideas are youthful idealism but there is a lot I agree with.

This is her quote:-

"I have felt the same way - I haven't seen enough of you in the last two leaves, but you always leave me wanting more, so I suppose it's just as well that way. I don't flirt with every airman I meet, and if I do, I get it from my mother. It isn't flirting anyway, it is just affection which, with me, comes out in peculiar ways. There is no need for you to be jealous. You're my oldest friend, and nobody will be quite the same as you, so to speak. I will admit that sometimes I show more affection to others than to you, but I have explained the more I like a person, the less I show it. You have annoyed me, often, by being so darned possessive when I start to fool around with anyone else, and at those times I haven't known whether I'm mad at you or myself, so we're quits. I shall confess, I have a habit called Pretense?! When I go to bed, if I don't go to sleep right away, I pretend something nice. But no matter who I start out with, in the beginning of my story, you are always the one I end up with. You fit into everything so easily, whereas, with anyone else, it usually gets complicated somewhere. That's, I have said, is because I have known you longer than the rest and I feel I can do anything at all with you."

"I doubt if I shall ever nod my head for many years to come" Meaning she will never say she loves anyone - "You see, I have never been 'BOY CRAZY' and have never thought I was in love with ten different boys at once. Love to me, is something sacred that one doesn't fool with. I have flirted with boys, but I have never gone as far as to even pretend to make love. I couldn't get myself to do it. As soon as I feel that I am getting too serious, it disturbs me, and I immediately become aloof, and even rude in my attitude towards that particular person. Marie, now, can say she's in love, and I know darn well she isn't. Though if Thor should ask her to marry him, she would be crazy enough to do so. Girls nowadays, are just too anxious to get their man and the old fashioned idea of loving your husband doesn't seem to enter their heads. If they can have a little fun with him, they seem to think that they would be happy living with him, for all their lives. I feel it takes a lot more than that. To begin with, you should know this man you supposedly love, through and through and you can only do that by knowing him a long time and under all sorts of conditions. You should know his faults and be prepared to cope with them. No, not just for the Honeymoon, but all through life. You should love him to such an extent that you feel your life is making his life pleasant. That takes a lot of love, and only the real thing could possibly meet those conditions. Whether I will ever feel that way, I don't know. It is hard in this world, with money playing such an important part in life, to marry a poor man. You can't live on nothing unless you've been used to it all of your life. But, any man I could ever love, would be the type who would have pep and enough ambition to make him work for better things, and have sufficient head on his shoulders to figure out a budget of happiness on what he earns.

"I shall go through life flirting, so you say, because, to me, any boy I wish to flirt with must be someone I like - as I would like a life-long girlfriend or a boy I had grown up with. I haven't known boys I could flirt with, until you and the other New Zealanders came. I hated boys because I never enjoyed myself with them and it repulsed me to have them even touch me. There were only two boys in school I liked, but as I was just too retiring at that time it never occurred to them to take me out. I hated dances, and I hated answering the phone in case it was some boy that bored me. When you came up that day, my whole outlook changed, and I remember telling Mum that at last I had found what I called real chums."

That is about the gist of it all, I think. You might think it funny quoting a very personal letter like the above, but I felt that you would like to know all about Diana and I think the above gives you a good insight into her character. All that is between you and I and the gatepost - The gatepost probably being Colly.

It is now 18/6/41, and my rank is now Temp/Sgt. as I can be quite safe in telling you to address my letters Sergeant/Observer Dixon. Sounds a lot better than LAC, doesn't it? To be quite honest with you, I must admit that I have not done as well as I might have in this course. What with a very lame instructor this course, I have been sort of resting after the strenuous course at Crumlin. I have loved bombing and gunnery though, and have often wished that it was real action. My practice results have been quite good, but I hate theory. In the exams I was about average with 61% in bombing and 64% in gunnery.

I will be able to tell you in a month whether I get a commission or not. I am sure I won't because the competition in our flight is too keen.

Yesterday the following people visited us :- Gordon Coates, Langston, Colonel Williams and Group Captain Isitt and a movie cameraman came with them.

They arrived when we Jeff and I were flying, and the first indication we had that they were there, was that we had to pose for the movie camera and walk across the tarmac with it turned on us. Keep your eye open, for it will be on at the cinema as a newsreel. When we got to the crew room, they were all there chatting - man-to-man with the boys. You are probably wild with me for not introducing myself to Gordon, but I didn't like to barge in and bring up personal things with all the boys round. Anyway, I was deaf from flying.

I was a bit disappointed in the man himself. Of course, being a friend of Colly's I was very interested. All the boys said that he looked half shikka and I'm afraid I was inclined to agree with them but, I do not believe you can judge anyone on such short acquaintance. I wouldn't give you tuppence for that little Labourite rat beside Gordon anyway.

To me, he looked just like an ignorant jumped up farmer whereas Gordon looked a real aristocrat. He was very tastefully dressed, and I very much admired his tall straight figure. What I couldn't get over was that he was so full of bull and rash promises.

Last night we had a chance of a ride to London and back - so we went. We didn't arrive back at camp till 3.30 this morning, but it was well worth it.

I have enclosed some photos of our aircraft. The ones pictured are the target (or drogue) towers.

Well, exams are well over now - flying is finished, and I'm a very tired little sergeant so ......,

Bon Soir, for now, Love to you all

Teg. XXXXXX

We will expect mail from home any day now.

DREAMING OF THEE

2nd July 1947

Dearest Mother, "I'm dreaming of Thee" today, my Love
> Because it is your Birthday.

I remembered yesterday and was going to send you a cable, but I was too late for the cable office, so I have had to wait till today, which I have just realized is the day after your Birthday. Right now it's 7.30pm 2/7/41 and here, 1.30am 3/7/41 in England, and 1.00am 3/7/41 in New Zealand. Now about the matter of photography- my photography is getting worse instead of improving. However I have enclosed a few that might interest you. Among the close-ups of us taken for the Star should be a photo of Jeff Reddell. If and when those photos are published would you please send a paper to:-

> Mrs. W. A. Reddell,
> 12 Bay View Road,
> NAPIER.

I am going to have a portrait of myself done in London Ontario, on final leave which is only about two weeks away. Incidentally, I hate to think of the final parting from the Thompsons. It's going to be almost like leaving home again - leaving to come out here was bad enough. Strangely enough though, I feel quite ready to leave Canada and get to England. Furthermore, I want to see Peggy. Tonight I'm getting a parcel away to you. There really isn't much in it - but a few nick nacks that have been mounting up in my suit case. There are a couple of souvenirs for Dem and Pete. I really wanted to get them something decent but I hadn't the faintest, so until you let me know just what they want or need I won't be able to get anything.

There is really no news to tell you at the present time - except about the 48-hour leave they gave us a couple of days ago. In my last letter I spoke of the heat we had been experiencing here. Honesty it was really terrible. The temperature rose to 108° the other day. Right up till the day before our leave, it was like that and we anticipated swimming and all sorts of things, but as is often the case, it clouded over, it rained and became miserable and cold. However we had decided on our rendezvous and even the weather couldn't change our minds. About 20 of us chartered four taxi's and set off for Clear Lake. A lovely tourist resort about 60 miles away. The place is really a part of Riding Mountain National Reserve and the little town on Clear Lake is Wasagoming. It is really like the Canada you read about - At the entrance to the reserve you pass through a huge arch made of logs and you are in Wasagoming.

It really isn't a town, it's a park with the shops and houses dotted here and there among the trees. I don't think there are any two shops in the whole town built side by side. Another thing about the buildings is that they are nearly all made of logs and look very very picturesque. The hotel where we stayed was very nice too. It was right on the Lake's Edge and had a lovely holiday atmosphere about it. When we had dumped our bags we set out to have a look around. We found out that there were available just about everything I like doing. Boating, riding, dancing, pictures, golf etc, etc etc. We also found a corker little souvenir shop, where I bought a few of the things I'm sending. Although the weather was still pretty cruel, we mapped out a super programme for our two days. It seems we can't get any enjoyment in this dam West because when we arrived back at the hotel, we received the sad news that we had to return to camp that night so we would be there to see our liaison officer who was coming to visit us on the morrow.

It nearly broke our hearts, because it was the first time we'd had two whole days off for about two months. To make matters worse, the weather was clearing, so we decided to make the most of the time we had left, so we went to the pictures in the little log theatre. After the pictures we went to the dance and about 10pm an officer and a couple of service police arrived to round us up. The officer, being only human, allowed us to stay till 12.30.

I slept nearly all the way home, but was still dog-tired the next morning, broke - it was a perfect day - warm sun, cool breeze and just a few lazy looking clouds. It would have been a big day at Clear Lake because it was Dominion day. A holiday. We also found that we were the only ones recalled the ones at Winnipeg and Regina were just too far away to collect. Well we waited and waited and Group Captain Isitt didn't come. They couldn't give us lectures with only half the class there so the day was wasted. He arrived this afternoon when we would have been home from our 48 hour leave. I hate this course and don't even want to pass it. However, whatever happens, I should be on the way to England in about six weeks. Thank goodness.

Well, Darling, I'm afraid this letter is a bit of a moan but I'll try and be more cheerful next time. I intended to write to Naenie tonight and enclose it in yours but I'm afraid I can't now because I have to go and shoot the stars - curse-'em.

Lots of love, Mum, and please don't work too hard. I don't see why you should get a job - finances must be pretty good now. Well, tons of love. Love to the boys and Colly and to Naenie and Michael George and Lin and Murray and the 3 N's etc etc etc.

Yours Teg (Sgt. Obs)

XXXX

Letter 15:-   8th July 1941
(Written on YMCA paper - ENVELOPE is from Hotel LONDON – Ontario)

Rivers Manitoba - Canada.

Darling One,

I have at last managed to throw a few words together for you to send to Naenie and I have enclosed it, Love, so you can read it if you want to.

I received your cable of congratulations about two days ago for which I thank you. I was a bit afraid for a while I wasn't going to get one because it was beginning to seem ages since I'd sent the one from Winnipeg.

A couple of days ago, a train load of Aussies and New Zealanders passed through here so we're expecting a big New Zealand mail any day now.

We're taking off on a night flight in about an hour, so I think I will stop now and finish tomorrow night.

Well here we are again. It's the next night and I might tell you we did not have the above-mentioned flight, owing to thunder storms.

There was a real wizzard of a thunderstorm here last night. Hail came down in pieces as big as sugar lumps, and the lightning was flashing across the sky lighting up the sky like flashes from big guns. After it was all over, there was a magnificent sunset about 9.30pm.

There is really no news except perhaps to enlarge a little on the enjoyable afternoon I mentioned in Naenie's letter.

The horse I had to ride was simply marvellous. A great strapping Thorough-bred with white fetlocks and a white star on his forehead - his name was "Star" —— before I got on him I was a bit (just a little bit) scared because I had been told how fresh he was and apart from that, they had a cowboy saddle on him, which I didn't really like the look of. However, once aboard, I felt perfectly at home and managed him quite well- He was the most spirited horse I've ever ridden. You know what lovely horses the Auckland mounted cops have? Well he was just like that and he pranced around tossing his head just like they do.

Well enough about horses, the swim we had was just lovely too. The pool was a real heaven on these darn Prairies.

I'm enclosing the latest photo of myself which was taken when we arrived in Rivers- The hotel in the background is the biggest and only brick building in the place. The others are all unpainted wood,

Love to you all and a big Hug and a kiss for yourself...

Yours...

Teggy Dix

ഐരോജരോജ

Letter 16:-   Sgt/Obs. Dixon.— T.A. NZ
C/- New Zealand High commission
415 Strand, LONDON - ENGLAND

18th July 1941,

Dearest,

Firstly I have another away-from-home truth to tell you - Then I shall get on to answering your letters. Point is, I've messed up my Astro navigation course, but contrary to my original ideas, I've completely surprised myself by electing to stay another fortnight, so I can get through. You see, when we arrived, they told us if you missed this course, you became a day navigator. I thought that suits me fine, so I sat back for the whole month and had a darn good loaf. Strangely enough, I did quite well in the exam and could have scraped through, but I went and saw the instructor and told him I wanted to do the course again. So here I am - the rest of the flight will be going on leave tomorrow, but I remain. I'm a bit sad about that, but I might catch them up in Halifax. <u>It is possible that I will be navigating a bomber from Canada to England when I'm through.?!</u>

Now I will have a look at your letters and see what there is to talk about. I have now received up to number 20 - two letters by the way marked number 19.

The first No.19 was from Christchurch, and there isn't much to say about that except that I don't know why the blazes you have to go to work - I think I might make you an allotment when I go to England, so you can have a bit of fun out of life instead of working your heart out. I'm having fun, why shouldn't you? You know you aren't a chicken and in both yours and Pete's letters, there is news of a recent slipping of your jolly old clutch. If you must work for god's sake and your own get something easy - writing a book for instance! I might mention Roma, old girl, I have not received the writing case and if our Mr.

Gresham doesn't 'shake the wire,' I'll have left the country. The letter from Wellington <u>Please</u> spell broadcast without an "E" and I'll do my best to get (receive) right and while we are on the subject, Thomson has not got a "P" in it.

I can imagine you popping into the radio to look for me. I had almost forgotten about that business. It seems so funny too, that just about everyone said how cold it is here (It was snowing outside at the time) - when actually by the time you heard the talk we were sweltering and still are.

About this business of making a record - I don't think it's possible - With the little time I have at my disposal, but I'll try.

I think both the Farmers and Air Force are too tough for you. Not too tough - but most unsuitable. Surely with your personality, old bean, you can get something easier than that. When you said something about my hard work, I felt a bit of a cad because as I said, I've had a loaf here. However I will certainly be working this next fortnight.

You remember how I used to be nearly dead, if I didn't have about 11 hours sleep a night? Now I can get away with 9hrs. Last night I had only 4hrs. When we fly at night, we don't get to bed till about 3am and sleep till 11am the next morning. There must have been something wrong with me this morning, because after a night flight I arose at 7am. I am so glad the purse is all I hoped it would be and you liked it. I'll be sending half a dozen pairs of stockings as soon as poss. Don't expect them to last long though because I've heard that the tropics takes the guts out of 'em and they run very easily.

You must have received plenty of snaps by now. Anyway, I'm doubling output even enclosing some more in this letter. I'm having an enlargement made of my best photo to date. It is only a river scene, but I think you'll like it.

It seems you must have taken too serious a view of what I said about getting pickled. Actually, it was nothing. I got pickled a few times before I met the Thomsons, and then never even had a beer for a month - I guess it was because I never had beer at all that I even mentioned it.

What made you think I had fallen for Kit instead of Diana? Smart arn't you, love? Seems I didn't need to tell you about it. However, I'd hate you to get this wrong like you did the beer. Kit and I are real pals, but she is no more a pal to me than she is to Jeff or any of the other lads. That bit of sentiment I said in one of my letters, I said simply because I have a romantic imagination and am a sentimental bloke. You ask what Mr. Thomson does, well he is an executive in a big advertising firm.

I received a very nice letter from Rae Jorgensen this mail - so pleased to hear Murry is in the Air Force. He is a pilot - I will definitely slap him on the back and say "Howdy Pal" when we meet. He might be my pilot some day, but I wouldn't mind betting he will be a fighter pilot.

That answers all your letters to date. In this mail I also received a parcel (sox, pad and envelopes etc etc) from the girls at R&G, and a parcel of biscuits, socks, booklet of text's etc., from the Milford Women War Workers. I'm doing pretty well with sox's now. I almost have too many. If you are doing any knitting, I'd like a huge thick wool, thick stitch, roll neck, grey pullover. It's something I have wanted ever since I have started flying.

Aroha and I still correspond - she is in Dannevirke with some relatives at present. She heard my broadcast and thought, as Rae did, that "Dreamin' of thee" was specially for her - this I'm letting them think - but it was really for all of you - It is my code phrase. At the time I think I was probably Dreaming of Thee - you.

Aroha has written me some wonderful letters and is knitting some (SOCKS) for me. Mum for next Christmas I still want that KIWI. If you can afford it, I want one. From you only - no one else - don't even suggest it to anyone else. Aroha is sending me a Tiki which she wants me to wear - I doubt if I shall - But I will wear your Kiwi.

I was listening to the radio today, and I heard a story about a little boy who had a step-father. His mother had divorced his father and the little boy knew who his father was. In the story the little boy was asking the Step-father about the mix-up which he couldn't understand, and it seemed to hurt the poor kid. It was rather sad. I never realised till I heard that play how much I appreciated not knowing about or meeting my father until I did. - just something else to thank you for. Thanks, Love!

I started this letter this morning and it is now evening. Except for five of us, Jeff and I included, everybody has packed up. They go tomorrow at noon. It wasn't till I saw them packing, that I realized how I was going to miss Alf and some of the others. I'm now in with a bunch of "blinking blokes" "Cor Blimies" "Limies" or should I say gentlemen of the R.A.F. They aren't bad chaps, but too many in a packet give me a tummy ache.

Jeff and I have been a bundle of disappointments to Kit and Diana lately. Firstly, for loafing our time away, which we told them we were doing, and now for not turning up on final leave when expected. However, I guess the last will make them more pleased to see us when we do get there.

That's all there is to say Darlin'
TONS OF LOVE
TEG   XX

Letter 17:-   24th July 1941

Hullo Roma, Old Girl!
Well, we have been about a week on this new course and I hate the place more than ever. It certainly seems lonesome without the men I have enclosed a photo of.

Thanks ever so much for the writing kit, which I received just yesterday. It certainly doesn't look very big, but it holds a heck of a lot.

Last Saturday, Jeff and I left almost before the boys did and we went away on a forty-eight to Clear Lake. The whole place was packed out and I've never seen so many half-dressed beautiful females in all my life. They weren't backwards either and were almost as sporting as New Zealand girls. The only place we could get to sleep in, the first night, was a lady's sitting room. However, it was quite comfortable and the next day, she gave us a room. While I think of it, I might mention the weather, although just a trifle too warm was marvellous - Cloudless days and starry nights.

Saturday afternoon we swam and went canoeing.
Saturday night dancing
Sunday morning swimming
Sunday afternoon sleep
Sunday night sleep
Monday morning sleep
Monday afternoon riding
Monday night dance
Tuesday morning returned home.

That was my programme and I can't enlarge on it much, except that where you see all the sleeping up there, I was so sick as a dog - I must have had summer sickness or something, anyway whatever it was it nearly spoilt my holiday.

There was one incident which I feel I shouldn't tell you, but as this is my diary and as I tell you everything, here goes. Don't kid yourself you are reading through the lines or anything because I'll tell you all.

On Saturday night, I picked out a charming-looking woman from the crowd and very soon noticed she wore a wedding ring and was older than at first glance or I had estimated. She was very nice and easy to talk to and we had a bottle of orange together and a very interesting talk. We only had one more dance and I took her home. We made a date for Monday afternoon and I returned to the dance.

On Monday afternoon, we went for a walk and on Monday night, we went for another walk - I kissed her tonight and that finishes the story.

She was an adventuress and probably a bad woman - she had a daughter of 13 and a son of 10 - she was quite well off, good looking and supposedly loved her husband.

Aren't women queer? I haven't been able to get over this episode.

I fall for some older women and some older women fall for me.

Well this woman was like that one remember, but this time I had enough sense not to fall prey to her . She nearly did fall when I told her how old I was. (over that is) :-

Another reason I've told you this, is because the incident is so unusual and yet has happened twice to me. I must attract randly old married women and boy oh boy, can I handle 'em ?!?

There really is no more news, except that I'm beginning to understand Astro a bit now and might get that ticket yet. I'm enclosing a photo of the flight, photos at Clear Lake and the ranch at Rivers and my old L.A.C. badges which I thought you might like for a souvenir.

That's All!! Love to all of you and tons for yourself.

 Yours Teg.

  (I Love you truly)

ೞೲೞೲ

Letter No. 18:-

R.A.F.
No 31. 0.T.U.
Derbert
<u>Nova Scotia</u>

C/- NZ High Commissioner
415 Strand, <u>London ENGLAND</u>
16th August 1941

Dearest Mother,

I have quite a bit of news stored up to tell you, but I will first answer your letters which I received just prior to leaving Halifax.

As you can well imagine, number 22 telling about Colmore certainly gave me a shock. You always get the rough end of the stick, don't you, old bean? Apart from the hardships of poverty and disillusionment that you have had to go through, that tender heart of yours has been wrenched torturously and considerably. Every time I have to go through misery, which isn't often, I know why I have to, but with you it just seems as if God doesn't want you to be happy. I felt sure you were almost set to be happy for a while, with a nice little house, £3 a week and only you and Pete to feed and Colly there to help you and make you forget where I was. He always was rather an enigma of a man, but this time he is more than a mystery. He must have had pretty solid reasons, I suppose, and I cannot believe he is so black-hearted as not to realise the heartbreak he has caused you, nor to suffer a little over it himself. However, I cannot forgive him for the manner and the time at which he did it. If it was something he had to do, I know he could have made it easier for you. Owing to my little bit of loneliness, I sure can feel for you at this time, and know the torture that you must have gone through.

Alone - even the word sounds cruel.

So far, all men have failed you and I remain a question mark. I feel because I am so much a part of you, I feel that these men have failed me as well, and I, like you, ask the question, "are all men lice"!?

There are just two men left whom I have great faith in, and if they don't make you happy now and always, I think it would be nice to see Christ come down and mop up the world. They will give you many disappointments, but if they ever really fail you- God help them - They are Dem and Pete. Yes, they are young and quite often difficult, but I look to them because I am weak and far from home, and we three are all you have, my dearest.

I have just read Colmore's letter again and although it tells me I feel the fineness of the man, but something inside says, "Why why why??" Conscience reasons - Blah Blah?!! Perhaps Lil had found out and threatened to drag about 60 people through a divorce court hearing.

I think that must be the answer, but me thinks t'would have been a better way. I bet you still love each other and if old Lil falls over a cliff tomorrow - take him back sweetest. I have nothing against Mrs. Williams, I just feel that she has spoilt a love that was too perfect to last even after 12 years.

You probably think I am sticking up for Colly and hate me for it, but I cannot immediately turn round and hate a man when I have loved and respected for years no matter what he does. I suppose you have thought the whole thing over a million times, but did you ever think of an answer to the episode of passing you on the kerb, when he seemingly looked right at you. Do you think that perhaps he was dying to stop, that he was even looking out for you, but could not bear the thought of standing there talking a whole lot of formal bunk with a third party, when all the time he would be dying to take you in his arms. My proposed answers to your love problem run like cheap love stories, but I am trying to take away some of your bitterness and you'll admit everything I've said is possible. There MUST be someone else for you, Mother. Perhaps someone who will give you all you've wanted for years as well as love. If not, remember there are still Three who love you dearly. - KEEP SMILING!-

"The moving finger writes; and, having writ, moves on";
"nor all thy pity, nor wit shall lure it back to cancel half a line,
Nor all their tears wash out a word of it"
"Ah Love! Would thou and I wish with Fate conspire.
To grasp this sorry theme of things entire
would we not shatter it to bits and then remove it
Nearer to the Heart's desire!?"

After that extra two weeks at Rivers, I passed the exams with flying colours. Of course, as soon as we left Rivers - Jeff and I headed straight for London, Ontario, as fast as we could go - We managed to scrounge five days' final leave and had a really wonderful time. It wasn't a final leave like the one at home - nothing can surpass the wonderful time I had in those two weeks. At London, most of the time was spent swimming, dancing and sleeping, I managed to work in a couple of lovely rides as well. As usual the whole family was wonderful to us and when we left, we gave them a chiming clock.

On the way to Halifax, we passed through Montreal, which was very nice, but which we did not see very much of. Alf wrote to me at London (Ont) and told me all about it, as I'm enclosing his letter. My news of necessity must become rather hazy here because Halifax is a place of military secrets. We were there about three days when a draft was called, which took all the New Zealand observers, except me. All our original flight, incidentally, including Alf, had left the day before we arrived. Anyway, this draft I spoke of, was sent to here for operational training before flying the Atlantic in a Hudson. The next day they grabbed me and sent me up too. The reason for the delay was because they had me mixed up with another chap who had syphilis. I didn't want to come here. I wanted to get to England as soon as poss and apart from that, I had a lovely girl in Halifax.

After a week's training here, I will be navigating a bomber across to England. That means that in about a week, I'll be seeing Peggy and son or daughter? By the way, how's my Godson?

When we were in London (Ont), I sent you some stockings and photos. I haven't received those things you sent me yet, but they should be here any day.

I've only received two letters from you so far this time, but there must be more on the way.

When I'm in England, I'd love you to send me some cigs and dark chocolate, I believe they're scarce over there and I darn near live on them sometimes.

I nearly forgot to tell you - We live in a Sergeant's mess here and are treated as our rank should be. (I know arrogance again) - We have tablecloths and are waited on at the table and even when the grub is lousy, you can eat it because once more, you live like a human being.

We sleep in rooms now, as well - four to a room, all the irks stand to attention and call me "Sergeant" when I speak to them. Of course, it is only the right thing to do, but sometimes I want to laugh when I think of men having to be polite and do what a kid like me tells them.

It will be funnier still, when I get a commission. I hope to get it soon after arriving in England, but I'm afraid it is just a hope.

Well Darling, that's all. Keep writing, smiling and Chin up - Not even the reasons that separate us are as great as my love for you, Dearest Mother.

      Yours

        Teggy XXX

ೋღೋ

Letter 19:-   Dated 4th of September 1941

On the Envelope is the art work letterhead and logo of HOTEL LA FAYETTE Buffalo, N.Y. (inside is a P.S. Don't let the envelope fool you)
Postage stamp Sept Montreal;-

Dearest Mother,

Well I'm certainly behind schedule arn't I? Here it is the fourth of September and not over there yet. However, it won't be long now because I'm waiting here in Montreal for them to call me, and any day now, I'll be flying across.

When I get there, I'm almost sure to be posted to the most coveted branch of the service, the Coastal Command, and will either be flying in Lockheed Hudsons or Bristol Blenheims. Right now, strangely enough, I'm living a life of luxury. The Air Force brings us here and gives us an extra $3 a day and tells us to live in Montreal until they want us. I'm staying at the YMCA and my living only costs about $2 a day - so I'm on a win. I'm glad things have turned out this way because I would have missed Montreal. Did I say I didn't think much of it? Why, I love it! Perhaps it is because I have never been in a really big city before, but there is something about Montreal that captures the imagination. Although it is rife with a lot of sin - a lot of the sin is covered up with Beauty, it is a city that really lives.

I've been here a week now and have seen and done a lot, so I will start from the beginning and tell you about the things I've come into contact with.

We left Debert last Wednesday, and very sadly, Jeff was left behind because of a cut he got while playing football. Now, as far as friends in the Air Force go, I am completely alone - I get lonely sometimes, but I have a girlfriend here and as you can well imagine that makes quite a difference. I met her on the train coming down from Debert and I've seen her every day but one, since. There is a lot against the girl, but there is a lot in her favour too. Without her, I think Montreal would have been a little overawing and I would have been a very lonely little boy. It is marvellous to have someone to show you around, but apart from that, I like her very much and I've made up for lost time on kisses and cuddles that I missed with Diana the beautiful, the sweet, but still Diana the cold. Ever since I've been in Canada, almost, I've been going with her and I've only kissed her about three times, so that my sexual energies and affectionate nature have been terribly pent up. With this girl I am at least allowed to be affectionate, although I've been told off a couple of times already, for being "Fresh".

The above might sound a bit silly to you but when I cease to tell you about such things - You'll know I have grown up. My sexual urges always were a problem, but only once have I slipped at not keeping them under control. Since leaving home I've been a good boy always. Kit has an idea what I was like and she said once how she was afraid for me with the "harpies" of London. Well she can forget her fears though and you can forget yours too. The thought of prostitutes always did and always will disgust me. Montreal is also lately lousy with them and twice when I've been with chaps in a French part of the city, we have been accosted by men acting as agents for brothels. I think the French must be about the dirtiest minded people in the world. The boys have told me about things they've seen here in Montreal that I couldn't even tell you about.

To get back to my story- Veronica Smith (that is her name) - Vicky for short, is rather a nice-looking girl with chestnut or auburn (NOT GINGER) hair, gray eyes and a positive dream of a figure. She has quite a good job in a cake decorating place, and must get a pretty good screw because she dresses lavishly. Finally, she is a Roman Catholic and just a bit common - her speech is really amusing sometimes. She is English, but from the time she was very small, she went to a French school. Consequently, she speaks better French than she does English. She very often speaks an English sentence with a French construction.

I have learnt a bit about French from her and as far as pronunciation goes, I might as well have not learnt Any French at school, all because it is all just so different.

When we arrived here last Thursday, I booked in with one of the boys at the Ford Hotel (one of the Biggest). That night, the city was just beginning to fill up for three good reasons. Firstly, thousands of American tourists come here every week-end anyway, secondly, the Duke of Kent was here, and thirdly, it was Labour weekend. I felt positively stinko after the 22-hour train trip, but Paddy (the chap I was with) insisted that I have a shower, a brandy and a feed. While we were having the Brandy, we met a very interesting New Zealander who had been for about the last five years studying in the States, and is now in Montreal teaching Navigation. Of course, that meant another brandy and I soon felt Tre's Bon. That brings us to the subject of drink, I've never seen anything like Montreal for drink (booze) - As Duncan once said - Nobody seems to get pickled; they just soak in it. You can get any sort of drink you want at cafes, night clubs, and hotels and they never shut till 2AM. After we had had a feed of Chops and eggs at a quite dimly-lit restaurant, Paddy insisted in showing me the "Music Box" in the Mount Royal Hotel.

I thought the "Music Box" was going to be a wonderful nightclub, or something, but it turned out to be just another boozing place - It gets its name from the fact that they have two Nickelodiums there and you can dance if you want to. Most people just drink. Did I ever tell you just what a Nickelodium was or does that puzzle you? It is something that makes money for its owner everywhere and anywhere all over North America.

They have them in just about every shop and restaurant you go into. They are really a slot machine / gramophone - They have a selection of about 20 records usually, and you press a button for the record you want, push in a 5c coin (Nickle) and by some ingenious system of electrical Machinery, your record is selected, put on the turntable and played.

I didn't think much of the "Music Box," so we went home to bed. The next day I was pretty busy going and seeing the Air Force to say, "Hullo I'm now here", fixing up my laundry and getting out of the Ford to come here to the YMCA. That night, I met Vicky however, and we went for a buggy ride up Mount Royal. It was great riding in a buggy. After a car it seemed so peaceful and when you have got nice company and the whole night before you, you don't mind dawdling. Mount Royal is really marvellous (especially at night) - It is really just like One Tree Hill and covers about as much space. The main difference is that Mount Royal is directly behind and above the City - something like Albert Park is to Auckland. There are roads all over the mountain, but only buggies and horses are allowed to use them. Everywhere there are rocks and trees (maple trees mostly) and winding in and out through the trees, are bridle paths and here and there are nice grassy patches and garden seats. About halfway up the mountain, there is an artificial lake where everyone skates in the winter. Near the lake is a ski shute where they have ski jumps like you often see in the pictures, a bit further up is a lovely garden that has flower beds laid out in the shape of a Maple Leaf and a Union Jack. and other similar things.

Right at the top of the Mountain is a place called the Chalet. It is really just a Tea Kiosk, but in another sense, it is a huge hall. It is Bigger than the Pirate Ship (on Milford Beach Reserve). It is used mainly as a restaurant, but is also used for big receptions and concerts etc. In front of it there is a large semi-circle of asphalt, the front of which is stopped by a very steep drop. From here you can see all the main part of the city, and the river and its big bridges. Montreal is an Island - the St. Lawrence goes right round it. I nearly forgot to mention- right on the very top of Mount Royal is a huge illuminated cross that stands about 150 feet high. When we came down the mount it was still rather early, so Vicky took me to see La Fontaine Parc (Fountain Park) where there is the most beautiful lighted fountain I've seen. It not only changes colour but it changes shape too and is really lovely. Here again is another artificial lake that you can skate on in the winter and go boating on in the summer. I'm afraid we much preferred to watch the fountain.

On Saturday, I just messed around most of the day and went to the pictures. In the evening, Vicky had to go out with her steady, so I had an early night.

On Sunday, Vicky took me to see the shrine of St. Joseph - Get settled ('cos this is going to take quite a bit of describing). Before I get going, I must say a bit about Catholicism and what it is like in Montreal. About 92% of Montreal's population (1¾ million) are Roman Catholics and there must be dozens of huge churches here. From Debert to here, nearly all the way was through the province of Quebec and I was positively amazed by the fact that even the very small towns had huge churches that would grace big cities. Strangely too, there always seemed to be a priest hanging around somewhere in all these little places. At one place we stopped, there was a priest and two nuns on the station, and I said, "Looks as if the priest has come to the station to kiss the nuns goodbye". I'm afraid Vicky didn't appreciate my wise crack and was almost offended. She isn't a terribly ardent Catholic, but she is ardent enough to go to a special service every Tuesday night because she is praying for something. When she gets it, she stops going to the special service and that's that.(!???)

For the simple reason, I suppose, that there are so many Catholics in Montreal, Sunday here is really just like any other day. Of course, most of the shops shut, but picture theatres and places of amusement do more business on a Sunday than any other day.

Well now, about the Shrine of St. Joseph. It is a HUGE CHURCH on one of the most commanding positions in Montreal. It was started by a man called Brother André who was a faith healer. Inside the church in one corner, there are piles and piles of king sticks and crutches left there by people who had come to this man and had been healed. They started building the shrine about 20 yrs ago and it is far from completed yet. The idea is that as they get more money more church is built on. The money does not come from the usual Roman Catholic channels, but it comes from anyone and everyone who wants to contribute to the building of the Shrine. Pilgrims from all over the world come to the shrine and a lot of money comes from them. As I said before, the shrine is very high up and leading up to it are literally hundreds of steps. Even when you get to it the steps go on up further almost to the top of the building. It is deemed a very wonderful thing and is supposed to show greater faith if one starts from the bottom of these steps and goes slowly up, kneeling on each and every step to say a prayer. The day we were there - there were hundreds of people of all class and ages doing just this. The most amazing sight of all, was little kids with their rosaries going slowly from one step to the next saying their prayers.

There were thousands of people about the shrine and Vicky informed me that about ¼ of them were American Tourists. They even have guides there to show them around, which I think is sacrilegious. But of course, the Roman Catholics are different. It seemed terribly weird when we went inside, because a lot of people were kneeling in the pews, while there were also crowds of sight seers wandering in and out and all over the place, and making a hell of a row. The main part of the church is built now, but about halfway up, a floor has been built in and above that (on the inside), everything is just bare rough concrete. This top part is huge and here you can see right up inside the huge dome. When all this upper part is completed, they will take out the middle floor and have a huge Church like Westminster Abby or Notre Dame.

A few years ago, Brother André died, and they kept his body in the church for a while, for people to come and have a look at him. Vicky tells me how for days, thousands of people absolutely swarmed up there to have a look at him. She went one night after work and stood in the crush for three hours, just so she could have a peek. Now he is buried in the church and people stream past his grave kneeling, and crossing themselves.

While we were there, they had a service on the slopes outside the church. The sermon was in French and of course, the service was in Latin, so I was rather bored, but this really amazed me. A bishop and his attendants rolled up in a big car, then as the Bishop walked through the crowds, he held up one hand and waved it from side to side, blessing the people. Everybody looked at him with awe, and as he passed, they would step back, fall on one knee and cross themselves. I don't want to seem blasphemous, but honestly, you would have thought the man was Christ Himself.

Immediately, across the road from the shrine, is a wax museum and this is where we went next. They take you down through dark tunnels, and in little sort of cubicles on each side, are scenes with wax figures in them. The figures are so natural as to be almost uncanny. If you look at some of the figures long enough, you can almost imagine that their lips are moving. Many different scenes are depicted, including biblical, ancient and modern history. There is also a wax figure of the Late Brother André and one of the present King in the uniform of Admiral of the Fleet. The most wonderful scene of all, is the one of the Pope and two Bishops.

Apart from the perfection of facial expressions, these figures are dressed in exact duplicate of their ceremonial robes, and the whole scene is valued at thousands of dollars.

After that, we decided we would go and see Belmont Park, which is Montreal's amusement park and is just like what I should imagine Luna Park was like. On the way there we passed through a residential suburb and I've never seen anything like the number of apartment houses there were. Nearly all modern ones too. I think about half the population must live in apartments. After we'd walked a wee way, we took a tram and that brings me to another interesting subject. They are a bit smaller than our trams but bigger than the Wellington ones. They have padded seats covered with a sort of fibre - half the tram seats are two by two and the other half there is just a long seat on either side. Smoking on trams isn't allowed at all and it simply isn't done to give up your seat to a lady, unless she's aged. Most of them have only a driver who punches your ticket when you get in, but some of the older ones have a conductor at the back so you get in at the back - all public transport vehicles in this country have a wizard system of doors. The driver or conductor just pushes a button and the doors open and a step goes down. The cost of travel in Montreal is very little - for 7c you can go from one end of the city to the other or in short, you can ride all day long on the trams.

It just simply means that no matter how far you have to go, it will only cost you 7c. If you have to change trams, they give you a transfer which you have to use within an hour. Near Belmont Park the scenery was quite countrified, and the tramway lines ran along a place by themselves like a miniature railway. It was quite close to some big Highway heading out of the city and all along this

Highway for about two miles there were dozens of little restaurants never more than about 200yds apart.

Drizzly rain rather spoilt our visit to Belmont Park, but we had a good look around all the same. It is really in a lovely spot right on the St. Lawrence river. You could have just about any sort of thrill you wanted there including dancing few drinking and rides in speed boats - on Sunday too, it was such darn miserable weather that we didn't stay long and so we tootled off home to bed ~ she to hers and me to mine.

The next day was Labour day as I slept nearly all the morning, and in the afternoon, I met Vicky and we went for a walk up the mountain. We stayed there nearly all the afternoon then we visited my favourite drinking place which is the most wonderful little dream of a place imaginable.

It is like a cafe really, but you can't eat there, You just drink. All the tables and chairs are made of chromium tubing and at one end is a very modernistic bar all glittering with glass and mirrors and chromium. The room is very dimly lit by concealed lights and as there are always only a few people there it is wonderfully peaceful and serene.

Later on, that evening, we decided that we'd go slumming - so we went and had a look at Chinatown and the old French quarter. You see some rear sights among the French, but I think the queerest is men wearing rouge

and lipstick. They have surprisingly few beggars in Montreal but they

do have old men who play barrel organs. On Tuesday I had nothing much

to do so I went and saw another picture show. Vicky had a couple of coupons for photos, so she insisted that I go with her that evening and have mine taken. We haven't seen the proofs yet but here's hoping. If they are at all respectable, I'll send you a couple. The last two or three

days I haven't done anything interesting at all much, so I think I'll close now.

About three weeks ago I received three letters from you and that is all the mail I have had in two months. I think it has all been sent on

to England. Well I hope you enjoy this wordy epistle old bean cos It's taken about two days to write.

Love to everybody and Tons for yourself.

   x   x

    x   x   FOR VICTORY

      x   x

       x

        Teg.

Letter no. 20:-   10th September 1941,
still waiting in Montreal Y.M.C.A CANADA

Dear Most Beloved in all the World,

I've been thinking about you a lot today so I thought it would be a good idea to write to you.

I still like Montreal as much as ever, but the most wonderful city in the world would become boring with no money and nothing to do. I've been here two weeks today, and believe you me, after two weeks of nothing to do and all day to do it in, becomes very tiring - especially with a war on. Our bunch ought to be in it by now and here's me sitting on my ass all day. I mentioned this before, but in case you didn't get the letter, I'll say it again. Send fags and chocolate to England, PLEASE - also if you haven't already done so and you can afford it.

I bet Peggy would appreciate a parcel of things that are impossible to get over there now.

I don't know whether New Zealanders realize it - I know Canadians don't and I'm only beginning to myself, but the lack of everyday commodities in England is deplorable. These Canadians make me mad. All they do is skite about their war effort and comparing it with Australia or New Zealand (populations considered) it's sweet Fanny Adams. I read in the Herald how the people of Auckland were almost sucked dry by the street collections. I'll have to admit that recently, Canadians bought millions of dollars' worth of war bonds, but just the same they haven't given half as much as they could. Another thing that burns me up is the thought of poor little New Zealand, almost bled to death of her man-power while here there must be millions of fit men who are just too indifferent about the whole thing to join up. They go around wearing "v" for Victory badges, but at the same time they crawl to Americans whom they want to win their war for them. You've probably heard a lot about Canada's war effort and will discount a lot of the above, but my argument is that she's not doing half what she could be doing. Gee, I'm proud to be a New Zealander. I think her greatness lies in her smallness and if she was any bigger or nearer to civilisation, she would not be so great. I think New Zealand is the greatest democracy in the world today. There are no overly excessive 'really rich' - and no one is left starving. People seem more equal and tolerant. I never was a labourite - I might never be, but if you saw the hours and the lousy pay and especially some of the lousy jobs people have here, you might still not say you like Labour, but by jingo's you would say that their ideas were for Good.

New Zealanders seem more proud and happy than most other people. I must say it soulds like I'm homesick, doesn't it? Well, I am a little, but now it's different.

I don't think I'll ever feel again, as I did for those first few tortuous weeks after leaving you and home. I have been homesick again since, occasionally, but its never been the same. I am too young to let anything worry me for too long and that is my greatest asset. I have become hardened to the world and I'm becoming more so every day. When I left home, the world seemed a very big place, but it's getting smaller. To wise and experienced men, the world must seem very small because it is the individual that is great, not the world. Also, it is the abstract things that are great (LOVE, PEACE, BEAUTY - and sadly, Hate). My great loves now are poetry and of course, music. I know, now that I have reached this age, that I should have been an artist of some sort, but artists won't win the war and anyway who knows? I still might be an artist some day - A poet or a musician? Perhaps a philosophic crank?! Or a writer of cheap love stories. Oh, by the way, though I still like the company of a woman now and again. Sick of listening to love tripe? O.K. sorry - I'll go to bed now. Are your two younger sons around? If so, give them both one of your most luscious beautiful hugs and kisses for me. I love you three so much it hurts. Just in passing, my darling Mother, how is your heart holding up now? All patched up again? I hope those two little men I put in charge of you aren't letting you down - If they are, take back those kisses and hugs. Remember, keep that chin held high - That's right -

Big Smiles ?!

 Goodnight Mother
  Yours Lovingly
   Teg

CHAPTER SEVEN –
ENGLAND AT LAST!

Letter 21:-

NOW IN ENGLAND At Russell's Water Farm
C/- NZ High Commissioner 415 Strand,
London ENGLAND
26th September 1941,

Dearest Mother (My Best Girl),

Well here I am at last in good Old England, with her blackouts and air raids - but still, with her Beauty- to start with - although I can't tell you anything about the flight - I must say that it was the most enjoyable flight I've had yet. Most of the way we were at 18000 and had to use oxygen - It took us 10hrs 50mins. On arrival, we were sent to a personnel recruiting centre where we stayed a couple of days, and from there we were given ten days' leave.

Of course, I immediately set course for Russell's Water Farm. I arrived in Henley at about 7pm and as the blackout was well on the way, I stayed at a pub for the night. The next morning, I was so impatient to see Peggy and young Duncan John Barrington McArthur that instead of waiting for a bus, I paid 10bob to come out here in a taxi. They are marvellous people - Peggy is a most attractive girl. Perhaps you have a photo of her - but she takes a lousy photo anyway and I rather feel she needs describing. She has most unusual hair that sweeps back from her forehead in graceful sort of curls. In colour it is mostly dark brown with a reddish tinge, but in the front, there are wide patches of corn-coloured hair that gives her an outstanding appearance. She has a high forehead with very beautiful eyes of a sort of speckly mossy green colour. She has a pert little nose (a bit turned up), a strong nicely shaped mouth and rather small beautifully white teeth. Now despite the advent of the baby, her figure is lovely - she is about your height and just nicely slim with, as Dunc has mentioned, very dainty little feet on the end of not particularly startling legs - she is terribly modern and simply adores anything modern and mechanical - aeroplanes, cars, etc., etc., just like Dunc. She has a wonderful nature and makes a great mother. Finally, she loves her husband and son absolutely and completely.

DREAMING OF THEE

Mrs. Phipps, or Dora as we all call her, is the dearest thing, who seems to work all day long and put up with the inconsistencies of her household with never a murmur - like a lot of mothers I know, she has always had to struggle, but by her struggling she has managed to give her children a good education. Just as we knew nothing about Peggy and her family when the two were married, so Dora knew nothing about Duncan or his family. You can realise it was a bit tough on her, but now she loves Duncan as much as we all do. In fact, everybody I've met about here seems to adore Duncan and because I'm his nephew and remind everyone so much of him, they have taken me to their hearts without question. There isn't much I can say about the rest of the family. There is the son, John (Peggy's brother) who is married, about 30ish and works on the farm. He lives along the road somewhere and is in the Home Guard - The old man is a typical old English Farmer - He has travelled extensively and is very well read, but nevertheless just the Old Farmer.

As you see, the Phipps are just a hard-working family - really just like any of us. They are really marvellous people though - The sort of people that make England – England.

I don't think Dunc has told you anything about them before - So I do hope I haven't been telling tales or anything. Now we come to the most interesting person of the whole household: Our new wee arrival, Dunc's son:- Duncan John Barrington McArthur. Of course, I don't know much about babies, but I'm quite sure he is the most wonderful child I've ever seen, I'm terribly envious - I wish he was mine - I'd like to steal him. The likeness to Duncan is absolutely striking. The only thing he has escaped is Duncan's cruel mouth. He has his eyes, and forehead, nose, jaw, body and even Cull's big feet. The thing that amazes me most about him, is his body. It's very long and beautifully proportioned; such a wonderful deep perfect little chest I never saw in all my life. He is a terribly good child. He never cries at night and not much in the daytime either. He is always smiling, and the smile is like Cull's, amazingly so.

Now a word about your big brother. Of course, by now you have heard about his being shot down on his 49th raid. He has done 35 major raids over Germany and now 49 in the Middle East. I don't know just how bad his injuries were, but I'm hoping that it has been enough for them to take him off operations for good. I reckon he has done his share. I don't know whether he'll ever knuckle down to being an instructor, but he will have to sooner or later. He is due back from the East about the beginning of November. He is a real hero and from things Peggy has told me, he should have more than the D.F.C. It is a fact that he should be a Flight-Lieut. and should have a bar to his D.F.C. He is on his way back from the East and should be here sometime in November.

It was tough on Peggy - his being away when Barry was born. Just three weeks before he arrived, she received a cable to say that Duncan was indeed missing - Of course the same day another one to say he was safe, but naturally it took a while to get over the shock. Poor Girl, so far, her married life hasn't been all beer and skittles. When Dunc used to go over Germany every other night, she said she never slept for six months. Since he has been East, it hasn't been quite as bad - but you know what a terrible correspondent he is, and she very rarely hears from him. Of course, I'm dying to see him - but I'm rather afraid he is going to be a very different person to the 19-year-old P/O who left New Zealand.

I've been having a wonderful restful time here- doing very little other than sleeping and eating. Last Saturday night, Peg and I went to a dance and following my usual habit, I met a very nice girl. Blonde hair and blue eyes. The strange thing about it is that her name is Diana. I think that my fate will definitely be a Diana or failing that, my first daughter will be a Diana.

Yesterday I went to London (England) which I am not particularly impressed with, and collected some mail which was very disappointing. Only one letter from you - No 27 (Airmail)- ? Where the hell the rest are, and the parcel - I just can't imagine, but I guess they'll turn up sooner or later. I also received a pair of socks and a Tiki from Aroha - that was all the New Zealand mail - Most disappointing. Don't worry about mail though, Sweets. Just keep writing. Some will probably take ages to get here and some will probably be lost, but I can bear it. I did not realize you were so hard up - So don't bother to send any of us anything right now - What I said about Peg was only a suggestion, and as far as I'm concerned, I really only want cigarettes and as they're cheap as blazes in Canada I can get them from Kit.

Remember the Greenstone talisman we sent to Cull? Well, he is terribly superstitious about it and absolutely will not fly without it.

When I arrived home from London, there was a memorandum from the R.A.F. telling me to report to my operational training unit. Well I'm there now and about the only thing I like here is the WAAFS. There are some really nice girls here, but to be quite honest, I don't really like women in uniform. It really does take away their femininity and on the whole, I think it is most unbecoming. Quite apart from the uniforms though, it makes one feel very proud to see how British women are helping their country. Believe you me, there is nothing glamorous about being in these Women's Services. I think WAAF discipline is every bit as tough as the R.A.F. and most of the jobs they have to do are pretty lousy.

There isn't much I can tell you about this station, because although I could damn near write a book about it, yes, with all the exciting details, I think it is quite possible that our great friend Mr. Censor might object. As far as not liking the place goes, I never did like new stations, and this being the first R.A.F. station, makes it worse. However, I think I will probably like it very much after a while. The most wonderful thing about this posting is that I am again among friends.

Eight of my original course are here, and with them is dear old Alf, Doug and Bill.

I believe Jeff has now arrived in the country, but I rather doubt if he will come here, worst luck.

The most important bit of news I can give you now, is that all hopes of the Coastal Command must of necessity be dashed. I am going on the same type of Aircraft as Duncan, and will be also playing his game, only of course in a different capacity. The aforementioned aircraft are absolute peaches and, incidentally are about the safest bombers there are.

From now on my letters will be a bit shorter - because my life is after all the air force, and there really isn't much I can tell you about that. However, I will no doubt do my best to keep up the supply even if they are short.

Give my love to my two fine brothers - and of course lots of love to the most wonderful woman in the world. When I meet one half as nice, I'll marry her, but that is many moons away now.

Love Teg.

₧₧₧

Letter 22:-

NZ High Commissioner 415 Strand
LOWDOWN, ENGLAND
15th October 1941

Sweetest Sweetheart (Mother) -

I've got sweet Fanny Adams to write about, but I rather feel that I should get going on this as more or less one of those "keep in touch" letters that we used to talk about.

We got the first weekend off here, so I ripped smartly back to Henley-on-Thames. On the Saturday night, Peg and I went to a dance and there I met Teddy Cameron's widow. You remember the nice boy with the big brown eyes, who showed us his pretty red rose. The point is, his widow is Peg's best friend and is positively a beautiful girl. A real English Rose. Apart from the dance on the Saturday night, the weekend was uneventful.

The following week we started work in earnest and since, have been on lectures for eight hours a day with only Sundays off. This week we have an exam and after that we spend all our time flying. Alf says he enjoys flying immensely here, but believe me, navigating in this country isn't exactly child's play. This course is only six weeks - so when you get this letter, I should have reached another of my goals - namely to get going on operations.

Do you remember an incident about a month ago, when a draft of empire airmen walked off the ship they were detailed to, at an East Canadian port? Well, Jeff was one of them and well, he is being kept at the personnel recruiting depot on ground duties with a reduction of pay. Happily, this will not be permanent, but it is particularly annoying because but for all that sticky business he would now be here. Do you remember the photo of me that appeared in the Star with my little message? I saw it the other day and I hardly remember saying all that.

The other day, I received a cable signed Simons Colmore. Do I dare to hope that you have come together again - but I rather feel the idea is a little fantastic. I was glad to hear you had received my parcels. Incidentally, I think they will be the last, because there is nothing I can send you from here, and while I think of it, a Happy Xmas and all the Best for 1942 to all of you over there.

I am enjoying England immensely and not working too hard. I must finish now because "lights out" is soon, so Toodle-oo.

Love to my brothers and heaps of love to you, my Sweet.

    Yours,

      Teggy

        xxxXXXxxx

♨♨

Letter 23:-

New Zealand High Comissioner,
415 Strand London ENGLAND
28th October 1941

Dearest Mother of Mine,

Since arriving in England, I have been doing very well with letters from New Zealand. Of course, they have all been very old, but that is not surprising as they all have followed me across Canada. They have nearly all been in to the numerous letters I wrote from Jarvis, which was the biggest letter writing phase I've ever had. I've had lots of letters from Dem and Pete, which I appreciate very much. It might interest you to know that you (of course) wrote the most, Dem next, and Pete next - so I think perhaps you three love me more than just a wee bit. From you, I have up to 28. So I think, as I haven't much else to talk about, I'll proceed to answer them.

Number 24 - I was very pleased to hear you had received the first parcel of photos and appreciated them so much. I also hope you have received all the ones I've sent since, especially the big river scene, which I am very proud of. You said you liked the one of me in Derek's uniform, well I'm glad you do because I wear air force battle dress now. The only difference with it, is that we wear a collar and tie and leave the neck of the blouse undone. Excuse my French, but I think it's bloody bad luck that your gloves didn't fit. Actually, we have been pretty lucky though because I think just about everything else has been O.K.?

I forgot what my No.11 letter was about, so I don't know why it was so marvellous and as for my ever being a journalist – Darling, you <u>are Dreaming</u>?! As far as bringing in humour goes, I don't know why, but I seem to have lost the knack. I am glad Herdsons appreciated their letter and I will try and write to them again. Do you know I got a letter from Peter H the other day. Ghee, that kid's clever - came top of standard 2. I hear our Pete is doing lots better also. Strikes me we are a pretty clever family all round.

I'm afraid there isn't much to comment on in No.25, except that Dem came 2nd in the half yearly exam, which endorses my remark above. In No.25, you mentioned Colly again - I have made comments before about the affair and now thinking it over, I don't know that I even meant what I said. When I first heard about it, it was my one desire to comfort you and to try and make you feel NOT too BITTER and disillusioned. For once I think my pen failed me miserably and it was because I had no clear thoughts about the matter. Here I must defend my lack of understanding by the realisation of the fact of my lack of experience. Some day when I am older and have had more experience, I'll write you an epilogue about it.

Now in Number 26.,you talk about having difficulty in knowing what to send me. In Canada, there was very little you could send me, but I might say now, anything (and I mean *anything* is appreciated). I don't want you to go spending a lot of money on me, but if you do want to send things, here are some suggestions. Eats of all descriptions, but if tinned, something that you can eat straight from the tin. Chocolates, cakes, biscuits plus fags and tobacco - I don't want you to get the idea I'm starving or anything because we get excellent meals, but it doesn't alter the fact that every chance I get, I'm eating and to get extra snacks is pretty hard. Most men's necessities aren't exactly scarce, but they aren't exactly easy to get, so anything you would like to send in the way of small clothes, including slippers, ties etc., would also be appreciated. Other things, while I think of them, are razor blades and chewing gum.

I will write to Wattie if I can find time, but when I'm going to find time is hard to know. The advent of the new law seems to have been quite a big think - Pete gave me the low down (very low down) on who was the first to do this and that, etc. If I remember correctly, Pete was the first to do "that," wasn't he? It must have been fun pushing Lena over ~ I only wish I'd been there to help you, because I used to itch to give her a heave, every time I went near her.

You said in No28, how you had become quite a society lass. I think that explains why I have been receiving so much attention from the Milford Women War Workers. You knew I had a parcel from them in Canada, didn't you? Well the other day I received a pair of soxs and a pair of mittens from them - both were very welcome and if you happen to know any of them, please convey a VERY BIG Thank You from me to them .....

BIG BREAK - WELL now: …

It is quite three days since I was at this letter, and in the interim, I have received another letter from you - No 23 plus a letter from someone else in Milford. The other letter was from Nancy Fenton, who has had me allotted to her to write letters and send parcels to, by the Milford Women's War Workers. It's marvellous actually, but I wish I knew whether she is a Miss or a Mrs. or young or old, or just what? However, I'll damn soon find out?! I have also received a letter from good old DUNCAN - He said very little as usual except that he has been given a job flying for Commercial Airways, and that he hopes to return to New Zealand very soon. He isn't banking on it, so don't you either!! It seems it is only a HOPE!

I was very gratified to hear you speak of warm weather in your last letter because all previous ones had been full of moans about the cold. I might tell you, Love, that England is BLOODY COLD - worse than Canada. It's a cold that sort of chews at you - Again in letter No 32, comes the subject of Eats - Oh no, please don't send me butter - we get all the "margie" (it is called here) we can eat and I can hardly tell the difference from the real stuff either. Jeff hauled out a tin of coffee and milk tonight and we have been guzzling it all evening. It's the easiest thing in the world to prepare and is very handy, just so you know! Another thing mentioned in No 32, was air mail. the 9pence is a waste of time and 6/6 is far too dear, so please don't bother about it, Sweet. We'll trust the Navy to keep us in contact. While we are still on the subject of mail and parcels, etc., etc., I might mention I received a parcel of tinned stuff from Granddad the other day. In case I don't get around to it - Please thank him and also Grannie for the other things you bought with her money, and which I hope to see soon.

DREAMING OF THEE

I've finished all your letters now, so here's some news. The most interesting thing that has happened lately, is that Jeff has caught up with me again and I am no longer the lonely little boy I was.

As far as the R.A.F. goes - It still gives me a pain in the neck, but things are moving fast and I'm moving with them. I am now in a crew and flying in Wimpys - believe me you - It's some crew- 3 of us are New Zealanders, there is an Aussie and a Scotchman and an Englishman.

All of us are Sergeants - In three weeks I will finally be on OPS and I will at last be able to do my Whack to keep Your's, my Brother's and the other people I love, some security - What it is to HELP to jam the cogs of the very Brutal Nazi machine.

As far as the social guide of my life goes, it will not surprise you to know that I am having a romance with a girl in the nearest town.

A few days ago, I got a black eye for my trouble to try and protect her from a very offensive Canadian. So now naturally, I am "quids in" - and so she is knitting me a pull over (keeping warm - ah what - smart work - ah What!?)

Peggy and I correspond regularly, and the latest is that Barry is cutting his first tooth.

The last interesting thing, is that I have bought myself a new Bike Hotieha cha!

I received an old cable from you t'other day saying "No news of you for some time, please telegraph" - I disregarded it because you must have heard from me quite a bit since you sent it.

Well I had better move off smartly to bed now - so my love Bon-Sour.

Don't forget, Sweet, I love you with all my heart

(It is a love that will go down in history)

XXxxxx (million ssss of e'm)

TEG

ॐ

ENGLAND AT LAST!

Letter No. 24:- *(actually, this letter was numbered 25, as it was received after the next letter, but I am placing them in chronological order for readability's sake.)*

Somewhere in England
27th November 1941

Hullo Darling Mother,

I am definitely a louse as Pete would say - No I haven't written you for ages, but I'm going to try and clear myself by sending this letter airmail. I'm also enclosing a photo of myself in battledress, which I hope meets your approval. Trying to think up news is positively stinko and I'm afraid I'm fast losing all my fans because I'm not writing to them. I haven't received any mail for a hell of a long time. The last mail was those three wizard parcels. The cake and chews from you and the kids - That was a wonderful cake, quite one of the best you've shaken out of the old oven yet and the chew was much appreciated too. At the same time, I received the parcel of peaches and cream contributed by Grannie Maugham for which - although you have already done so - I would like you to convey my thanks to her. The third parcel was a Christmas parcel from the girls of Ross and Glendening's millinery workroom and contained all sorts of nice things, including some very sweet messages from my old friends there.

There is very little Air Force News of which I will now divulge. Quite a few weeks ago now, I was put in a Crew - and Boy Oh boy, what a crew we are! Two New Zealand pilots, an English front gunner, An Aussie wireless operator, a Scotch rear gunner and of course yours truly Navigator/obs :- So far, every flight we have done has been most successful and I can only hope that they will continue to be so. When we have finished here, we will have a further short course at another OTU, then we will be flying out to the Middle East.

Actually, we are behind schedule owing mainly to the bad weather and we were all becoming a little "Cheesed off." Just in passing, I might mention that for the first time since I've been in the Air Force - I am now satisfied with my job and more efficient at it. Another reason possibly, is the realisation of my responsibility as a navigator. I feel the crew depends on me to take them there and bring them back - which isn't really true because we always have our K/Op and his infernal wireless set, which I hate the sight of- That might all sound a little conceited, but it is a great change from having a navigator's inferiority complex, just hating to "get airborne", and always wishing I was a Pilot. I would still very much like to learn to fly- but I have no desire left to be a pilot. It is not till one starts to fly in these big kites, that one realises what a wizard bloke a pilot has to be. If my self-confidence remains and I keep hard at it, I do rather hope you will be eventually able to address me Pilot Officer (in about 6 months).

113

Another thing, there has been great controversy lately about giving all Air Crew double wings and I do hope it comes off. I would feel much better with something like this

N for Navigator
O for Ops, etc.

Further up the page I said something about being "Cheesed off" and a little further down, I used the expression "get airborne". These bring me to a very interesting subject: The Air Force "language". "cheesed off" actually means Fed up - it used to be "browned off"!!?? but for some reason or other, they now prefer "cheesed" - now the term "get airborne" means to, of course, get off the ground and flying. The funniest and stupidest expression I've heard, I think, is the one, "you've had it" or as it is usually said, "You've bloody 'ad it Choom." It simply means that if you've missed on something you've wanted, you just have to consider yourself as having had it. This stuff is typical of the English spirit at present - They sure do without a hell of a lot, but they don't moan about it, they just shrug their shoulders and my "we've had it" ~ The old expression "get cracking," is used a lot, but it is sometimes modified to "get weaving" or "get mobile" - There are a lot of other very Air Forcie ones too, like "taking to the silk" and "taking evasive action" etc. etc.

But enough about expressions – let's talk about New Zealanders. In Canada we used to get terribly annoyed by people's ignorance of our dear little country and the things she is doing, but in England we are known and respected for our Wizard war efforts, and New Zealanders are always in the news with Decorations etc. etc., at the present time. Of course, the New Zealanders are top-line - front-page news for their doings in Egypt - I think New Zealanders are the most popular of the Dominions personnel and of course this makes one feel very proud. This station is almost a NZ OTU now, and when I see the new batches of men rolling in, I often wonder when poor little New Zealand will be sucked dry of her manpower.

Sometimes through my dreams, I think that perhaps after I've done my Ops in the Middle East, they might send me in a crew to fly home - and relieve the men on the flash new Hudsons you've got out there. I would have flown 2/3rds around the world and I would be home. The Great longing desires I used to have, to return home are much less now - It seems the wound has healed, and I really have the wanderlust, plus the fact that flying has just got into my blood.

As old Dick Lavender said, after any Wanderings I will thank God that I've got you and New Zealand to go back to and he is definitely right - But I know that I'll have a hell of a job too, at settling down. All the places I've so far been to, seem so full of life. And there seems to be **soape** *(sic)* for everything. To read about London and all the things and places in it, once made you dream - long and wonder - but just recently, I have read a book about London and it seemed funny to think it was only at the time sixty miles away.

A couple of days ago, we got a 24-hour leave - The first leave since I've been here - I made a stupendous effort, and by travelling about 8 hours of the 24, managed to get to Russell's Water and herein lies a sad story. It is mainly my own opinions and I'm not blaming anybody, so don't tell any of the following to Deidre or anybody, because they are my ideas and probably wrong. In short, Duncan's marriage is beginning to look hellishly shaky and I am fast forming the opinion that he is a bigger Kid than I am. Peggy has not heard from him for approximately 3 months, and strangely enough, I have a letter from him written in September. He has not yet acknowledged to Peggy that he is a father - I can not believe that letters from him for three months could or would go astray. What a man?! I really can't understand him. In his letter to me, he gave me quite a lecture on marrying young and very broadly hinted that he regretted his marriage. I have had the same lecture and the same in letters from Peg too, so I ask you, doesn't it look shaky? What gets me, is that even if Duncan is sick of Peg - has he no interest in his son!? Oh mother, what a child. He will be a god among men. When I saw him the other day, of course, he was 9 weeks older and how he has grown. He's much fatter and bigger in every way and his beautiful little face (always smiling) is beginning to look more intelligent - losing the very young baby look. I more than adore him, he's almost an obsession and to be quite honest, he was the real reason I went all that way to Henley in my 24 hours. If only he was mine?!

I have a hell of a feeling I'll never have children because I love them too much. Most of my visit was rather uncomfortable because Dora (Peg's Mother) was trying to pump me about my letter from Duncan, and there is nothing worse than an enraged mother-in-law. I was very non-committal and I told her nothing for fear of putting my foot in it. Any time Duncan was mentioned, there was a moan about him. Of course, it is to be expected in consideration of the way he is carrying on, but I can't stand it and for my next 6 days' leave, I think I will go and see some of Kit's relations. I left Henley that night at about 7.45pm and was going to meet some of the boys in London - I missed the boys somehow, but I had a glimpse of London that positively enthralled me. I was supposed to meet the boys in the Regent Palace Hotel, and oh, what a place the Regent Palace is from the Merky blackout I walked into. A positive Fairyland. The huge vestibule of the Hotel was beautiful, luxurious with big marble pillars and thick carpets. It seemed a combination of Old and New to make a Wizard ensemble. Everybody there seemed to be an officer or was very smartly dressed. As a sergeant, I felt about as big as sixpence and having a sty in my eye even knocked about 4pence off that. There was a lovely office at one side which seemed to be full of beautiful women. It was very awe-inspiring, but I slowly advanced and was made to feel amazingly at ease. It was the girl in the office, she was wonderful ~ possibly reminded me of you. She was no girl; actually, she was about 28 and she spoke so very well. Not London or Oxford Accent, just English as it should be. The boys were not at the Regent Palace and they had no rooms which was probably just as well because it looked awfully dear to me. The charming "off the ice" directed me to the Winston, which was much more in my line. The next morning, I rode on the underground all by myself and quite amazingly, didn't get lost.

Last night, I went to my first fancy dress ball in the local town. Of course, I couldn't go as anything, but it was fun just the same. What was most interesting were the judges. They were lords and ladies and you should have seen Lora Newman's daughter; she was marvellous. I believe that no one who isn't, could look like an aristocrat. Remember what you once said about people being similar to horses and that people of fine breeding were like thoroughbred; I am greatly in favour of that idea, and if I can't get some thoroughbred blood back into our stock, it can't be for want of trying. Remember how I used to argue with you about the subject of breeding? Well, now it is one of the worst bugs. I haven't met any reel high-class people yet, but I will sooner or later. As you can see by the way I've messed about, I had more to tell you than I thought, but the last was written a good while ago.

Well keep the home fires burning, my love, and I'll keep the Eastern Fires burning or (start them when I get there).

Give my love to Dem and Pete

Tons of love Darling

Yours

Teg

"In the made of your love I have found a world so new"

₧₧₧

Letter 25:-

C/- New Zealand Nigh Commissioner,
415 Strand, London – ENGLAND
6th December 1941

My Darling One,

I sent you a 4/6 airmail a few days ago, but I have received parcels and a letter from you since and I want to thank you for them.

Firstly, I have just received a letter (9d Airmail No 33), A parcel containing chocolate, cigarettes and butter, and another parcel containing <u>THE KIWI</u> - A Cake and some chew. I also received a parcel of Cigs and Hankies from Don- thank you a thousand million for all the lovely things, my Sweet, and in particular THANKS FOR THE KIWI! Which was much nicer than I had remembered, and which will always be with me. I seem to have received a lot of parcels from you lately - Please don't get over-enthusiastic and go breaking yourself. Last night about six of us got together around a big fire and guzzled coffee and milk and New Zealand Cake. A Wizard combination - but a hellish dream provoker.

12 December 1941

It's damn chilly and late, but it is six days since I started this letter and as I'm in a very slight letter-writing mood - I thought I'd better finish it off. I've been getting bags of mail lately (not literally, just an old R.A.F. saying) - Quite a few Christmas parcels from :-

Kit, Vicky (Montreal) - and the Milford Women's War workers. The way people look after me from afar is simply devastating - (in a good way of course) - I'm afraid all they get in return is a few pages (or should I say lines) of Bullish such as this ..., doesn't seem enough somehow. Another thing I received recently was a cable from Mavis Herdson - Oh my conscience pricks me a bit in that direction too - I haven't written to them since the first time - however a letter/card ought to bridge the difficulty for a while.

Now about your letter, Sweetheart - two or three things rather shook me. First of all, I feel a bit of a cad for sending you things for so long and now having to stop. However, I know you understand. Secondly, the fact that Dem is now as heavy as myself, is rather a smack in the eye and Pete being taller than Dem is also a bit amazing. In your letters you can talk about as much as you like about those Kids - I just eat it all up. I wish I was with them at this stage of their journey through life, as I feel I could be a great help to them now, whereas I won't be much use later on. I shouldn't worry though; I must have been forgetting that they have the best little mother ever. I read with interest about your joining the Air Force, but why the blazes don't you spell comittee like that instead of like this: committee.

Of course, I don't know whether you are in it or not, but if you are – all the best and don't work too hard. I suppose you are assistant section officer or something by now. The blinking Air Force must be in our blood. I suppose the boys will be joining the Air Training Corp, next?

You finished that letter by saying - It was aweful - but believe you me, it was a beaut?! While I think of it - Yes, I love you too. In fact, I'm thinking of marrying you?! (hahahaha)

As far as news goes - There ain't. NONE!

I am still at the same OTU and doing bags of flying. We have nearly finished though, and will soon be hitting the trail for the Middle East. Duncan is supposed to be back from there now, but evidently isn't because I haven't heard from any of them for quite a while. My Christmas started weeks ago with parcels and should be good on the day because I'm going to a Party at New Zealand House.

I will be thinking of you then, my Love - Well that is all now. May God Bless You and guard you all, my Dearest - I see you too are in the battle zone, but God will guard you.

My love to you and my brothers –

Chins up all of you - pray hard - work hard - but have bags of RELAXING FUN TIMES TOO.

    Yours

        Teggy

P.S. How's my Godson? - please convey Kind thoughts and happy wishes to him and his mother.

This is an image of my Grandmother – then a NZ WAAF and her youngest son, Pete – I believe my Father was still at boarding school when these promotional Airforce photographs were taken to appear in the Herald and Star. Pete and my father were as Terry put in his letters, far too young to enlist, but every boy who had family already fighting were used in some way in the War machine and this image is a prime example.

Young Pete Simons is signing and Gran is sitting with the mock uniform registrar.

AIR CADET UNIFORMS ISSUED: A member of the Air Cadet Corps being fitted with a uniform at the Air Force city headquarters yesterday.

Pete standing in mock uniform of Air Cadet for promotion shots.

CHAPTER EIGHT –
SOMEWHERE IN THE MIDDLE EAST

121

DREAMING OF THEE

First letter
Middle East Command
Letter 1

"B" Flight - 37 Squadron
ROYAL AIR FORCE
MIDDLE EAST COMMAND
20th January 1942,

Dearest Mother,

I have been putting off writing to you for ages - Why? - God knows! Of course, I have been travelling around a lot and not receiving mail, and as you know, such conditions are not conducive to good letter writing,

It was at my first OTU in England, that I last remember writing, so I will continue my story chronologically from there. After much sweat and toil, we finally beat the weather and got our necessary training finished and then - Started a glorious week in London. Once more, I had to say goodbye to Jeff and Alf, but friends seem to be made to part from - most especially during War time with Nick and Ian (my pilots). I stayed at the Regent Palace in London and had an absolute smashing time. They were in with rather a wild young set, consisting mainly of Pilot Officers - and Air Training Service Girls. The first night in town, we went to an exclusive little night club just off Piccadilly, where I met a charming (very Charming) ATS girl. The next day, she showed me a lot of London and I enjoyed myself thoroughly. Firstly, we went to Trafalgar Square and had a look through St. Martin in the field. One of the oldest churches in London. We then took a bus across Lambeth Bridge, from there was this girl's favourite view of London and I must say, it was rather inspiring. Seeing it gave me a slight understanding of an Englishman's Love of London. (or "the smoke") as we call it. Looking one way, you had a scene of the Parliament buildings, which one sees on postcards and looking the other way you looked right down the river past all the warehouses etc., and in the distance you could see the chimneys of the industrial centre through the smoke and fog - Everything seemed OLD and enshrouded in History, but above all, floated in the mist with the sun glinting on them, the symbols of the terrible current history. The barrage balloons! We walked back over the bridge, and as we walked, she explained to me the Englishman's love of traditions and how it hurt her the way most of the men from the Dominions move, more or less. England isn't a country of individuals; more a country of families and classes and in my opinion, it will take more than a war to change it all. Being a country of families is (it seems) why they cling to their traditions and habits. I think everything about the country is either hereditary or inherited. With us, as with the other Dominions, our country is not old enough to have developed traditions, and we have or are a country of

122

individuals, and have been so, right from the start - because:- was it not men who wanted to get out of the rut, that founded our Dominion? Individuals - men with open minds and guts! Anyway....

We walked through Westminster Abby and looked at all the monuments and memorials there. It did not take much imagination to be able to picture the coronation with all its pageantry and the tradition which I have just pulled to bits - but cannot help, in a measure, appreciating. From the abbey, we walked through St. James Park and across the Mall, from where we could see Buckingham Palace. We then proceeded up the Prince of Wales Steps, and so back into Piccadilly. I would have liked to have had a closer look at the palace, but we didn't have time, as we had to meet the rest of the crowd for lunch.

London is a hell of a place to find your way around, but the taxi service there is the best in the world, so if you ever do get lost, the easiest way out, is to call a taxi. The way they know all the places and the way they drive through the Maze of traffic in blacked-out London, is absolutely Wizard. I've heard it said that the back of a taxi cab is the most romantic place in London. Do you know Ma, I think you are right?!

During that glorious week, I saw a lot of good pictures, went to a couple of dances, a couple of night clubs and bags of nice eating houses. Unfortunately, I did not get to see any of the famous London shows, but I guess I can take a couple of them in when I get back.

I got to know the West End fairly well, and believe me, there are some wizard places there. Take, for instance, the Regent Palace Hotel- One would hardly credit that there were such places merely to live and drink in. The palace part of the name is very apt.

I think the nicest place I went to, was the dining room of the Trocadero, they had a lovely orchestra there and what with snow white linen, shining silverware, and dozens of French waiters dashing about, it was positively wizo.

About the third day in London, I went to New Zealand House and got some mail, and oh the joy. About three letters from you. I'm afraid my joy was soon turned to sorrow.

Can you imagine the blow it was to me to hear for the first time about Duncan and Peggy? As I read, I was really shaken, and I admit I was close to tears. The whole affair from start to finish is ridiculous, cruel, and positively low - I presume Duncan wrote to Peggy and told her he had finished with her, and that his letter was lost!? I still think it is ridiculous, though, because he had no reason to stop loving her, let alone completely estranging himself from her, and I am serious when I say I have fears for his sanity. The news put me in the biggest quandary I've been in, in my life. Whether I should tell Peggy or keep out of it altogether, was the biggest question I've had to answer for myself yet. I still hadn't answered it when I caught the train for Henley, and I still hadn't answered it when I arrived at Russell's Water.

I am not trying to boost my part in it, nor am I trying to defend myself if I did wrong, but think of what a job it was. For about four months, Peggy had had no word from the one she loved!? The father of the most beautiful child on God's Earth. It seemed her love did not weaken, and her thoughts were always of him, while every ribbon and frill for Barry's clothes was put on with the thought of, 'I wonder if his Daddy will like it!?'

I kept off telling Peggy the sad news up and until she finally cornered me, and then it had to come out. I told her that Duncan had completely estranged himself from her because he considered she had been unfaithful to him. I did not tell her that he had come to hate her, and I did not tell her there was indeed another woman. She guessed the latter and I denied it. Naturally, she was absolutely heart-broken because she really did love him (or so she said)- Her love quickly turned to hate, and she wished him dead, while she cursed herself for loving and trusting him so much.

She then threatened that she would have his commission taken from him, I believe she had the power to - not for this affair, but for some previous (supposed) rottenness of his? At the time, the atmosphere was way too charged for me to defend Duncan at this juncture, so to this threat I made no answer (I did not have one). A couple of days later, however, I wrote the best letter I've ever written, absolutely imploring her not to do what she had suggested. Whether the letter did any good or not, I don't know, but you should know by the time you receive this~ I myself am quite convinced that Peggy was innocent of any charges Duncan made against her (at this point in time), and so far as I know, she was never anything other than a very unselfish loving wife. With reference to Duncan's statement about spoiling Barry's life, there seemed to be an inference that he thought Barry was not his child. If he ever did suggest such a thing, he is definitely nuts. Peggy told me, how for a time he thought of nothing but the plans for his future? Also, he was loving?!

This is what she told me:

That Duncan was indeed loving and kind to her, right up till the time he left England when, by then, the baby was well on the way?!

Quite apart from all that - as I said before, this affair raised its ugly head, Barry's likeness (in my humble opinion) is amazing. Peggy thanked me for telling her the sad story, BUT I am afraid I left very low and was rather pleased that I was leaving England too - where I can busy myself in the Middle East. (And make sense of this).

SOMEWHERE IN THE MIDDLE EAST

After two more days in London, we reported to our new station. This was just before Christmas and we spent the entire Christmas on the camp. We spent Christmas Day most enjoyably in the sergeant's mess with WAAFS as our guests. I once recently said I didn't like WAAFS, BUT I have acquired the taste. Right now, I would give a week's pay for the company of one. You will realise why, later on in this letter.

I often wonder if you finally got into the WAAFS, and if so, how you are liking it.

Near the end of 1941, we took off and set course for the Middle East. Our first stop was Gibraltar, where we were overjoyed to find that there was no rationing or black-outs. When the weather was favourable, we took off for Malta. Malta was a very picturesque place - with its stone buildings (Like a Holy City), horse-drawn vehicles, and setting of the blue of the Mediterranean. It was here that I first experienced an air raid. The first two or three to me were very thrilling, but I soon got used to them and took them as a matter of course.

We had quite a nice time at Malta, but as usual, we did not stay long. When we moved this time, however, we went by boat. It was quite a blow to our pride to have to come down to boat trips, especially as the trip was so different from my first trip; as opposite as heaven is to hell. When we arrived in the Middle East, we were in a personnel depot for a while, and then we were posted to 37 Squadron ~ The squadron that Duncan came out with, and did his 49 raids with. We are at present, the blazes way out in the Desert - about 200 miles from the nearest habitation - that sounds like the end of the earth, but it really isn't so bad, with the good company I am in. Strangely enough, in this far corner of the globe, you can buy sparkling Waitemata beer, and that makes up for a lot. Don't send anything to me here, please, because in the cities, on leave, we can buy anything we want. We haven't done any ops yet, but it won't be long, and we are now all really looking forward to it.

The only city we have seen out here yet, is Alexandria. It is a very cosmopolitan place, but of course, the majority are wogs (standing for Worthy Oriental Gentlemen). WOG is a very common term and means just about any dark-skinned person in the Middle East - Here in Alexandria, it was very clean and modern, and although we didn't get to know anybody there, we had quite an enjoyable time with pictures and cabarets, etc. I haven't had any communication with Duncan since I came out here, but next when I go to Cairo, I will dig up some clues concerning his whereabouts and find out just what is the matter with the silly devil. Right now, I really don't know how I feel about him - when I read your letter and heard Peggy's story, I despised him. However,

I never did go on one-sided stories and really, I suppose, I only know half a story, so it is just not my place to condemn or criticise.

As far as I have been able to surmise, he (Duncan) is in the British Overseas Airways Corporation (must have been some deal with the Air Force as he was still in active combat situations), and this explains why he is or was in Lagos (the White Man's Grave).

As my candle is now burning low and I am getting a numb bumb, I think I had better close.

From this Airman to that Airwoman

all the love in the world

Yours

Teg.

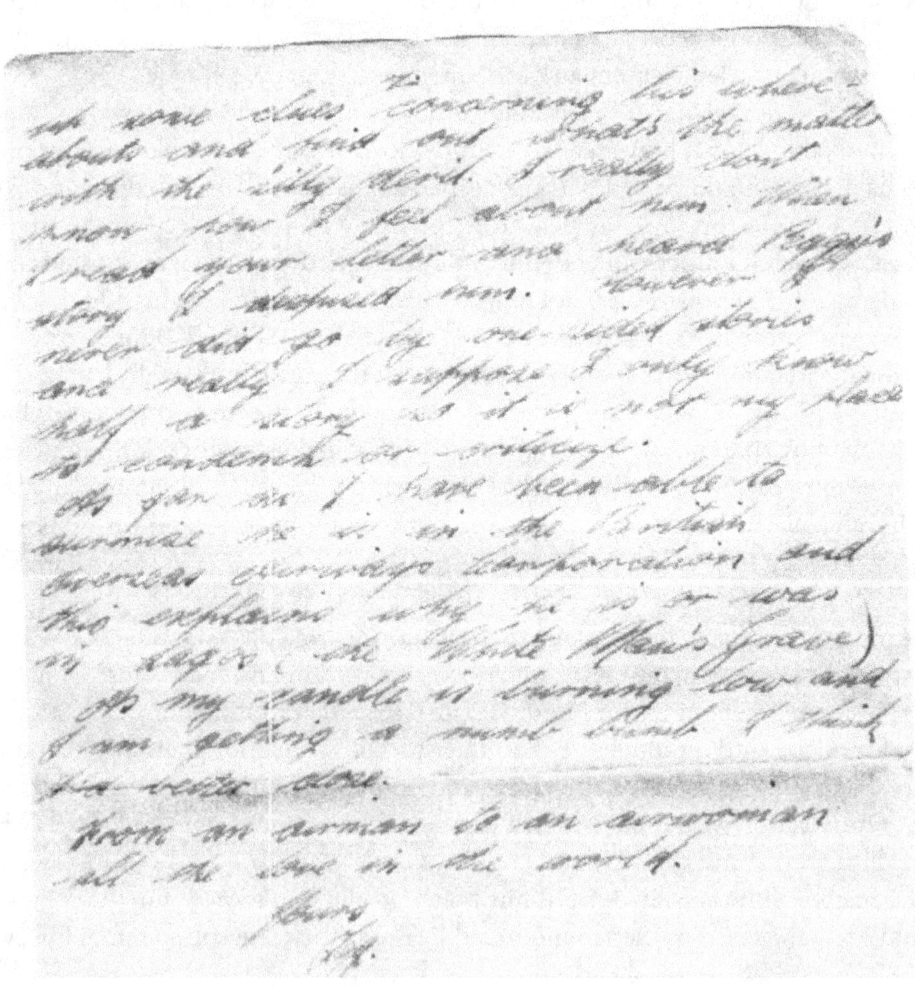

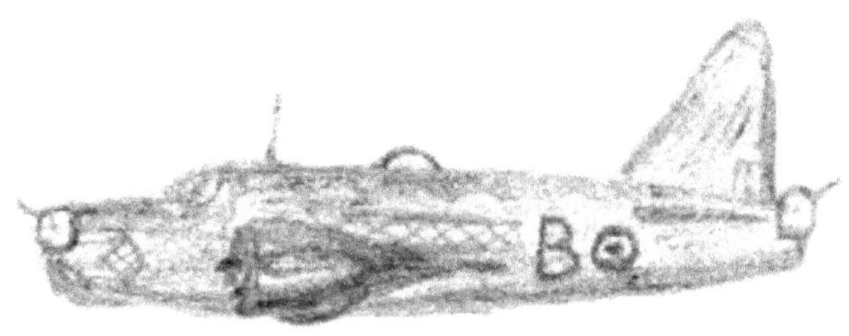

This image was drawn as part of the letter on the previous page.
Below: CABLE GRAM sent to Pete for his birthday FEB 1942

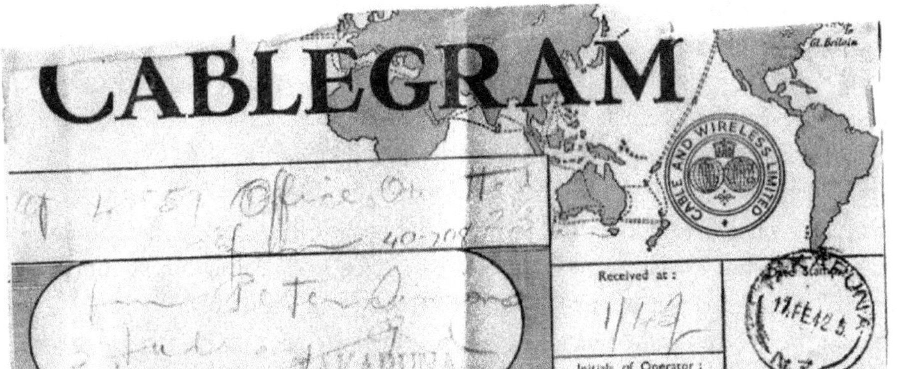

CABLEGRAM

CABLE AND WIRELESS LIMITED

TAKAPUNA

NEW ZEALAND POST OFFICE TELEGRAPHS
(IN CONJUNCTION WITH CABLE AND WIRELESS LIMITED)

Received at:

Initials of Operator:

17 FE 42

N.Z.

NOTE.—This form must accompany any inquiry made respecting this telegram.

The cable reads: Birthday Greetings, Pete
My new address is No. 37 Sqdn RAF Middle East
Terence Dixon

Letter 2:- from the Middle East   11th March 1942

C/- Royal Air Force Middle East Command

Dearest Mother,

So Again, it is now many moons since I last wrote - so I suppose I am in the cart? Not a terrible lot was happening since I last wrote, but what has happened has been very interesting.

Firstly, I have now met up with Duncan & until recently, we have been stationed not 10 miles apart.

Do you remember how there once was a time when I said I would never censure anybody for their wrongs until I had heard both sides of the story? I wish like blazes that I had kept to that ideal with the Duncan / Peggy affair. You see I only had Peggy's story and consequently I rather blackguarded old Dunc rather sadly. Now I have got the low down, I don't actually blame anyone and wish I had never ever heard of the affair.

Duncan said that Peggy more or less swept him away (having met her I can see this happening), then after he had become married to her, he had found out (the hard way) that she was inclined to be Rather Loose and consequently, he set about himself to estrange himself from her - I think his first move was posting out here (well out of it) and from then on, he said he tried to make it die a natural death, as if it just was any ordinary love affair. I am afraid he didn't realise that it wasn't any ordinary love affair and he seems to forget that there is a child. Up until the time he left England, he was very attentive to Peggy and apparently never gave her any cause to doubt him. Of course, I am young and very easily deceived, but still in my opinion, Peggy was not such a wicked woman as Duncan would have us believe, and although old mothers are trusting and loving and also easily deceived, I rather think Peggy's mother, Dora, should know her own daughter, whom she lead me to believe she had complete faith in. She also told me that she only let Duncan marry Peggy because he talked her into it. Another thing I saw about Peggy - That as a mother herself, she left nothing to be desired.

The whole thing in my opinion was that Duncan found Peggy a very good sport and became terribly infatuated. She probably would not surrender to him and with her woman's wiles she probably got old Dunc where she wanted him and so did trick him into marrying her. After all, she is, in my view, a typical English sophisticate - 1942 model — which also (isn't a very moral or sober type) - and also as Duncan says, is a very clever woman. What put Duncan against her, was that he really, a little late, realised he had only been infatuated and tricked, and he also tired of her just as someone tires of someone else at that age, unless there really is Love both ways. To make things worse, he found out a little late, that he had NOT married a virgin, and he met quite a few men who had boasted (her sporting nature) before the marriage and before he was aware. In defence of Peggy, I would say that she tricked him into marriage because she felt she loved him completely, and also, I do not believe she has been unfaithful to him since their marriage and child, but of course, of that I am not sure either. I still like Peggy, but naturally must choose between her and Duncan, and since I have met up with old Dunc again, I have realised he is one of the few people in this world, I really do Love. You therefore know my choice.

(this is where the saying blood is thicker than water slips in)

Now about Duncan himself - Before I met up with him, I wrote him a very censuring letter – luckily, I sent it to a very obscure address and now I am hoping he never receives it. The way we met up again was rather unusual - actually he found me ~ You see I wrote a letter to Peggy, which was censored by Flight lieutenant McFarland who is one of Dunc's best pals, and the next day, Dunc walked in on me. He was up until recently, an instructor at a station about 10 miles away. I expected to meet a man aged beyond his years and worn to a shadow after a long illness - perhaps even a little dippy - but thankfully, instead, I met the same old Dunc with that same big smile - yeh - the pal - I joined up to chase after. Apart from his suffering from illness, he has suffered mentally, and of course, socially over his domestic trouble and he does feel that even his own family is against him. When I met him, you were his only backer in the family and after we had had a big talk, he even thought that you and I were against him. Out here in their rotten little social circles he is well known and well liked, but even here they talk - So he loves the desert and operations, where he can get away from everything. Now he has just received his Flight Lieutenant and is again back on operations - his address is: 108 Squadron - R.A.F. - Middle East. If you write to him - TELL HIM YOU LOVE HIM. Cheer him up and don't mention either his mother or his wife - please don't lecture him - but tell him we all make mistakes and that everything will be ok. Try and undo the wrong he has done to himself and the wrong Peggy has done him - and indeed the wrong l have also inadvertently done him .

(seems our dive to be with family or in a family has driven this terrible affair to this end).

One of the first people I met here, after Duncan of course, was Mary- Mary being the woman as you described as being the Dorothy Lamour, the enchantress. Well, I'm afraid Dorothy Lamour just isn't in the same class - The girl is absolutely beautiful. She is only 22 days older than myself, and is sweetly unspoilt and although she has lost none of her teenage charm, she is semi-sophisticated. Her mother is Greek, and her father is English, and she is very dark. She has a perfect figure including bosom. Before I go further, I must explain (in case you have any doubts) that between she and Duncan there is nothing more than a beautiful friendship - Perhaps she loves him and perhaps he loves her - that I don't know. When Duncan told me to go and see her, he said, "Boy you're going to meet a real virgin."

Although I have only known her a very short while I do think quite a lot of her myself. Her people are very nice too and although it is strange to hear her mother speak it is lovely to go there for the afternoon. Mary herself speaks beautiful English. Another chap and I were there for the evening last night. We had a lovely tea and then went to the pictures we came home about 8.30pm and then had dinner, then about 10.30pm we went home. At dinner we were waited on by a WOG (worthy oriental gentleman) servant and we had a lovely meal which included lovely wine and which we finished off with some beautiful Jaffa Oranges. They are positively wonderful fruit. They come from Palestine where you can buy them - at 4 for a penny. These Jaffa Oranges are as big as two ordinary oranges and taste like a mixture of an orange and a pineapple.

As far as news about myself goes, there is very little to tell. After about a month of doing nothing, we were returned to base. I have done a couple of ops so far and enjoyed them immensely. Should you have any fears about your first-born's safety you better drop 'em because we are all terribly efficient and I have the most amazing luck, especially with your Kiwi dangling from my pocket. I had to take it away from around my neck because it used to peck me and give me eczema.

I am enclosing a recent photo of Duncan and one of myself (note the kiwi)-

By the way, how are the WNZAAF's? I suppose you will be running off with a Wing Commander any day now. I am dying to hear how you like the Air Force - In fact, I am just dying to hear from you - It is getting near three months since I had a letter from you, but of course it is not your fault.

Bye bye for now —

tons of love Sweetheart.

All my love as always

Teg.

⁎⌘⁎⌘

Letter 3:- Middle East

8th April 1942,
37 Squadron ROYAL AIR FORCE
Middle East Command

Dearest Mother

For some reason or another letter writing becomes more and more difficult - I have quite a little to tell too. I have a lousy memory right now and I don't keep a note of things, so I don't quite know where I left off last - so I hope I am not repeating anything .

Duncan is now a Flight Lieutenant and is also a Flight Commander. His new address is care of the 108 Squadron - R.A.F. Middle East Command. I saw him the other night for the first time since our original meeting up over here. He wrote me that he would be at Mary's place and although I was worn out, I dragged myself down to meet him. He was wonderful and despite his many experiences, in my eyes he has changed very little. We didn't have much chance to talk, but we recalled a few of the happy times and the silly things we did in our boyhood - for instance - Uncle Cecil telling me to climb through the keyhole - The week Wattie, he and I spent on the Launch and the time I got my foot caught in the picket gate and fell head downwards at Parua Bay?! You have yourself, probably felt the cruelties of society and position and now I am feeling them a little myself, just because I was too lazy to get myself a commission. During this war the distinction of class between officers and men hasn't been so bad in England, but the further East one goes, the worse the snobbery gets - out here, they have their lousy little social set - The Officers have all the best women, the best clubs and hotels and nobody without a King's commission can get a look in - and that's democracy?! The Port Tewfik social set is a typical example. If I had been an officer, I could have had a marvellous time and been introduced into the club and the sports, but it just can't be done. Everyone I've met at Mary's place, has been an officer and outwardly I feel a slight inferiority complex, but inwardly I feel well, why should I - because I am doing so much and, in some cases, more than any of them. As usual, I can see their side of this argument too. If the men were allowed everywhere the officers go, it would be tough on the officers because so many of the damb fool "other ranks" don't know how to behave.

The night I was at Mary's with Dunc, their friends came to take them to a party. Another Flight Lieutenant, D.S.O, D.F.C. and bar, and a squadron leader. They wanted to take me with them, but you see, I didn't wear that little bit of ribbon, so I couldn't even go out with my own Uncle. There was rather a funny instance connected with that particular Squadron leader. When I went to see

Dunc once, I strolled up to the office and asked the officer standing there, if he was about. He was only a youngster, but a Squadron leader, so he dressed me down for my omission to salute him. When Dunc came out and introduced me as his nephew, it made the young squadron leader look silly. Later Dunc said, " Don't you usually salute Squadron leaders? But, Oh yes, I forgot you are a New Zealander?"?!! They all joke about it now and most particularly the Squadron Leader himself. You know, I am working like blazes now for a commission, but whether I'll ever get it or not, is another question.

Duncan gave me rather a problem that night. His navigator is going back to England, so he wants to move heaven and earth to get me in his crew. Ever since I started training, I dreamed of getting in his crew and he always talked about it, but now there's a possibility I'm going to refuse. The main reason is that with him, I won't get my ops in. He has done about 51 now and won't be doing many more, and at present he does about one in two months because as flight commander, he has enough to do on the ground. If I stay with my own crew, I will get them in at the present rate of two or three a week, and soon we will have Ian (my old Captain and present second Pilot) back as Captain. I am very attached to Ian, who is a good pilot and if it is at all possible, we will stick together right through. At present, I have done 8 ops. As Dunc's navigator, I would probably get the desired commission and be pretty well off, but I think my decision is a good one.

The fact of Duncan introducing me to the Mahons has been a wonderful thing because they are all wonderful to me, and I spend a terrible lot of my spare time there. Recently, Dorothy and Bobby have been home on holidays and I had a lot of fun with them. Dorothy is 16 and Bobby is 14 yrs old.

Recently we were lucky enough to get some leave, so we went to Cairo. We didn't exactly have a marvellous time because that is rather a hard thing to do in this part of the world. We certainly got about a bit though, and in my next letter I'll tell you about it and send some photos. It would rather spoil things just to tell you a bit - so when I have time, I'll write you a book on it, like I did in Montreal. I sent you from Cairo a box of stockings and a marvellous piece of brocade, which was probably a bad buy, but I could not resist it because it was so beautiful.

Incidentally, I met Fred Simons in Cairo *(Fred is Terry's stepfather, Kawe Simon's brother)*. We did not have much of a chance to talk, but I suppose I will see him again sometime. When we got back, your letter No.44 was waiting for me.

I think the last letter I received from you before that was no 34.

So, there must still be quite a bit of mail on its way still. Before I received your cable, signed WAAF Simons, I wasn't sure if you were actually in it and until I received No 44, I didn't know Don was in it. Just in case <u>IT</u> the mail doesn't catch up with me, please repeat any news of importance since about last September. And also say whether or not you received that portrait from Montreal. There is absolutely nothing you can send me here because there's nothing I want, unless perhaps for next Christmas, you'd like to send me a flat (holds 20) chromium cigarette case - I lost the one Rae gave me in the kit, which was left somewhere between Canada and England. This flying places is good, but you are always only allowed 30 lbs of kit and out of my original issue, I have a shirt and a pair of flying boots left.

Could you please send me Mavis Bagley's address. I am a godfather and I have done absolutely nothing about it so far. You might give me some advice on the subject also.

Thanks a lot for the photos. I couldn't quite figure out who the girls you were with were, but that's not important. The uniform looks pretty good, but it isn't as smart as the English WAAFS - The Hat for one thing - however it suits you quite well - and I am proud of you. I noticed with alarm that in that photo taken on the beach, that your gray hairs have multiplied, but I suppose we've got to be mother and son sooner or later, although I now look a hell of a lot older now you know, and we can (appear) as brother and sister still.

A rather sad accident happened t'other day. I opened a hatch in the top of the aircraft when we were flying and as I was raising it to close it, the suction pulled it out of my hand, and it knocked out a couple more front teeth - upper left no.2 and the left eye tooth. I really look a mess now, but I will soon have a couple more fake ones. Well that's all the news for the present so I'll say good night. Please don't worry about me because I'm happy; I have not succumbed to the woes of the East and I'm as fit as a fiddle.

Give my love to Dem and Pete and Colly and get them all to write and send photos of themselves too.

All The love in the world,

    Yours

        Teg.

℠℞℠℞

Letter 4:- Middle East

20th April 942,
37 Squadron - Middle East Command

Dearest Mother,

There is not much happening around here lately - but it's time to write again - So here I am. We've been having a bit of a loaf lately because our Captain has finished his ops and we haven't got a new one yet. We've been trying hard to get Ian as Captain, but I'm afraid Pilot Officers get first chance and I think we will be having one for Captain.

We've been having real tropical weather lately. The temperature has been around 115°F mostly, and it is terribly muggy, so you can imagine how we feel most of the time. We go swimming at Port Tewfik quite often and the water is absolutely wizard. Incidentally, Mary is an absolutely wonderful swimmer and although I have not seen him do it, I believe that Mac Duncan is a very good diver. I've been seeing the aforementioned person quite often lately. I've taken up tennis a bit and although I haven't bought a racquet yet, I manage to scrounge quite a few games. I think I told you about my losing two more front teeth. Well I had two added to my old plate and now I look just the same again except that I have only one gold filling instead of two. Last time I wrote, I said I would tell you about Cairo later - well this later is here - so Here we go-

It might surprise you to know that one of the nicest places in Cairo is a little bit of New Zealand - In other words, the New Zealand Forces Club. They have their three different dining rooms: one for Sergeants, one for Officers, and one for men. They have a canteen selling New Zealand goods, a library, information and post office, Sleeping quarters for Officers and men, and a Huge lounge. It's a wonderful place and a great advertisement for the country because men from many different countries visit it. There was a New Zealand bar there too, but our favourite drink probably makes your mouth water. For 2 piastres (5pence) we could get a whole tumblerful of pure orange juice - no water or sugar added. It's a lovely drink and we used to get through quite a few of them.

One of the first places we visited, was the Cairo University, which rather upsets one's idea of a university. All the students are Eastern people, who pay nothing for their tuition and live at the University. When I say live, I mean they sleep there just wherever they happen to be, and they buy their food from Hawkers on the streets. As far as washing goes, I don't think they do? The building itself is terribly old, and is built around a big courtyard. It is cut up into rooms and each room is set aside for a different country - Abyssinia, Morocco, Turkey etc. etc. There are no furnishings at all except grass mats on the floor and in one very large sort of common room there are beautiful Red Persian carpets which were presented to them by King Ferouk. They learn to read and write and languages, but most of all they study the Mohammedan Bible. There seemed to be no fixed classes or anything, they just sat about all over the place on the mats and sort of chanted their lessons at the same time swaying backward and forward. One of the most interesting things of all, was a fairly big library the books of which were all printed by hand.

From the University we went to the Bazaars, which were positively intriguing. Where they are situated is mostly considered a Native quarter and there seems to be thousands of people all over the place. Something like Queen Street on a Friday night. This is not surprising because in the area of Cairo, it seems no bigger than Auckland and yet it has a population of over a million people. The Bazaars themselves are contained in two narrow lanes, one about a hundred yards long and the other about two hundred yards long. Jammed close together are the bazaars ~ some of them just little stalls and others are medium sized shops.

Their wares hang about all over the place. There is a great variety of stuff none of which is very useful being mostly souvenirs and curios.

And a lot of it is terrible junk, but some of it is quite valuable and rare. Some of the places make the things they sell - There was a kid there making beads on a home-made hand-worked lathe. They said that with his crude apparatus he turned out 600 beads a day. At another place was a chap doing designs on brass - he also had very crude tools, but was indeed turning out wizard articles. We went into one place where they had the most beautiful silks I've ever seen. The boss was a Greek or something, who spoke seven languages and was the best salesman I ever hope to meet. Firstly, we just let him show us half the shop and we swore black and blue we weren't going to buy anything. I absolutely itched to buy one particular piece of brocade, but the price was exorbitant. It was about 6 yards square and was of royal blue and gold - The blue predominating. The design was gorgeously worked - lotus flowers about the size of your hand and the fascinating thing about it was that it changed colour in different lights. The chap offered us tea about 6 times, so finally we accepted. It was Persian tea and we drank it from queer-shaped little glasses, incidentally it was excellent. After about another half-hours' arguing and beating down the price, I bought you some stockings and one of the boys bought a kimono. After that, we left the bazaars smartly, for fear our resistance would weaken further. We then took a garry and went to the New Zealand Forces Club. A garry, by the way, is simply a buggy.

In all the towns out here, you find just about as many garries as you do taxies and as you can guess, I nearly always choose the former. Most of them are drawn by spanking Arab horses. With my last letter, I sent you a photo of an Egyptian Mounted Policeman. Those horses are just about the best I've seen, I think. As you might have noticed, they are almost pure white and the reason they always look so proud is because they are stallions. They are wonderfully trained too. When I took that photo, the chap just gave a low whistle and up went the horse's ears and he was all attention. When these horses are 12 years old, they just shoot them. Mainly because at that age they are getting too old for service and they don't want to see them used for garries or anything. One day, I happened to be at the YMCA and a tour was about to start, so I snipped in smartly and joined it. The first place we visited was the Sultan Hassan mosque. There are about 50 ancient mosques in Cairo and about a hundred altogether. The Sultan Hassan mosque is 600 years old and is not used now. It is just bare stone, except in one place, there are designs in coloured stones and gold. These are now a bit defaced and the vandalism is supposed to have been done by Napoleon. In the wall of the mosque on the outside, is a cannon-ball embedded into the stone. This was fired by Napoleon's soldiers when they made an attempt to rein the mosque. On the other side of the road was another ancient Mosque in which is the tomb of Khedive Ismail. We did not go there, but instead went further on to visit the Citadel. The citadel is a sort of Fort and is on the most commanding position in all Cairo. It was built in the 12th Century at about the time of the third Crusade, when Richard the Lion Heart fort in Palestine. It has been changed about and rebuilt through the centuries and was used by Napoleon when he was in Egypt.

It is reputed to be built of stones taken from the smaller pyramids of Giza. In the enclosure of the Citadel is a Mosque and place of Mohammed Ali. The Mosque is one of the most famous in the world and is one of the newest in Egypt - as it was not completed till 1867.

It is made almost completely of alabaster - which was taken from the second pyramid of Giza. The floor is completely covered with beautiful Red Persian carpets, similar to those in the university. About half way up is a gallery where the women pray - women are not allowed to pray with the men. Further up, there is a row of stained glass windows which extend right around the building - They are the most beautiful glass windows I've seen. Their beauty is not in the intricacy of the designs but the vividness and richness of the shades of glass. At one side of the Mosque there is a semi-circular part cut away - it is about a yard across and a yard deep - This part is all beautifully inlaid with coloured stones. The idea of it is that it points the direction that the Mohommedans have to face when they pray, because they always must face towards Mecca where the prophet is buried. You find that little circular part in all mosques. In the mosque, is the tomb of Mohammed Ali who was at one time a ruler of Egypt. Behind the mosque is the palace that he used to live in. It is in very bad repair; all the rooms are still there, and we could see where the harem used to live and there was within there a sunken bath. From one of the windows of the palace you could get a view of Cairo and see miles up and down the Delta, while right over on the other side of Cairo on the edge of the Desert, you could see the Pyramids.

From the old palace we were driven through the Cities of the Dead, which are sort of towns comprised completely of tombs. The Arab rulers of the middle ages are buried there along with the ancient Caliphs and Mamluks. Some of these tombs have been restored in modern times. This place was eerie enough in the daytime, and I shouldn't have liked to go through there at night. The tour then went to the Bazaars - It was my second visit, but none the less interesting. Our most prolonged stay in any one place this time was in a Perfume shop called the Palace of Perfumes. It is really a world famous shop and all this perfume - King's formulas are supposed to be secret - such things as Tutankhamen Pharaoh sent, Morning Glory, and Flowers of the Sahara. They are sure intriguing smells but not the sort I would like to get a whiff of from my best girl. They are so heavy and strong, and they last for ages. They gave us all a little advertising pamphlet which I kept and now still stinks like blazes. I nearly burst out laughing at one thing they advertised. I'll quote it to you, and it will give you an idea of what a low lot of devils these people are:-"Ambarpaste the elixir of youth is perhaps the most Oriental of all my preparations. The effect is enchanting and seductive and the taste delicious. Although delightful for all ages owing to its curiously pleasant flavour and its blood warming properties, the genuine Amber paste is a veritable open sesame to elderly people, who would for a time re-enter the portals of the Realm of youth."

This time I had a good look around the Bazaars and this time I also managed to keep all my cash - It was my third visit to the Bazaars that brought the fatal crash when I weakened in buying the brocade I sent to you. On the 2nd visit, this time, we went back to the YMCA and that was all there was to that tour.

The last day we were in Cairo we visited the Pyramids and strangely enough it was, for me anyway, the least interesting tour of all. When we arrived, we had the options of hiring a horse, donkey or Camel to ride around on. Ian and I chose horses as you can see from the enclosed photo.

Firstly, we visited some ancient tombs. We had to crawl almost on our hands and knees through a tunnel to get to the vault - there was a solid stone coffin in which was a skeleton. Around the wells were the stone carvings that you so often see pictures of. Our next visit was to the temple of the Sphinx and the Sphinx itself. The temple is made of ABSOLUTELY COLOSSAL Lumps of Granite, the biggest one being about 8 feet long and 3 feet square. Most of the temple has no roof and is just rows of pillars of granite. From there we went to the Sphinx which is beside the Temple. It is down in a sort of Pit and is made of small bricks, It is really better preserved than one gets from photos - You can still see the shape of the Lion with its tail and paws etc- We really hadn't time to go inside the Pyramids or climb them, but I'll give you a bit of information about them which you might find interesting. The large Pyramid (The pyramid of Cheops) is 4,850 years old. It covers an area of approximately 13 acres. It's height about 480 feet, blocks of stone contained - 2,300,000 - the average size of each being 40 cubic feet and their weight about 2½ tons - most of the stone was cut from the plateau on which it stands and from the hollow where the Sphinx is situated. The pyramid was once coated with a very fine limestone which was taken from quarries on the other side of the Nile. A lot of course, grained red granite from Aswan 500 miles away was also used for the interior. It is actually a tomb and inside is the now empty stone coffin.

The second Pyramid that of Chephren is the same age as the Sphinx about 4,800 years. It is 471 feet high and was once covered with alabaster, which if you remember, was taken to build the Mohammed Ali mosque. It is also a tomb and also contains an empty stone coffin.

The third pyramid of Mycerinus is much smaller than the others and is made partly of limestone and partly of granite. Seems the stone coffin was lost at sea on the way to England.

Now a few words about Cairo itself. It is quite a modern city which seems rather strange with all the ancient things about it - Like all cities out here, it is very cosmopolitan and as I said before, very crowded- There are some quite good shops there, an opera house and a lot of cinemas, a few good hotels and dozens of restaurants, clubs etc. While we were there, we joined a Sergeants and Warrant Officer's night club. It wasn't too bad either. It was beautifully laid out with two bars and a lounge and nice Dance floor. They had a very good five piece band and always put on a very good floor show. They had a hostess system there which wasn't bad, but just a little too expensive. If you wanted a girl to dance with, you had to buy her a drink. They always had some special drink which was probably just coloured water and which they received a commission on. They weren't bad types, but they were all sorts of strange nationalities and the one I had a few dances with, could only speak a few words of English. The female question is the worst drawback to this part of the world. At a guess, I should say there can't be more than one European woman to fifty European men here at present, and believe me, they are hard to get to know. A bit different from good old England, where unless you are a woman hater, it was just about impossible to go without a girlfriend- I'm a bit fed up thinking and worrying about it, but I often wonder how Duncan's matrimonial affairs are going to work out. I don't think Peggy will ever divorce him and I don't think he *could* divorce her. Even if he was free, I don't think he would marry Mary? or not - she just about worships the ground he walks on, but I really don't know how he feels.

If he did marry Mary - then another problem would arise because I doubt if New Zealand would appreciate Mary as much as Dunc would want them to. You see, even without the browning of Egypt's sun, Mary would still be rather dark and you know what people are like about such things. You probably don't think so, and it might surprise you to hear me say that in my opinion, New Zealanders are in many ways very narrow-minded and unworldly, mainly because, I suppose New Zealand itself is so far from the centre of the world. On the other hand, New Zealanders at home are the most moral and temperate people I've come in contact with. Maybe it is the effect of the war - I don't know, but it seems English people are just the opposite. The reason for it mostly, I think, is that so many women are in the services and this spoils them, so with the women of the country being spoilt the backbone of the country is getting weak. I'm getting a bit deep here?! I don't mean the country's morale is going to the pack or anything, and I do admire the women in the services. Indeed, Britain's backbone was probably never as strong as it is now, but the people are slipping in little things that in ordinary times make a country admired. That's a mess isn't it - I do wish I could do a proper job of expressing myself. Don't imagine I have any fears for you in your uniform - It would take more than a war to change my Ma. I suppose there are thousands of girls in the WAAF at home now. I picked up a weekly news the other day with photos of WAAFS in it, and right away saw two girls I used to know very well. One was a girl who asked me to my first party in Herne Bay. I'll never forget that party - I debated for an hour whether I should wear a tie or not and finally went without one. All the other boys there had on dark suits and naturally ties?! That night I fell in love with a girl with blonde curls. Thinking of those times now, reminds me of the only time I've been in love. That was with Nancy Stonppe when we lived in Herne Bay. I was 13 and she was 11. You should have seen the sheik she gave the go by for me - she was very sweet in those days even if you didn't like her mother. I went and did the dirty on her and according to Beth (her sister) I went very near to breaking her heart. Tis sad, but true, that when I left New Zealand, she was getting very hard and more and more like her mother. It is a sweet memory; my sweet and short youthful affair and I often wonder where she is now and what she will be like when she grows up. Did I ever tell you that story before? Perhaps I didn't. You know, Roma, old girl, you must have learnt a lot about me since I have been away, eh?

Thinking back over those times again reminds me of something and what the air force has done for me. Ever since I started work, I always seem to be with chaps older than myself and I was always wanting to do the things they did. For all sorts of reasons, I couldn't, and you told me my time would come. I tried ever so hard to be patient and wait for my years to catch up with my age and my favourite comforter was the song:

"There's a good time coming be it ever so far away."- The time came when I joined up and two of the most enjoyable times I'd had for years, were on final leave. One night, when I took out a pretty little girl from Smith & Caughey's who I had wanted to take out for ages, and another night when we had the dinner party at the Waverley. The only thing that worries me now is, after the war is over, when they sound the last "ALL CLEAR." I've thought up dozens of ideas - so far, I have still got plenty of time to think up some more. Of course, any advice you or Colly have to offer on the subject will be very welcome.

I have a very strong complex at present - I don't want to come back to New Zealand! If I have the chance, I'd be back tomorrow like a shot, but I have the feeling that once I come back, I will see no more of the world and I must admit that seeing the world has got into my blood. I want to see England and Canada again and all sorts of new places as well. As Mr Lavender told me once, I'll thank God that I have you and New Zealand to return to when the time comes, but there's that funny feeling!?

About 3 pages back, I was talking about Mary and side-tracked on the most uninteresting subject "me" and "my thoughts" - If Dunc took Mary back home to New Zealand as his wife, people who didn't know where she came from, would say she had Maori blood and people who did know where she came from would say she had Egyptian blood. I have probably told you of Mary's charms and believe you me, I did not exaggerate. In fact, the more I know her the more I like her. A great number of men worship at her shrine and still she remains unspoilt. If it wasn't for about 300 "ifs" including "If I was in love with her" - I'd marry her myself. Perhaps I have a special big piece of my heart reserved for mothers because I have such a wonderful mother myself. Anyway, Mary's mother is also a rather marvellous woman. There's just something about her one can't explain. I think it has got something to do with her complete unselfishness and strength of character. I have been at this for a day and a half now - and so I think I have just about written enough.

I am on the scrounge again - Last time I wrote I said there wasn't anything I wanted out here, but it has come to my notice that should you have a few spare hours away from the Air Force and your favourite squadron Leader, how about baking me one of those super colossal cakes of yours.

I'm sorry to say I haven't been too well lately, with the hot weather and one thing and another, but neither has anyone round here for that matter, I have been a bit constipated and have had a few boils, but they will soon be gone, I hope.

I have enclosed a photo of Duncan which Mary gave me. It isn't bad but it isn't good and one thing about it you see - He still looks very young. Actually, he has been looking a bit pale lately and seems to be going a little bald on top, but he's pretty ok, I think. The other day Ian and I went down to Mahon's and he and another flight lieut. and Spanky MacFarlane (Squadron Leader) our flight commander were there. We had quite a bit of fun with them. Ranks were either disregarded completely or joked about and as I was feeling on top form, I kept throwing cracks at Dunc while he threw them back. I shook him rigid a couple of times because he thinks he is such an old timer compared to me, however he paid me back by almost embarrassing me once. He had been terribly worried about me going about with a gap in my teeth and he was pleased to see I had some new shiners. It's funny how each of us worried about the other.

I have also enclosed a couple of photos of our visit to the pyramids. That is Ian with me on the horses and the photo was taken right beside the BIG Pyramid. In the other photo, the foreground is the temple of the Sphinx and behind that is the peak of the second Pyramid - In the middle of the Sphinx you can't see its front paws because stones in the foreground hide them. At the right is the Big Pyramid and the dots below it are people closer than it to the camera, giving you some idea of its actual size.

Well I hope you have enjoyed reading this as much as I have enjoyed writing it. For the latter part of it I have been right in the mood and just felt as if I was talking to you.

Refer to this letter when you receive it because seeing it (they Pyramids), is the biggest most interesting thing for a long time and I would like to know whether you do receive it or not.

Give my love to Dem and Pete and Colly and all the love in the
World for yourself

Yours

Teg

₧₧

Letter 5:- Middle East   25th April 1942,
                                                                          37 Squadron
                                                           Middle East Commission

Dearest Mother,

I have just received your letter No46 - so despite the fact that I only wrote a couple of days ago here goes. I don't know where letter No 45 has gone to but I suppose it will turn up sooner or later.

I'm terribly sorry you had to go so long without receiving any mail, but it was just a slip on my part and won't occur again. Since I've been in the Middle East, I have been fairly constant. As far as your letters are concerned 35 to 43 inclusive have not yet come to hand, but are probably on their way out from England. I am glad you gave me a bit of gen about your WAAF duties because I was rather in the dark about it all. The ranks you have, certainly are different from England and I still can't figure out what WA stands for. By the sounds of things, you will have a commission before I have one as assistant section leader is P/O I believe, and isn't very far away. In England in the WAAFS (bless 'em the lovely creatures), they have ACW2 (second class aircraft women) ACW1, Corporal, Sergeant, senior sergeant (flight sergeant) then commissional ranks, starting at assistant section leader. I'm glad to hear they are going to give you service caps because although the old felt suits you quite well, I do think the service cap will be more becoming. Your doing all the thinking for the adjutant sounds rather typical of the air force. In the RAF they call it "binding". By the way, I would definitely advise you to remind the adjutant about recommending you for promotion if he forgets. As a matter of fact, Ian and I are thinking of reminding Spanky (our flight commander) about recommending us for commissions. However, we have an officer Captain now, and if he is an obliging type, he might do something about it.

I did not know before that Pete was at tech. Good luck to him. Ask him if he can get a bit of spare time away from homework to write and tell me all about it.

The house sounds pretty good now and I'd certainly like to have a look at it, but that is just one of those things that's coming be it ever so far away. I should be getting my promotion to flight sergeant soon and when that happens, I will allot the extra pay to you to help save up for the bust up you talk about when I come home. Since I last wrote, we have shifted into the desert again. Unluckily, our crew again had to travel by road, and I had my tummy just about turned inside out, but I managed to get my arms legs and face nicely tanned (not burnt) - This time being more or less "old campaigners," we came up much better equipped. This time we brought camp beds with us and a good supply of tinned eats. Another thing better about this trip, is that it is now summertime and although it is rather hot, it is a nice dry heat and so far, quite bearable. It is a bit tough that we won't be able to go visit the Mahons again for some time, but I suppose we will get some leave sooner or later. Before we left, Ian and I were in big with the Mahons and I think we would have gone dippy if we hadn't been able to visit them occasionally. Of course, Mary might have had something to do with the pleasure of the visits, but I and Ian are quite definite to each other that she didn't, though why he should want to pinch a photograph of her, I haven't the faintest.

I am going to have a hell of a job to know what to write about out here. As a matter of fact, this letter is finished already. However, I should have plenty of time on my hands and I will write fairly often.

Love to the *kids and Colly (* whoops not kids - men)

Yours lovingly

    Teggy

Letter 5 continues

Luckily, I did not post that letter yesterday because today I received the biggest swag of mail I have received since I left Canada. From you I received 37-38 and 44 which makes me think you might have sent two No. 44. Number 37 was posted on October 29th, so it took 6 months to get here but "Maleesh" (Arabic for "Never mind") - I got 4 letters from Dem (Bless him) - 2 from Nicky - 1 from Dorothy Clark - 1 from Wilmar - one from Don, and most ironically, two Christmas cards- one from Kit and one from friends in Halifax. Damned amazing old Dot Clark writing to me. As a matter of fact, I couldn't remember who she was until I got about half way through the letter. Appreciated Dem's letters immensely as always. I can hardly grasp the fact that he is in fourth form and Pete is at tech. Dem really took that letter I wrote him to heart - so I hope the advice I gave was good. It seems a lot of my letters have rather cracked me up a bit, so I hope you won't be too disappointed when the same silly old dreamy Teg turns up at home again. I think it's because my thoughts go on paper and my thoughts are usually better than my actions.

Well, now to answer your letters. In No 37 you told me how the house seems to be decorated with my photos. I was pleased to hear how much you appreciated "Storm Clouds" and I am so glad I had it enlarged. Photography doesn't interest me quite so much as it used to, but I'm stimulating the interest a bit and even thinking of buying a better camera. Light gets in on some of the negatives with the old one and I'm just getting a bit fed up with it. Duncan, by the way, now has an Exakta reflex camera as well as a movie camera. I'm sorry you never saw the film I was in - maybe they didn't publish it, anyway I'm glad you saw the one of the ferrying across the Atlantic.

I'm so glad to hear that you approve of my marrying Diana, but you're a bit ahead of me, old bean! Why I'm not even in love with the girl and believe me I've got bags more women to meet and give the once over (maybe) the twice over - before I make the final plunge - boy what a plunge!

There isn't much more to comment on in No. 37, except that at the time of writing your garden sounded very nice and you were all in anticipation of being called up.

In No. 38 you acknowledged my brooch and a very "dear" letter from Canada. I presume the dear letter to be the long one describing Montreal. Please, in future, generally refer to something about a letter so I'll know which one it was. By the way I still don't know if you received the portrait of myself from Montreal. Just in passing moustache (must ask) you to spell committee - like so - rather than like so committy.!?

In one of my letters (about a year ago), I must have shot some line about having an artistic temperament. Maybe I'm right and you seem to agree with me. You suggested some things we might take up when I come home, and you had some pretty good ideas. Right now, my ideas are all over the place, but I rather feel that I must be something more than a Warehouseman when I start again. I'm an absolute fool with money and I'll never get anywhere unless I make some. Quite apart from that, I don't want to get into a rut again. Funny thing - I'm almost sick of the Air Force, I think!? But perhaps, I'm just sick of Wimpys and being a sergeant. That's one thing about the Air Force though - There is nothing surer than that things will change sooner or later.

Seems you're in big with everyone, except Aunty Norma and Nganie. Y'know, it's time people woke up to your admirable qualities and just shut their eyes to your few little tantrums - it's mostly people that caused the tantrums anyway. You had better tell Nganie that they too had better realise what a wonderful woman you are, or they've had me. - That'll wake em rigid!

The gist of No.44 (the second) is mostly about the Air Force the ATC and Dav. Sounds pretty good this Dav bloke, but I think I would prefer one of his daughters specially way out here in the desert. Stop that Dixon - "Dreaming of thee - love or be"?!

Now to get back to Dav - string him along Ma - you'll be a cinch for a commission - but stick to old lieutenant Colmore Williams even if he lets you down and dented that great big heart of yours once. He may be a rotten old sod, but even rotten sods are sometimes the best inside. Anyway, he is my Pa even if he is a stern old b....r! or should I say Lobster-faced B....r! Give him a good swift kick in the pants and congratulate him on his commission. By God, I'd even salute him if I was there to do it.

When you said Nganie was going to have a baby, I had to take another look at the letter just to see how old it was and make sure it wasn't Michael you were talking about. You also could have knocked me over with a feather when it finally sank in. By the way, what is Michael's second name and please don't forget to send me Nganie's address. I've forgotten who Miss Broadbent is and how about getting me some gen on Nancy Fenton. Y'know I might have something there, if I didn't put her off by my first letter which was written during a very mischievous mood.

In No. 44 you got onto the subject of clothes... Uniform I mean - Well out here in the desert we wear just about anything as long as it looks something like a uniform. At present, I have blue battle dress, Khaki battle dress and KD suits and shorts etc. Incidentally, I've just handed in my blue uniform because it was too much to carry around. We also wear with certain things - sort of suede bootee affairs. Nearly all the officers out here wear them, and we sort of copied them. They're really boots and have thick crepe rubber soles. They're absolutely wizo - I don't know how I'd get on without em in the desert. You offered to send me some buttons. I can never have too many buttons with NZ on them, and just in passing if you could rake up a couple of pairs of real pukker office type New Zealand issue pilot's wings for Ian, he would appreciate it immensely. He usually wears RAF wings now and apart from the principle of the thing, their wings aren't as nice as ours. I'm always telling him off about it.

Just before I finish off, I'll tell you a funny story. All along the line you and I seem to have had trouble with loo's. In Levin, I had to cue up for them, in Canada they didn't have any doors and of course at home there was Lena. Now out in the desert our tent is so situated that we have to walk 3/8ths of a mile to get to aforementioned conveniences. Thus, after almost running 3/8th of a mile to get to the one way and walking back you have covered 3/4 of a mile - A lot of the boys have got the runs at present, and what is usually called a "convenience" is badly mentioned out here. So badly mentioned, that not that many hours ago, I staggered blindly through a sand storm for 3/4 of a mile - transacted NO Business what so ever due to a false alarm and staggered another 3/4 of a mile back to the tent - what a life!! By the way, I was sober, the sand storm caused the staggering – No, No Not "Chuckles with Terry" this time, but "Chuckles with Lavvy". The Canadians would call that last crack "Corny".

Well that's all for now my Sweetest of all Sweets.

Yours lovingly, Teggy

Letter 6:- Middle East

6th May. 1942
c/- 37th Squadron
Middle East Commission

Dearest Mother,

Wonders never cease - When I returned from 7 days' leave yesterday, I found another big pile of mail waiting for me. From you I received 39, (no Number), 41, and 45 as well as the CAKE with the photo and the pullover from Dem and Pete. I also received a photo from Rae, letter and photo from Aroha, a parcel from R & G millinery workroom, a parcel from Mary Campbell of R & G, a letter from Pete and a couple of letters from a girl in Montreal. Not bad what!!??

Incidentally it nearly all came from England and was ages old.

Before I go further, I'll answer your letters. Your letter No. 39 refers mostly about your going into the Air Force and I've (We've) discussed that before - You also acknowledge the photos from Montreal - At Last! - I thought you were never going to - If I remember rightly, I sent a couple of photos, but you omitted to tell me what you did with t'other. Nothing at all to refer to in the (No Number) one except to congratulate Don on getting into the RNZAF.

On No 41 you get on the subject of Peggy McArthur and family. I'm afraid it's a subject which I do not wish to discuss and has given me enough worry already. I haven't written to Peggy since I re-met up with Duncan - mainly because I wouldn't know what to say. My failure to write probably makes her think I'm a louse too, and maybe I am. I don't know how Duncan will ever straighten the mess out. All I can do is hope that somehow things will turn out, and we'll all live happily ever after. With being up here in the "blue" (desert) I have not seen Duncan for quite a while.

I'm sorry Audrey got more mail from Alf than you did from me from England, but his was all 4/6pence Air Mail, and although I could have afforded it - you could not have afforded to answer it the same way, so there wasn't any point in doing it that way. I was very pleased to receive letter 45 because I was wondering where it had got to. I was pleased to hear that Nganae was on the job and I would like you to congratulate her for me. I was also pleased to hear they're also changing your head-gear. Thanks for the photo taken at the ATC Store - The old heart jumped a bit when I saw the boys in uniform - then I read what was on the back. I suppose they are itching to have those uniforms themselves, and they are certainly smart. I sincerely hope this 'DO' will be over before the boys are old enough and I have a feeling it will be. The cake was also Jolly-lutely wonderful and the pullover is just what I dreamed of. Although, just about useless out here it will be wonderful when I go back to Blighty.

Well, that just about answers everything, so I'll get on to the news. About a couple of days after arriving in the desert, we were sent back to Cairo on leave. Ian and I left Cairo the next day and went down to Port Tewfik to see the Mahons. It's wonderful going down there. The Mahons always seem to be so pleased to see us, and they are always very genuinely sorry when we leave. We had a quiet evening with them, and it was most unfortunate that Mary had a date with a Naval Officer. The next morning Ian and I went to the beach at about 9 am and swam all morning. I haven't enjoyed a swim so much for ages. It was one of those perfect days when the beach is the perfect place to be. At Tewfik there they have quite big baths fenced in with diving boards etc. The officers have one end and the ORs have the other. As there was hardly anyone there that morning, we used the officers' end. We used their boards and Gym equipment and even their solarium. I'm going very easily with my sunbathing and haven't peeled yet, so I'm keeping my fingers crossed.

We're rather lucky here, every afternoon they take us down to the Mediterranean for a swim. We had lunch with the Mahons that day and then returned to Cairo. That night we went to our favourite little night club and knocked back a few. The Barman there is a positive wizard at making John Collins. Don't get the idea I drink much, I'm actually being very good. The following day we didn't do much more than loaf all day, and then went to the pictures in the evening. The day after, we went to the 2nd NZAF camp where we made recordings of greetings to you. If you listen to the radio on Sunday mornings about the time you get this letter you will probably hear me spout my piece. I said more this time than last, but I was so jittery by the time I got to the end that I couldn't get "Dreaming of Thee" out. When we had finished our speeches, we went for a swim in the Freyberg baths and did some sunbathing. You can really have no idea of the heat in and around Cairo. It was quite impossible for me to wear anything more than shirts and shorts and sometimes even that was too much. At night, bedclothes were quite unnecessary even when sleeping under an open window.

On Sunday, Don (my wireless operator) and myself went to Mena House swimming baths. Mena House is a tourist hotel about 500 yards from the Big Pyramid. Their swimming baths are marvellous, but for outsiders the price is colossal. It cost 3/3d to get in and about 1/- for a cabin. Although it was hardly worth the price, I had a lovely swim - I won't bother to try and describe the baths —- instead I will send you a couple of snaps in my next letter. That evening,

Don and I went to a dance at the Cairo River Club. There were quite a few girls actually, but they were all escorted and so trying to get a dance was like trying to reach the moon. At about 9 o'clock we were fed up, so we went to the picture.

We were supposed to return to camp the next day, but they didn't send an aircraft for us. It was rather handy really because there was a new picture on that we badly wanted to see. The following day, Spanky came down and picked us up, so here we are again. Our tent could hardly be better: we have two primuses - coconut matting on the floor, plenty to eat and drink for sly meals - as a matter of fact, if we had H&C laid on and electric light and a wife each, we'd be about right. The weather at present is stinko. It's what's known as Khamseen *(Khamsin)* weather with terrific heat and high hot winds that cause that hateful state of a dust storm.

I just thought of something that might interest you. Do you know I have almost forgotten how you all at home speak. I mean what your voices sound like. As you will find out from my broadcast, my voice is still as bad as ever.

I've come to the conclusion that most New Zealanders speak rather well, but if you strike a particularly pronounced New Zealand accent it's just awful. The other day, Ian and I were sitting by some New Zealand girls in a restaurant. Their voices were almost as bad as Canadians - most of the New Zealand girls over here are rather bags as a matter of fact, but I saw a New Zealand VAD the other day, that I could fall in love with just as easy as winking.

Since I started writing, more mail has come in and I received parcel No. 5 from you - Thanks a million, Sweetheart, but I hope you have received the letter since telling you to cut out sending parcels. Quite apart from the money I quite realise the time, thought and care that those parcels have cost you.

Enclosed are some photos taken in Cairo. All completely lousy but still quite interesting.

Well, I must away now and dive into the rest of my correspondence.

I'm glad you think Rae is improving because I have fallen for her a bit again after seeing the photo she sent me, although I wouldn't be surprised if she spends most of her time with the American Navy.

All my love to the big four :- You, Colly, Dem and Pete - If they fought the war everywhere as well as you (everybody) in New Zealand are fighting, it would be over by now.

Tons of love and kisses and then some.....,

Yours

Teggy.

Terry found doing these broadcasts that would be played on the New Zealand National Radio at home very stressful and often forgot what he wanted to say. As you can see, this time, he typed himself something to go by:

TERENCE DIXON

Hullo, my friends in Auckland and Christchurch. A big cheerio to you all. If my friends and relations in the W.A.A.F. and R.N.Z.A.F. are by any chance listening to the radio instead of doing their fatigues…

Love to Mother, Dem, Pete and Colly. I have been hearing great things about you four. You must look great in uniform Mother, but do not work too hard. I was pleased to receive quite a lot of mail from you recently. I am very fit and I am surviving the heat and flies pretty well. I must finish now, so lots of love to you all. Kia Ora.

ഇരുന്നുരു

Letter 7:- Middle East

37 Squadron
Middle East Commission
23 May 1942,

Dearest Mother,

It's a couple of weeks since I wrote, and in the meantime, I have received quite a bit from you. On the 14th I received a parcel of Ovaltine, coffee and milk and some fags. It was very much appreciated, but I hate to think of you spending money on things we can really buy ourselves out here. When I go back to England you can start again, but out here it is just a matter of whether you spend the money on yourself, and I'd rather I did the spending here. On the 17th I also received Dem's Birthday cake which was an absolute beaut and it had not deteriorated a bit with its long journey. On the 21st I received a birthday greetings cable from you and now today, which is 23rd, I received letter No. 43, which has come out from England. Thanks a lot for all the above it has put a Wizard guilt on the Gingerbread lately. The same day that I received your cable I also received one from Wilma who has become pretty good with correspondence lately. I see from the address on the cable that she has been called up - Good luck to her - Good luck to you All!

Before further ado, I must answer this last letter of yours. You mentioned a parcel of coffee and milk, biscuits and fags etc. Well I don't think I have received that one yet because I know I have never had a parcel containing biscuits. You asked if I ever received the four tins of Greys tobacco that went to Canada and the answer is NO!? In this letter you were feeling a bit browned off with Colly, the old Lobster face, but from later letters it seems things aren't so bad again!? You sent some lovely snaps with that letter of Tinopai and the house and the Hydrangeas etc ... I couldn't remember for a while who David, Joan and Wendy were, but it soon came to me. The house and garden looked lovely and brought back a bit of a longing - but I soon came down to earth again.

Duncan's bad luck must have been a terrible blow to you as it was to me. I did not let it worry me too much and I have been as optimistic as possible about it. I hope my cable cheered you and stopped a bit of your worrying (as I suppose you probably did anyway) - I have done all that is possible to find out what - but nobody really knows. He had bombed his target and then nothing more was heard from him. There was **a rumour** that the Rome radio made a statement that there were two prisoners of war from a crashed aircraft over that target that particular night, but that is definitely nothing to go on. We can just hope and pray that he is alright and until we hear to the contrary - It is the best thing to believe. I went to his base the other day to see if I could get some little thing of his, but I had left it too late and all his stuff had gone to The Committee of Adjustment. Down there, Spanky MacFarlane (our flight commander) introduced me to Flt/Lt. Ralfe-Smith who you might remember. He did everything he could for me - but there really wasn't much he could do.

(still same letter but it is now 31st May 1942)

I'm sorry there has been such a gap, but we're really been busy of late. A couple of days ago, we operated two nights running and even now I'm a bit tired. Looking at the above date you probably wonder now what sort of Birthday I had. Starting from the beginning I'll give you an account of it - At 23:58 on 29th I dropped a load of "Blows for Democracy" on an enemy target. I didn't realise it was my birthday until about 04:30 when I had to look at the date for some reason or other - I wasn't too happy at the time because the old Nav had gone a bit duff.

The realisation cheered me up a bit. Later we were being briefed in the Officer's mess and Spanky introduced me to Dunc's old Wing Commander, who shouted me a beer. I never realised before that beer could taste so good so early in the morning. I had a yarn to the Wingco about Duncan, but he knew no more than I did. I slept most of the day, but the heat and the flies weren't conducive to getting good rest. It turned out to be pay day which brightened things greatly. I.e. did some local flying about 19:30 and when we returned there were two parcels and a letter waiting for me. Can you guess what they were? Your photo

Your Birthday present and Your Birthday cake. You couldn't have timed it more perfectly. Even at home I never got things on my Birthday.

Despite the fact that you didn't think the cake was up to standard - We thought it was of the best we had had. Mick and Ian want to convey a special thanks to you. I don't like to think you going to so such trouble for me, but seeing you have I really think the appreciation was worth it. Since I've been away from home, I have often thought of buying myself some slippers, but have never done so. The ones you sent are absolutely ideal and fit just as slippers should fit. Please thanks to the boys for the tie, Chocolates and fags but don't thank them for the razor blades - I've got so many of the damn things I don't know what to do with them. The chocolate was the best we have had so far because coming direct it hadn't melted. We were going to have a few beers to celebrate but the beer was awful so we left it - We were just going to eat my Birthday supper of sausages and peas, which Mick had prepared on the primus, when the 'Jerry' came over - We were going to leave it - but someone suggested that we take it to the slit trench. We got about half way, when the old bugger let fly we all dropped to the deck and those beautiful, wonderful sausages and peas took off and went flying, so not one little sausage and not one little pea did we partake thereof. Ian and I went to sleep in the sh (nearly made a faux pas) slit trench and at about 01:00 this morning, I woke up and the blighter was on top of me in a very loving attitude.

I didn't like to wake him, he looked so comfy, but I was damned <u>un</u> comfy with him pushing my ribs in one way and then a dirty great stone pushing them in t'other way - I lay and reflected a moment and thought what a bloody silly thing this jolly War is. Last night we had bombed him, and he had probably lost his supper and gone to sleep in a trench - Me now, you next sort of business like a silly lot of kids. More ridiculous when you come to think that I could have been walking along the beach at home with family or wooing some lovely New Zealand lass on such a beautiful moonlit night, with the same old moon in the sky. Finally, I did wake Ian and we went to bed and that was me birfday- and so now I am 21 - 20 years and one day ha?! "Sand Happy" they call us. Right now, Mick is so sand happy that he is trying to make a fly trap. It is just too complicated to describe: consisting of a glass, match box, mirror, a pineapple tin of kerosene and a bit of meat paste., but it is so useless that now he is catching flies to put in it to fool the boys.

Despite all the messing about, I'm very Happy and as fit as I've ever been. I think the Desert agrees with me.

This is a poem which Mary sent me on my Birthday and which applies to us - I've changed the word friend to 'lover' which I think sounds much better.

DREAMING OF THEE

Fond words that bring remembrance
come winging far and fleet,
From lover to lover awaking
old memories warm and sweet
My thoughts and prayers are yours today
with love from one who's far away.

Yours ever with love
    Teg.

    (Vestigia nulla retrorsum) *Never Step Backwards*
    P.S. := I do hope you like the enclosed photography

ഇൻരുൻരു

This letter to Pete only arrived after news that Terry had gone down. I put in in here, as it fits in chronologically. There were other letters that also arrived after Terry's death. Receiving such letters, after his death, may have been another reason in the end, that my Gran's health went downhill.

From Sgt. Terence Dixon
NZ 404678 R.A.F. Middle East -
37th squadron
1st June 1942

Dearest Pete,

I haven't yet much to say, old bean, but I thought that after your valiant effort of writing, it might tickle you a bit pink to get a letter (sorry, Note) from your bigger Bruvver. Seems things are going along pretty well at home, but blow me down, the old woman isn't half doing a spot of work. Actually, she is probably doing a darn sight more than I am, but she writes and says how she thinks of me working like blazes. I really don't work like blazes at all and I have told her so, but a fond and proud mother cannot be disillusioned.

Old Mum writes me wizard letters an' ye' know, I think she loves me a Bit and just in case I don't make it quite clear in my letters, you'd better tell her for me that I love her too. All my notes to you must sound rather a load of bullshit, but I must say this: I am very proud of my two brothers and if I never have a son of my own, I will be satisfied with the knowledge that I have such a wizard pair of brothers. You might let Dem read this and I say to him that I share in his

152

triumphs (or would like to) of both his sport and learning. My hopes in both your futures are very great, and my desire at present is to be back with all, where I can be of some use to you.

I won't bother to write any news in this because I have quite a few letters to write and the news would only end up being a repetition of what I will be writing to Mother.

My love to both you and Dem and give Mum a big Kiss for me and Kid her for a moment that you are myself.

Yours
  Teg.

P.S. Thanks a million for the Birthday presents - The tie was a beaut and cost you more than you should have spent on me - Ian who is a "gentleman" says on the subject, that it is the best tie I ever had.

෯෬෨෯෬

Letter 8:- Middle East   4th June 1942
                                                    37th Squadron

Dearest Mother,

Only 4 days since I wrote a nice long letter to you, but perhaps this will make up for the times when I didn't write to you for too long a time at once.

The main object of this epistle is to answer 47-48-49-50 and 51 which all arrived at once on the 1st of June. Most of what is in no.47 I have already answered in previous letters mostly about Don and Nganie and Colly. The latter seems to be turning up trumps again and I quite enjoyed reading that letter of his you sent me. Next time you write to him send him my love and wish him all the best from me. All through No 47 you moan (bind we call it) about not having received any mail from me. I am really terribly sorry about that and will do my best not to let it happen again. I think the trouble is that I feel every letter to you must be a super one and it always looks to be such a big job and one which I must leave plenty of time for. I'm getting out of that habit now and if some of my future letters are a bit shorter, they'll still be super ones. I have become very good with correspondence lately, but to a lot of people they have become very brief letters - you know. 1½ pages to Nganie, 1¾ pages to Wilma (brief) sort of business.

You asked what we do for women in the Middle East. I think I have discussed that rather fully before and I don't mind telling you again. It's a bit of a cow (or something)- If I didn't have the Mahons and Mary to go and see I would be almost "blackened out" ask what Colly says. I fail to see the connection between Mary (who is wonderful) and a Swiss Egyptian lass, so Duncan must have had another girl friend.

THIS IS NOT OFFICIAL IS NOTHING TO GO BY AND IS ONLY A RUMOUR

but I heard today that the entire crew of Duncan's plane are prisoners of War. If it is true, you will know long before you receive this and if you haven't heard anything please don't think any more about it.

I hate to think of you cleaning buttons - lousy job. Why don't you get Pete to do it for you? I think, by the way, that it is time you got a commission with all this work you are doing. All the WAAFS in Blighty in such positions are Assistant Section Leaders.

In letter No. 48 there is really nothing to comment on because it was all about Duncan and other subjects which I have already discussed very fully. 49 like 48 is just a chatty letter but with it you sent some snaps which were very good and very much appreciated. In the one of the Marstons - who is the extra child which is seated on Pat's knee and is Pat married to Cliff??? The ones of the boys and their acrobatics and the family group all in their Sunday best are best - Wizzard. The one of Dem and Pete sitting on the beach is also exceptionally good and, by the way, I rather like the way Miss Dorothy Jeffreys winks at me from the photo. She could do me a lot of good away out here in the blue?! Dixon behave yourself! Sorry Ma, that was a futile attempt at a wisecrack. Did I tell you I didn't like the portrait you sent me. So sorry, but I much prefer the snaps. Unless they change their ideas a bit, I think the days of portrait studio photos are over. In that one of you they took away all of the wrinkly little soft bits that I love so much and are so nice to kiss. Hope you don't mind my being so frank about the photo. I really don't dislike it altogether.

In letter No 50 you speak of Easter. Funny thing I hardly remember there was one. I think someone probably mentioned something about it at the time, but we never gave it a second thought as we were "just kept very busy at the time. I'm glad to see they gave you a spot of leave. Too bad I wasn't there for Don's 21st. It was very nice of him to make those few little remarks about me. I can just imagine Nganie bursting into tears. I do hope she doesn't do that when I come home.

Excuse please - we've had just a little interruption here. We've just had a wizard supper of sausages and peas. Australian sausages and New Zealand peas. Both from a can but absolutely cooked to a turn by Mick over our little primus. A nice cup of tea too. Do you remember how we used to be so put out if we ever had to have a cup of tea with condensed milk? Well strangely enough, I never have a cup of tea that hasn't got condensed milk in it these days, and we never notice it. Milk seems to be quite a problem in Egypt. In the cities they have cow's milk, but it is always boiled and in restaurants they serve it to you hot.

To get on with answering your letter. You did finish off that letter with a lot of questions which I have already answered. No. 51 – Yes, I was terribly glad to hear that you had at last received some mail from me. Re the trip out - your first guess was right. I was terribly pleased to hear of Dem's further successes - You certainly have a real bright son there. You still seem to be working terribly hard. I am ever so sorry I didn't acknowledge a lot of your letters, but as I only started my correspondence book a little while ago, I can't tell you now, what I have acknowledged and what I haven't.

There is no further news so I must finish now. As a matter of fact, I've got a job to do as well.

Give my love to all my loved ones and all the love in the world for yourself.

Yours Ever

Teg

P.S. :- The possibility of my returning to NZ as an ATC instructor is not as fantastic as it sounds - but don't think about it too much because it's still a terrible long way off.

ഇരുങ്ക

Letter 9:- Middle East

37th Squadron
Middle East Commission
15th July 1942

Dearest Mother,

It is ages since I last wrote, and much water has passed under the bridge in the interim. My only excuse is pure laziness. I wonder how I can do it to you when I receive so many letters of such fine quality from you. The latest lot received yesterday were a funny mixture. Some from England and one direct. I will answer them here as a sort of feeler or forerunner to the main part of the letter. The first one was written on the 17th December 1941 and marked No. 41- It was stale I suppose, but very interesting - I'm glad to hear that Dem and Pete are being so good to you and that our wee house is becoming so beautiful.

You spoke of a bad summer and were hoping that I wasn't feeling the cold too much. Seems funny now you are in the middle of winter and I'm just about a grease spot in the sand. We are still somewhere in Egypt and the heat and humidity is terrific. Certainly, I suppose the pipes were in the sun, but I turned on a cold tap today and the water came at a heat I could just bear to keep my hand under. Most people still think I'm not very tanned - but all over except for my lower abdomen, I'm the darkest I've ever been in my life. As you said in your letter, it is hard to believe that the War has come so close to little New Zealand, but I'm proud to see the mighty spirit of you at home that has shown itself in both yours and Don's letters. The spirit that will keep our paradise Islands intact should the emergency arise, the spirit that holds the Hun in the desert, the spirit that is represented on the sea and in the air and the spirit that even the Hun himself praises.

You hope that it won't be too long before I return - Time marches on! And it is the better part of two years since I left you all, but the longer I'm away the sooner I'll be back - It's in my bones and in my heart. Oh yes. It permeates my very soul - I will soon be back to you.

Your next letter was written on New Year's Day, and was numbered 42 - At the very hour you were writing - I was flying on my way to the Middle East - It seems so very long ago now.

Thanks for enclosing Don's letter - I was also amused with the Dear Roma! There is really something great about that boy despite his little failings - Only since coming away and receiving his letters, have I realized what a real friend I have in him. His letters are wonderful and really put mine in the shade ~ His sense of humour and depth of feeling and imagination are colossal. Apart from quality, the number of his letters is only second to yours.

(side-tracking a bit) Sitting right here in this room with me, also writing letters, is one of the best friends a man could wish to have. It is Ian Medwin, our skipper. He is 25 and a self-made man who has always taken life by the throat and shaken the best out of it. His morals are like clear running water, he is as honest as the day is long and his code of living is one, that like rare jewels, is so seldom found. He is a Wizard Pilot and one of the most popular men on the squadron. Ian and I are rarely seen apart, and I am jokingly referred to as his Yes-man. He respects my position in the aircraft and trusts me implicitly. He looks after me like a big brother and considers me his responsibility.

I owe a lot to him and always shall - even my life as I shall tell you more about in a minute.

Ah, has your son painted the picture of a perfect partner in this wicked world? Rest assured My Sweet! I've made him sound like a saint, but he isn't. He drinks and smokes and appreciates lovely women as much as anybody and like everyone else has numerous failings. Well I have to say it is hot work writing letters! I've just had a beer and I now feel much more up to the job.

You have recently received a cable (probably) reporting me as missing in action and after that a later cancellation. Of the whole story I don't know how much I can tell or should tell being very much in the dark as to what is considered a military secret, however here we go, and the censor can cut away if he likes.

Last month during the disastrous advance of the Hun, we were detailed for operations over the enemy front line. Our bombing was a complete success, but after turning off from a ground strafing attack, we were attacked on the port beam by an enemy night-fighter. He gave us one long burst of cannon and machine gun fire and as he turned away, he was so close that Ian recognised the type of plane and clearly saw the enemy markings. The port motor and wing immediately caught fire, and parts of the wiring which burst into flames
- it entered the wireless and so quickly the top of the cockpit was blown away. I attempted to extinguish the fire, but it was hopeless. Ian ordered us to prepare to abandon the aircraft but although we were ready, in no time we had just lost too much height to jump so instead we braced ourselves for the crash landing which was now inevitable - It was night (and we had moonlight) and Ian brought her down on a reasonably level patch of desert on her belly. The jolt was no more than the ferry hitting the wharf very hard. There had been no panic because there wasn't time.

From the time we were hit till the time we crashed was about 3-5 minutes. So, you see - Through Ian's cool-headedness and the superior handling of a half dead aircraft, we were all unhurt and I shall always remember the part he played. We left the kite blazing and hours later we could still see her aglow in the distance. Unfortunately, we were behind enemy lines, but as desert fighting is so scattered, we were lucky enough not to see any Huns and after walking/ running pretty fast for about 3 hours, we were picked up by a forward British Patrol. (Now don't worry) but Three of the boys, including Ian were slightly hurt, and they were taken over by a medical corps. The other three (myself included) started off on the long hitch-hike back to base, which in the interim had been moved back another 200 miles. We did it in very lucky stages and arrived back on the squadron almost three days after we had left it. Now I don't need to tell you - The rejoicing was GREAT! We drank in the Officers' mess with the CO (I was given a double brandy which nearly laid me low) and we were immediately sent on leave.

DREAMING OF THEE

I had a glorious restful three days with the Mahons at Port Tewfik and then returned to the Squadron — (Incidently during those three days, I first became interested in Dorothy) By this time, Ian and the others had also returned, and we were all given an aircrew medical exam ~ my first since November 1940- and I passed it! Yah, still fit, Ma! We were all pronounced fit but were given another seven days leave - Palestine tempted us but the magnetism of beautiful sweet Mary and the lovely devilish Dot at Port Tewfik were too strong for Ian and I, so off we went. The train was too slow for me, and I was terribly impatient until we finally burst in on them. Another home away from home with a Mother and two lovely girls. We put up at a hotel where we only spent about 9 of the 24 hours every day.

Our usual routine was as follows ~ Along to the Mahon's about 08:30 and Dot and I would go down to the beach where we would meet Ian. Unfortunately, Mary worked during the morning from 9am till 1pm.

As I have said before, down there they have a beautiful bath house for the Officers and civvies and a wooden shack for the men. This time Ian and I decided not to be mugs and boldly used the officers' end. We wore good class clothes which looked rather different from the issue and wore no badges of rank or service at all. We got away with it, even if the little rat-bag manager did look askance at us a couple of times. I'm glad we did because we would not have been able to accompany Dot and Bobby otherwise, and I'm sure it would have spoilt my whole holiday.

That beach bath house and surroundings are really lovely. The swimming pool itself is a fenced-in stretch of water which has been dredged to about 20 ft below the diving boards to a safety depth near the edge for children. As the change of tide is nothing compared to home, it makes very little difference. The diving boards are varied in heights and super, and here I might remark that my swimming and diving has much improved. From the water's edge there is at least a hundred yards square of beautiful white sandy beach, which is raked and smoothed every morning. From the beach you go up sort of marble steps to the beautiful modernised bathhouse, which is also made of this modernistic white stone stuff. There is a bar and a verandah cafe overlooking the baths, while on the roof a solarium, all around are lovely lawns under shady trees, and we used to lie there and read or fool about all morning. At one o'clock, we used to meet Mary, and all go home for lunch. As you know only mad dogs and Englishmen go out in the mid-day sun, and out here the siesta custom is strictly adhered to (except by the forces), so down there we used to just snooze every afternoon. Perhaps I should say attempted to snooze because with the Ma and Pa asleep, we had very little peace from the girls or should I say we gave the girls very little peace - or what have you?? At four in the afternoon we used to have tea consisting of bread and jam and cakes and gallons of tea (I'm a worst tea swizzler than ever) - Mary used to go back to work from 4.30 till 6pm and then at about 7.30pm we had dinner. After dinner, we went to an open-air cinema near-by, then after the pictures home to bed. It was a very lazy sort of leave, but we did not tire of it for one minute of the time.

I think I have described the Mahons to you before, but at the time I didn't know them quite so well. They have improved with knowing them and Mary is truly one of the finest girls I've met yet. To me, she is like a big sister. Ian has become rather smitten with Mary - So much so that it even worries him a little.

Perhaps I am a cad for chicken-stealing, but Dot (who is only sixteen) and I had a lot of fun. She is short and plump, but well-proportioned and really nice looking with absolutely marvellous hair that the sun has bleached into three different shades that blend into one another. She is one of these "grown up too young" lasses and boy was she dynamic. You once asked what we did out here for women – well we try all sorts of things even chicken stealing. Dot has been taken out by everyone from a sergeant to a squadron leader and has been proposed to a couple of times already. Yes, she is a little spoilt. We hated coming from that holiday, but we are now settling in again, and we will soon be cracking on the job again.

While I'm on the subject of the Mahons and Port Tewfik etc., just cannot get Duncan (Duncan) out of my mind.

It is no use keeping it from you that although he is still posted "missing believed killed", the fact is that he was actually killed. I'm sorry mother that I have had to tell you because like everyone else, you must have had hopes. My hopes were high right up until I went to Head Office of personnel records, where they told me that they had a report from another member of the crew who was now a prisoner of war. Despite this report, still he had to be posted "missing believed killed" because the report was not considered enough concrete proof. I do realise that the whole sad business had been a terrible blow to you, but I hope it will not worry you too much.

Yes, I do know I have side-tracked a long way from answering your letters, but I will do some and finish off, No42 had a real kick in it, as you say the Air Force has changed you like it does everyone. That letter sounded as if you are being handed out a few bad breaks instead of receiving them all. It was a real fighting letter mostly about Colly and all his nonsense. From a more recent letter I see he is turning up trumps again. Too bad you had such a lousy Christmas while I was having such a peach. As old Lil says, we think the sun shines out of our bottom eh? Perhaps it does, because we get closer to the sun than anybody else! (being in the Airforce) - I don't think I need say any more about that ignorant remark at least a few intelligent people realise the job we do.

The next letter was No. 52. posted on April 30th 1941 (42?) and again was mostly about Duncan (Duncan). Poor old Duncan I'm afraid he was in a hopeless mix up. I think he was in love with Mary, but he didn't want to break away from Peg although he did fill Mary with talk of getting a divorce. At the same time he was writing to Peg patching things up (or so it now seems) - It is said he also had more girl friends than just Mary out here - as far as women were concerned I believe Old Duncan didn't have a clue because they fell for him like Palms before a Hurricane.

It is said Peg thought he loved her again and that his estrangement was simply due to his previous crash landing (and escape) while Mary thinks he was still madly in love with her. Poor little Mary she is so sweet and innocent she even sent an anonymous parcel of baby clothes to Peg. She has a heart as big as a house. It is a terrible pity she is so dark - she worries terribly about it too.

(From the beginning of my answer to No 52 is a paragraph that perhaps should not be there. However, I just can't help myself from telling you everything. The above is only acknowledged to you Ian and myself, so let's keep it at that).

Along with those letters of yours I received 21 other letters from various people. I got quite a few from Nganie in which I learned that Joyce Skinner is engaged - Oh too bad that! I got some wizard letters from Don and some from Canada and England and believe it or not, a Christmas card from Nganie and George (Christmas in July)?!!!

I just remembered you said something in your last letter about my being worried over my attack of Gyppo tummy. It is nothing to worry about my Sweet - I've even had it again since. Everyone gets it - It's just a sort of summer sickness - It seems to hit some worse than others and I am proud to say I haven't really been ill since I've been in the air force.

Well I must away now and write to a few of the others who are no doubt clamouring for letters.

Don't forget Sweetheart you're still my best girl and even if my writing home does slip a bit we will never drift apart - This mother-son combination - because We are an amazing pair.

All my love

Teggy

Give my love to the boys and maybe Colly if he is behaving himself!?

The Auckland Star, Friday, S

AUCKLAND FLYERS IN DESERT ORDEAL

SHOT DOWN IN FLAMES

Pilot From Hamilton Wears Winged Boot Badge

Special Correspondent
United Press Association—Copyright
Rec. noon.   LONDON, Sept. 24.

Wearing the small, winged boot badge, indicating that he has been shot down and had then returned to his own lines, Pilot-Officer I. G. Medwin, of Hamilton, has returned to England from Egypt. He was shot down during June when the Germans were advancing towards Mersa Matruh.

The officer said: "Our job was low-level bombing and strafing at night and we were giving it. A German column had just pulled out when a Messerschmitt got on our tail and raked us with cannon shells and bullets, hitting the port motor, the wing and fuselage, and setting fire to the aircraft.

"I had a bad moment when I looked round and saw the kite ablaze. I thought it was the end, because we were too low to bale out, while we were unable to reach our base, but despite the dark we managed to pick out a likely looking spot. Then we made a crash landing in flames.

Flight Sergeant (now Pilot Officer) T. Dixon.

"My second pilot was K. Andrews and the observer T. Dixon. Both are Auckland flight-sergeants. I managed to get the plane down, but Andrews was injured badly. I managed to keep walking. We had to keep a sharp lookout for German columns which were walking round, too.

No Food and No Water

"We had no food and no water. It was lost with the plane, but after five hours we met men from the King's Own Regiment who were minelaying. They had lorries and took us to Mersa Matruh. Andrews was like a man possessed the way he kept walking despite his injury. He sometimes staggered as to fall, but so long as we kept him on his feet he kept going. He was getting on all right in hospital the last I heard, while I and Dixon recovered after seven days."

Pilot-Officer Medwin has carried out 33 operations. He was shot up eight times, including five when over Bengasi while minelaying. A shell once went through the hood of the plane between the two pilots, miraculously missing both.

Warrant-Officer W. Bruce Heney, North Canterbury, saw Pilot-Officer Medwin shot down. "I saw the plane flaming but didn't realise whose it was until the next morning, when I found Medwin's tent empty," he said. Warrant-Officer Heney has carried out 40 operations, many of them when Pilot-Officer Medwin was operating. They raided Rhodes, Greece, Crete and Libya.

Sergeant-Pilot L. G. Moors, Auckland, has also returned. He has carried out 40 raids, including 13 in succession against Bengasi.

Terence Dixon, aged 20, is the eldest son of Mrs. R. Simons, of Audrey Road, Takapuna, and has now gained a commission in England. Pilot-Officer Dixon left New Zealand in 1941, trained in Canada, and spent 13 months in England and the Middle East. He was educated at Auckland Grammar School, and prior to his enlistment was employed on the staff of Ross and Glendining, Ltd.

161

Letter 10:- Middle East   27th July 1942
37th Squadron
Again deployed somewhere in the Desert
Middle East Commission

Dearest Mother,

Again, it is high time I wrote, but isn't so bad this time as it's only ten days since I wrote you a 12-page letter. You can well imagine that I have very little to write about over such a short duration of time in which we have done so very little.

I received 2 letters from Diedre the other day written on 31st May. Naturally it was a wretched and rather heart-wrenching letter in which she asked me to tell her all about Duncan. I have probably put my foot in it again, but seeing she asked me I considered it the wisest thing to tell her the unhappy news I had got at the personnel Base Records office. The Greatest tragedy has caused us all much unhappiness, but please now, let's just let us try now to forget that it has happened, and make ourselves think as we would have a child think, that he has just gone away for a while, and we will meet him later on.

Please don't worry about me either, at present I am fit and happy and when I have finished my operations here, which will be soon, I may have a chance of going to the U.S.A. For our feat of walking back through enemy lines, it is possible that we will be accepted also as members of the "Late Arrivals Club" for which we are allowed to wear a little badge consisting of a silver boot with a wing on it. Apart from that I have a faint suspicion that Ian has been recommended for the D.F.C. but as yet, nothing is definite about that. Apart from flying we have done very little lately except that on a day off a couple of days ago we went down to Port Tewfik. I.e. had to hitch-hike there and back and only had about 6 hours with the girls but it was well worth it.

We went swimming in the afternoon and shucks I thought I could swim but you should see little Mary Mahon (she is not little she is nearly as tall as I am)! She is like a blinking speed boat in the water and dive! She is like an arrow going into the water. Ian and Dot wouldn't come in ~ Ian because of his inability to swim much and Dot because she wanted to keep him company. It was about eight o'clock of a very warm evening before we returned from the swim and as it was far too late to go to the pictures. After dinner, we stayed home and played the gramophone out on the verandah in the moonlight – Ghee, You should see these bright Eastern night,s they are just gorgeous! I was almost back to my old form that night and sang "The magic of your Love".

SOMEWHERE IN THE MIDDLE EAST

As always "though this lovely night will end" as it did far too soon, and we went back to the hotel. We got up pretty early the next morning and did some very lucky hitch-hiking back to camp.

Mary and Dot are a great pair. They are both sensible, loveable and almost beautiful. The four of us make a very happy quartet.

I've got your photo on the wall above my bed. Nobody believes it is my Ma - You're too beautiful. Well I must away now and have a cup of chai (tea)

All my love Sweetheart

Yours

Teg

ॐ

This next letter was given to a friend returning to NZ as Terry hoped it would fit in to his regular mail as an added up-to-date bonus - so not given a number or in sequential order in the box. (Clearly, Johnnie travelled by ship with Terry's letter)
STAMPED   Auckland   12.15am   5th October 1942

The letter is dated and written

3rd August 1942

Darling One,

It has been suggested to me that I write to you and send the letter per a very fast safe method. I have really nothing to say except that I love you just as much as ever. It occurred to me that a far better method would be to get Johnnie Goddard (the tall dark and handsome) young man you see before you, to go and see you. I don't want this to sound too much like a letter of introduction, but I might as well tell you Johnnie is a very good friend of mine and can tell you much more of our comings and goings than I can in a letter. He and I both came to the Middle East at the same time and we have both been to all the same places. I have done 26 op's now and should be well finished with my first operational tour by the time you receive this letter. I very much doubt if I will be fortunate enough to return home like Johnnie when I've finished. It seems they only need wireless op's at home. A lot of observers and pilots go from here to the U.S.A. and it is quite likely that I will also be doing that.

I more recently became a member of the "Late Arrivals Club" and now proudly wear the emblem of the flying boot on the pocket of my tunic!

163

It is a sort of honour bestowed upon those brought down by enemy action in the Desert and return to base long after their estimated time of arrival. After our walking and hitch-hiking we were three days late.

I am also writing the usual letters so I will just leave this as it is. Keep the pecker up old bean - maybe they will soon decide that they want some navigators over there.

All my love my sweetheart Yours
Tegs.

Order of the Boot:

A winged boot forms the badge of the Late Arrivals Club for airmen who walk home from air battles.

ဆားဆားဆား

Copy of a letter Terry wrote to a friend: Alf Drew. This is a letter Alf sent a copy of, to Roma, later on. The P.S. at the end is what Alf commented to Roma.

dated 9th August 1942
sender: Sgt. Terence Dixon NZ 404678
37th Squadron, RAF Middle East Command.

To Sgt. A.S. Drew NZ 404560, RNZAF
C/- NZ Hours, 415 Stand, London, England

Dear Dekkar,

Excuse my continual use of airgraphs, but as you know there is really very little to say and they just about meet the bill, I received yours of the 10th July today. Too bad you weren't posted out here but believe me your present position has many advantages over the Middle East. I have met Jeff a couple of times out here and now he is pretty busy though recently he was lucky enough to get a couple of weeks leave in Palestine. Unfortunately, I haven't managed to get up there yet - but I have been able to pass some very happy days with friends of mine in Egypt.

Not long after I wrote to you, we were unlucky enough to get holed by a Jerry Night Fighter and we made a crash landing behind enemy lines. We were lucky it was night because we managed to walk back to our lines without being seen. By hitch hiking we finally got back to base about 3 days late. For this we became eligible for the Late Arrivals Club and now we wear the badge of this club - a little silver winged boot.

We had a week's leave after that, and Ian and I stayed with our friends in Port Tewfik. We had a lovely time down there swimming, sunbathing and just sleeping. One seems to need a helluva lot of the latter out here.

The weather is always terribly sticky, and we haven't seen rain for some six months. Well, all the best old bean, look after yourself.

Have Good Luck, your pal Terry.

P.S. Around about this time there was an American comedian who used to have a slow, crazy Texas drawl, Terry was so intrigued with my ability to take off this character's way of speaking he started using it as a nickname. As you can see, Jeff picked up the habit too!!!

₧₨₧₨

Enclosed within Letter No. 11:-
Still on op's somewhere in the Desert

Middle East Commission
37th Squadron 16th August 1942

Dear Dem and Pete,
As far as you are concerned, my cherubs, I have just one letter from each of you to answer,

One from Demmy - and sorry written on 12th January 1942 which has been to Blighty (England) and back. Seems you had a rather strenuous Christmas Holiday (that was last Christmas and you are probably reading this next Christmas) - I suppose the hard-working holidays are putting the muscle on you. I've hardly done any real exercise since I have left Levin and I'm as weak as a kitten - You'll be able to clean me up with one hand behind your back when I return.

I seem to remember some mention of a female in that letter - well nice work! Makes life interesting, doesn't it? But watch out that it doesn't interfere with more important things.

Now young P.K. (*short for Pete*) - A letter from you on 2nd May 1942 nice and newsy - just the gear old boy - keep it up please and as often as possible without letting it interfere with your studies.

I think I mentioned this before but just in case - Congratulations Dem, old sport, in winning the senior champs. Definitely a wizard piece of work or as they say in the RAF with a plumb in their throat "Jolly good show old boy"!

Too bad you are having so much trouble with French, Pete old bean, I wish I was there to help you. Here's a hint. Do all your ordinary thinking in French and ask yourself occasionally, "How would I say it in French?" Do that and learn all the vocabulary you can and the grammar will come to you.

Now Boys, I presume you are still doing a good job of looking after our Ma. Keep it up boys my thoughts are with you All.

Love Teg

⁗⁗⁗

Letter 11:- Middle East

37th Squadron
Middle East Commission
16th August 1942,

Dearest Mother,

I'm afraid this is going to be rather a clueless letter because I have never before sat down to write to you with such a little bit to say and yet haven't written since 26th July 1942 - nearly three weeks. I think the reason I don't write to you so often as I should, is because I must really get settled down for a couple of hours, this way I can give the letter my whole attention, and it seems very seldom that I can get those two solid hours.

The last lot of New Zealand mail has been very disjointed and also disappointing. It has been straggling in for nearly a month now. In it I have only received mail from you and Diedre and a scenic photo from Don. Evidently that particular photo was referred to in a letter which I did not receive. Now I have a faint suspicion that some mail has been lost somewhere. Before I wrote you last, I received a parcel from you and forgot to mention it. Thank you ever so much. Those biscuits were particularly very appreciated - I ate nearly all of them myself - So yes, a Guts. Unfortunately, the butter content of the shortbread had made it melt a bit and gave it a peculiar flavour, but the coconut biscuits, although they were very broken, were scrumptious.

The latest letters from you are No number referring to Duncan (*Duncan*) and No. 54 - 55 unless the unnumbered one is supposed to be 53 - that number has been lost?

Number 54 was a long and interesting letter which I just about devoured. You spoke about my Birthday and how I was catching up to you.

One thing for sure is the last couple of months have certainly added a couple of years. I was even taken for 26 the other day. Sometimes I really feel it too. You haven't exactly been getting any younger either. I can not help noticing in snaps you have sent me, just how gray your hair has been becoming. I wouldn't say it had made you look any the less attractive though. Perhaps on the contrary, it gives you a rather more aristocratic appearance - not to say you didn't look aristocratic before the streaks of gray. Further on in your letter, you mentioned that quite a few airmen seem to be returning to the Dominions – Well, Lucky Blighters! A couple of weeks ago, a few young New Zealand wireless air gunners left the squadron bound for the South Pacific Paradise. One of them didn't even want to go because he has a wife in Scotland. Another of the boys is an Aucklander, so I asked him to come and see you. You've probably already met him by now if his word is as good as his intentions were. Just to make sure he would visit you, I showed him the photo of you in your uniform - Believe me it made a difference. Is there any chance of my returning??? I'm afraid you must take the chances as almost Nil my sweetheart. Someday they may decide they need a super Air/navigator out there, but I am sure, Not this trip. Apart from hoping for the aforementioned miracle to happen, I am also hoping I might be sent back to the Great North American Continent.

Too bad Rae was turned down for nursing, but if she is in the WAAFS now, I guess she will be happy. I wrote to her a few days ago. It's a damn shame she is so small it must spoil her for a lot of things. Despite the fact that you never thought she had much in her, I personally think she has definitely got something in her that a hell of a lot of other women haven't and for her years, I think she has a great depth of understanding.

The WAAF seems to be just what Nganae needed in life. According to your reports and judging by her own letters she has changed considerably into a much more sensible and interesting person; Whereas her letters once bored me, I now find them quite interesting.

(This is an absolute wizard time for writing - Mid-afternoon everyone asleep and all is very quiet - I wonder how long it will last).

In reply to Number 55, your job seems to be getting better and better as far as position goes, but surely such a responsible job is worthy of a higher rank, even if it is the NZWAAF, you should be at least a senior NCO if not a commissioned officer.

Old Colly seems to be quite an angel these days - give him my love and wish him all the best.

I've come to the conclusion that we used to sleep too much. You say that you are getting used to short sleeping hours. Last night we were on operations and I didn't get to bed till 4am. I got up again at about 08:45 for another breakfast and I have been quite chirpy all day.

It's amazing what you can do when you are accustomed to it. It's ages since I sent you some snaps, but I hope to rectify that very soon.

There is no news whatsoever, so I'll fold up till next time. All my love Sweetheart

Yours

Teggy

ഔഇരഔഇ

Letter 12:- Middle East

37th Squadron
stationed somewhere in the Desert from Egypt still
MIDDLE EAST COMMAND
19th August 1942,

Dearest Mother,

At last, after what seems an age, I have finished my first lot of operations and now I am rather resting on my laurels wondering what they will do with me next. It is a queer feeling, knowing that for quite some time, one will not be flying through the night to these beautiful and horrible targets and yelling through the intercom, "Bombs Gone!" It is really hard to diagnose one's feelings about operational flying and I think about 90% of the air crews feel the same. You hate the whole bloody scheme just like all war, but there is something about its thrillingness that gets to you also.

For the last few weeks, I have been terribly "browned off" and I was glad to finish, but I have faith (yet I am a fatalist) and I won't mind doing the next lot when the time comes. The reason for my writing so soon after my last letter is that I have just received another letter from you with which was enclosed Colly's letter. Your letter was No 57 just where number 56 is I can't imagine. This letter is the Longest I have had from you in ages and although it has rather striking complication, I enjoyed it thoroughly.

I was very glad to hear that my mail is coming through OK. Again, I say sorry for the gap when there was none from me, but that seems to always happen when I do a lot of moving about and cannot settle down to writing. Unfortunately, it may occur again soon - but I will try not to let it happen.

I am rather pleased (selfishly) to know that Duncan's death had actually been confirmed to you all before my fateful letters to you and Deirdre arrived, to tell the tragic news. Perhaps I am not so hard-hearted - I cannot bear the painful duty of breaking sad news - I did know that Duncan had been reported missing before my letter of May 6th, but in an effort to be diplomatic I said nothing until one of you said something first. Many false rumours flew about - I even heard once that he was definitely safe. I have said before that we must drop the subject - And once more I shall - I didn't get any real gen about him, but I just heard the other day that Gavin Goldfinch was on this squadron just before I joined it.

I'm glad you like the look of Ian. As I told you a couple of letters back, he has been a very good friend and a great help to me in many ways: You ask me if he is musical - Did I not tell you that before joining up, he was recognised as one of New Zealand's best amateur baritones? His singing quite puts mine in the shade, but it never worries me, and I still croon or burst out in song whenever I feel like it. Ian was also a representative table tennis player (he beats me 21-2 and that 2 is just given out of the goodness of his heart). He is also well above the average at tennis, but he can't swim or dance. Although very shy of those last two he does long to be able to do them - We'll train him ah. His address is Te Aroha Street, Claudelands, Hamilton. As far as I can gather his family is one of simple living folk who have strived nobly and have reaped the benefits of their hard work. Perhaps you would call them a typical small town, comfortable, middle class New Zealand family. They are a family of two sons and a daughter — The other son (a P/O observer sent home from Canada for home service) and the daughter - they were both recently married.

I should think Mrs Medwin (Ian's mother) a very sweet woman - very highly principled I would think and a little old fashioned and just seems to be living for her children.

Lately I have seen Jeff Reddell a couple of times, although we haven't had much time together. Did you receive the enlargement of he and I on horseback - I'm sorry it yellowed - It must have been the negative.

Alf still in England and operating with the New Zealand 75th Squadron. If you have a spare moment you might write to him. You definitely had the wrong idea about Flight Sergeants. - Flight Sergeant is the next rank to Sergeant, no matter what the trade, and is due to being in Air crew 6 months after becoming a sergeant (you don't always get it then, but often receive it later backdated). Jeff was a Flight Sergeant before leaving O.T.U. There are also quite a few W.O. first in air crew. It is (in air crew) the next rank to Flight-Sergeant and will be what I end up as, failing a commission- so just a slight swift kick in the pants for you, my sweet. You say "Don't go consoling Mary by marrying her." Why must you think that every woman I admire I might marry - I am not a silly impressionable girl! Don't think! This is an old oft discussed subject between us, ah. I have always said that such thoughts are far from my mind, but I grant you that if I ever really found the woman I could marry, I might have great difficulty in stopping myself. However, I have never met such a woman yet and I have never been truly in love. Perhaps I haven't the capacity, but I pray that I have and will have.

My ideal of the love I would wish for is a love like ours (between mothers and son plus) - They say that love between mother and son is difficult and so my above idea would seem fantastic, but although there is a mother-son love between us there is also something more (like a sixth sense) - perhaps because of your youthfulness when I was born - Now when I think it over I am wrong about any new love of mine being like ours because in that case, when I did fall in love it could mean I was replacing you by another woman and that shall never be. There must be a subtle difference somewhere, and I fancy this is where the Sex issue "rears its ugly head" and here in my youth is a question I have never yet been able to answer, despite people I have known and things I read - perhaps you can tell me? Just how much does this sex business actually enter into Love and of course a happy lasting union between two people? Is sex love? or is love sex? (I think not myself) - If a woman fails to satisfy a man physically or vice versa, is their love and their unity doomed?

...oooOooo...

Well I had to stop writing last night because I got very tired... indeed very tiring - I tired myself out with over-thinking, I think!

This morning I read DRO's at breakfast and found that I had been promoted to the exalted rank of Flight-Sergeant. Of course, I won't get paid for it for quite a while, but it is nice to have it. It was back-dated to the first of January 1942, so one of these days I should receive a nice big bit of back pay, which I will send home to you.

Today Ian and I went to Ismailia and did some shopping. Ismailia is one of the nicest places in Egypt. I would even go so far as to say some parts of Ismailia are really beautiful. There is a terrible lot of vegetation about and it has about 20 acres of Park land, a lot of which consists of big bushy Australian trees. We picked up the enclosed photos and I think they showed that I have not entirely lost the art of photography. The better one of the two of the Gyppo sailing boats I am having enlarged to 9x6 in order to make another picture for the sitting room and I will send it on when it is ready. I am also going to have a studio photo taken of myself up to date complete with my crown and "flying boot".

Tomorrow we hope to be going to Palestine to see all the holy places, so the next letter should be quite interesting.

Joy of Joys - on arriving back in camp, I found another letter from you (No. 58) waiting for me. You now definitely have the monopoly on New Zealand to me - For ages yours has been the only New Zealand mail I've received and the last two have been wizard letters too.

I was very glad (ever so glad) to hear you had received the parcel and the big photos. I was beginning to think they had gone astray. After buying and sending that brocade I thought it rather a silly gift, but I think maybe you did appreciate it.

I am addressing this letter to your section leader in anticipation... Congratulations, old thing, you certainly worked for it. I think this is about the first time your slaving ever was given recognition. You might tell them for me though, that they haven't got a clue out there as far as ranks go in the WAAF's. Why don't they take a line in the RAF WAAF's. It is a military organisation, isn't it? Then they must have proper ranks and officers. To think that you should be called a section leader, but only have the status of a corporal is definitely off the hooks!? In the WAAF in Blighty (England) the rank section leader is equal to F/O and a corporal is equal to a corporal.

You say that you are getting thin - not from too much work, I hope. Well I weighed myself today, and I am only 9-10lbs - Don't worry about it though, I am probably better off for it on the lean side.

All through this letter I have been thinking of a very difficult subject and I have been hedging around it, but now as it is the last thing to be discussed it must be discussed.

Ah I have been the only one to depend on Colly - However my star must have waned, but I'm still not backing out - The people who are so against him are rather prejudiced, don't you think? However, having had time to chew things over, I do realise that his actions of last year are truly unforgivable and must appear to anyone with half an eye, the absolute height of selfishness and lack of feeling. <u>BUT</u> there really is no explanation as to why he caused you so much heartbreak and an explanation there must be . Well now, if the explanation is a simple one of an attempt to drop you - Then it would see that you are wasting valuable years of your life, wasting your love and wasting all those things which you give without knowing, all this on a man who is not worth them. Is he not worth them!????

Sometimes I very, very much doubt it (if he is worth it)? But I don't know him the way you know him? I even doubt if you do. It would seem he is definitely a blackard. He or his actions have even proved it, but still I feel there is something more deep that we can not understand. His letter, like himself, was a mystery - It gave no clue. He may as well have just written and told me about the bush and the beaches and caves and made no mention of you. I did not appreciate his flippancy about you after the misery he has caused you and though many a true word was spoken in jest? Well, is he just having his game? It sure was a long game? The whole affair must add up to about 14 years now. (I must have been about 6yrs old) you often make reference to my loving him? Do I? I don't know? I first realised his presence at an impressionable age and have always respected him because of his intelligence, position and personality. It has often been said (to or in front of me) that he has been like a father to me and now when you think about it, there has never been any real reason for that statement. If a person had a choice of fathers, he would be a strange one to choose, don't you think? We've never had a chat all together - just he and I alone.

The task is done; the laws are plain to see. But one thing each must carry in his mind, A talisman to understand mankind – An "Open sesame" - a magic Key - I often wish I had the talisman and the "magic key" It would make things a lot easier. - I don't know Colly, but now I'm afraid I don't know Dave either, although he sounds quite a fine type. A fine type is perhaps an ideal type!? I say seize the opportunities whenever they come - The once missed chance may never again befall. The winning throw comes not at every call, Nor trumps by the sound of life and drum...., The whole trouble is that you still love Colly, and if you married again could you caste him forever from your life and never again give him a thought? It would be essential - Never before has such a golden opportunity for happiness and security offered itself to you, but before you do grasp it, you must realise that should the bottom fall out of what it offers or should you be unable to caste out Colly, (once more) you will probably be worse off than you ever had been.

It seems ridiculous that I should be saying these things to you. It almost sounds as if I am trying to give you advice, but I'm not really. I am just telling you how I feel about it all. Really, I think perhaps the best thing to do is to leave things as they stand until after the Scrap's over. (The Scrap being the bloody War).

By that time things ought to have worked themselves out.

Well as this is the second night I've been writing and as it's pretty late on the second night I had better finish off now.

I hope you aren't letting life worry you too much -and are taking things just as they come ~ I think it is the only way to go with this big Mix up.

Give my love to the boys and all the love in the world for yourself.

Yours

Teggy   xxxxxx

SOMEWHERE IN THE MIDDLE EAST

This letter is really Terry's Middle East Commission Number 13th Letter (but this letter was written to his best New Zealand old school friend) Clearly Don and both my Gran conferred after Terry's loss and there was much grief and shock and of course the information sharing.

sent on 21st August 1942

Dear Don,

I haven't received a letter from you for quite a while, but even so still your name glares at me from my book of words as having sent me a photo, thus I have finally brought myself to acknowledge same. Apart from that, I have the same old tale. "nothing to report" - I do wish they had an aerogram system to New Zealand. On them you can just say "Hullo 0 - how are you? Kiss'n foot - love and kisses - Goodbye!" BUT with a letter you feel a bit twerpish if you can't reel off at least a couple of pages.

Damit I almost forgot the purpose of the letter - Thanks a hell of a lot for the photos of the Spitfires and the Alp's - Did you take it? If so, you must be getting pretty good at that game (photography), and maybe you'll soon be telling me things. I lost interest for quite a while, About the only things that seem to be worth photographing are military objects and of course that's "VERBOTEN" - While we're on the subject ~ how about sending me a photo of yourself. I just about forgot what that ugly mug of yours looks like. I took some snaps of typical Egyptian scenes the other day and some of them turned out quite well, I've sent them home to Mum and I suppose you'll probably see them sooner or later.

As you can see by the heading of my letter I have recently been promoted to flight-sergeant ~ It doesn't mean a great deal, except that I should soon be getting a bit more pay. How's your promotion getting on? I wouldn't be surprised if you were some terribly exalted rank by now. I see by Mum's last letter that she seems to be doing rather well with a private office and a whole lot of people under her, etc. Pretty smart girl, don't you think? A few days ago, I finished my first tour of Duty of Operational flying. It's a great feeling to know that you (us) will be off the game for a while. I'm afraid I was losing interest (and concentration) a bit towards the end. If I'm lucky, I should soon be posted from the Middle East. As to where I am going, I haven't the faintest notion. If I am unlucky, they might keep me here as an instructor - Oh!! I would be annoyed. - I may get a chance to go as an Instructor to where Kit and Diana are (I'd love to see them again), or I might be sent back to Blighty (England) – Incidentally, there is somebody there I wouldn't mind seeing again either. One chance in a million of coming back to New Zealand, so I'm not even entertaining the idea.

At present, we aren't doing much. We are more or less enjoying a bit of a rest from flying and realising that at last we are off Op's. We really enjoyed

173

operations, but we took such a hell of a long time to finish our lot, that we were getting the browned off feeling. We had a bit of bad luck at different times which stopped us operating for periods. Twice we had a change of Captain and as in each case, a new one wasn't immediately available - quite a bit of time was wasted and then of course we had the crash landing after being shot by Jerry.

Tomorrow I'm going to visit yet another country. We're going to spend a few days in Palestine, so next time I write I ought to have a bit more to talk about.

Keep Writing - By the time you get this letter I will have cabled my new address - if any -

All the Best

Yours

Terry

ഇൻൽഇൻ

Present address :

          RAF - Head Quarters

          Middle East Commission

to post all mail in future to   C/- New Zealand High Commission

          145 Strand, London

          ENGLAND

          3rd September 1942,

Dearest Mother

I haven't the time or patience to write a decent letter just now, but I thought it would be a good idea to dash off a couple of pages because there will be quite a break between this and the next letter, as the next letter will be coming from England.

Before being posted from the squadron, I was lucky enough to be able to visit Palestine. I think it is the most interesting country I was lucky enough to be able to visit and have yet visited. It is steeped in history ancient and modern - It will be quite a big job to tell and describe all the things I did and saw in Palestine, so rather than dash it off now in my very unsettled frame of mind, I'll leave it to a later date when I can make it an interesting and descriptive letter like the Montreal, Canada, Cairo etc., letters.

I also have a lot of photos and souvenirs to go with the letter, and they all need a story with them. The most treasured souvenir is a New Testament with polished wood covers that I bought from a shop in Bethlehem - 10 yards from the Church of Nativity.

When we returned from Palestine, Ian and I only stayed in camp about a day then we tootled off to Port Tewfik to see the Mahons.

It was really most fortunate that we went down there when we did, or we mightn't have been able to see them again. We'd only been there about two days, when our postings came through. Luckily, we had told one of the boys where we were going, and he gave us a ring so the next morning we got up at 5am and tore like blazes back to camp.

I'm not sorry I am going back to Blighty, because I do want to see the old place again . I certainly didn't see much last time. Quite apart from England itself, I am dying to see Peggy and Barry again.

I guess I'll hardly know the boy. Last but not least there is a very charming little WAAF back there who's kisses are divine and who thinks I'm a much nicer person than I really am. Boy, what an allure!

You will probably be amazed at the Christmas present I sent you. So inappropriate for a WAAF. However, you have wanted just that all your life. I must admit too, that it was much the case of the brocade all over again. I had the cash in my pocket - but where was the power of resistance? In case you haven't got the parcel yet - it is a <u>triple string of pearls</u>. The other day, I also sent you a parcel of books. They are books I have picked up here and there and as now, our kit has to be down to minimum for our next journey, I had to get rid of them. Unfortunately, there is one missing - Kit sent me a book of poems of the English language - a wizard book - I lent it to someone and that was that.

Well, I must away now and see what the club has for lunch.

Love to the boys and bags of it to yourself.

Lovingly

Teg

This was, sadly, the last letter Terry wrote home, that we know of. 11 days later, the plane he was on as a passenger, had an "accident" just off the coast of Gambia. In this next chapter, we will read the communications that ensued, official letters, and some letters of condolence from various friends, colleagues, and acquaintances.

CHAPTER NINE – REPORTED MISSING, POSSIBLY KILLED

Thro' peril towards the stars they soar
Thro' winter's wind, thro' tempest's roar;
O Thou, who ridest on the storm
With Godly grace their hearts inform.
    Eternal Father, hear our prayer
    For those who battle in the air.

So much the many owe the few;
With strength from Thee their arms endue,
And let them feel 'midst war's alarms
'Neath them Thy everlasting arms.
    And ever in Thy watchful care
    Keep those who battle in the air.

Their deeds are writ in glorious flame
That puts the foreman's rage to shame.
The sweets of victory let them know;
Be Thou their guide where'er they go.
    Our Father, heed our thankful prayer
    For those who battle in the air.

But if the silver cord should break
And one Thou to Thyself shalt take,
Grant that he may not pass in vain
And give him rest from toil and pain,
    Thy peace, O God, be his to share
    Whose fight is ended in the air.

By J.C. Marlin, K.C.
Weyburn, Saskatchewan

Although both Duncan and Terry had survived crashes on ops, as you have read in Terry's letters, he still had a very nonchalant attitude towards his life.

Terry learned of Duncan's death, and tried to get more info regarding what had happened, and even tried, sadly too late, to get some of Duncan's effects, before they were sent to his "next of kin", being his wife, Peggy, with whom he'd never annulled the hasty marriage.

Ironically, in the end, his own death was not while he was "in action". They both eventually gave their lives for their countries, and for the Mother Country, Britain. You've read Terry's letters, in which he tried to relay the news of Duncan, and also tried not to think about it too much. Understandably, he couldn't let grief get in the way of his work.

As noted in the previous chapter, some of Terry's letters only arrived after Gran had already learned of his death. These letters coming in out of sequence and stamped READ by the censor after Terry had gone down, must have been another reason in the End that my Grandmother's health went downhill.

How painful it must have been for both Gaga and my Gran, to have lost these two young men so soon after each other.

For some time, in fact many years, both women, Deidre (Gaga) and Roma (my Gran) were desperate to find out just exactly what had happened in their sons' last hours.

There was naturally a telegram followed by correspondence both internal and external in which my Gran tried to work out the actual sequence of events…

In this chapter, I have included scans of the actual communications regarding Terry's death. And in the next, we will read of the communications regarding Duncan's death. In some cases, for simple readability, I have done transcriptions of the letters.

As you will see from the communications that follow, Terry was on a seaplane (Flying Boat), and on his way to England for some much deserved leave after completing his first tour of duty. He never reached his destination. More information on this is given in Chapter Ten.

REPORTED MISSING, POSSIBLY KILLED

** This letter was written on 29th September 1942*

Dear Mrs. Simons,

I am writing to offer you my deepest sympathy in the presumed loss of your son, who was a passenger in the B.O.A.C. flying boat "Clare", when it made a forced landing in the sea, about 70 miles North West of Bathurst, GAMBIA, on the evening of the 14th September, 1942. He was on his way back to The United Kingdom after having completed a tour of operational duties out here.

The cause of the accident is unknown, but it is not believed to have been due to enemy action. Searches of the area in which the flying boat came down have failed to reveal any sign of the aircraft or its occupants. If any more information should come to light, I will pass it on to you.

I am afraid that I did not know your son very well, as he left the Squadron very shortly after I took over the command, but on looking up the records and talking with those who knew him better, it becomes obvious that he was not only very well liked in the Squadron, but that he had done an excellent job of his work while he had been with it. His loss has been a considerable shock to his many friends still in the unit.

I am,

Yours Very Sincerely,

(L. Renkin) Wing Commander, Commanding; No. 37 Squadron. R.A.F.

Christmas card from the Mahons in CAIRO received by my Gran sometime AFTER Terry's loss. Post Stamp on back reads 10th November 1941, so this took nearly a year to arrive!

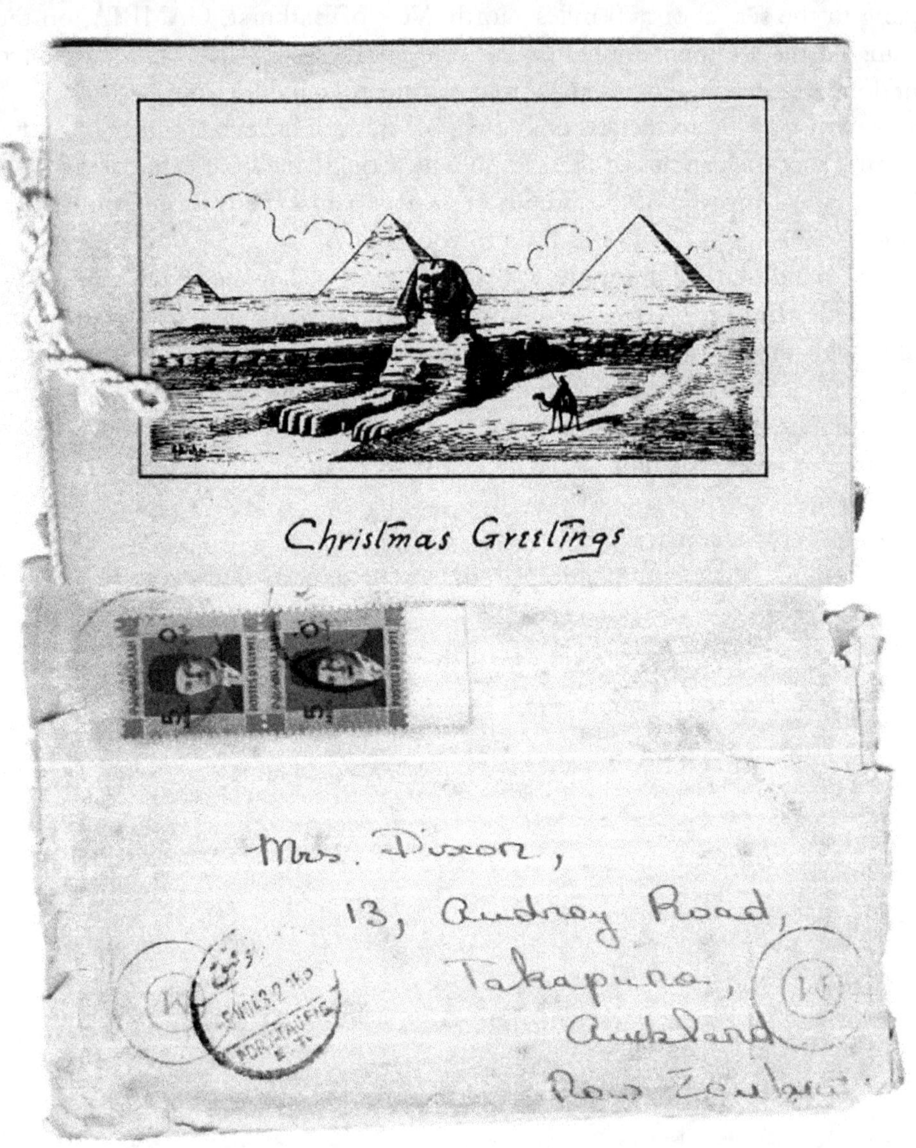

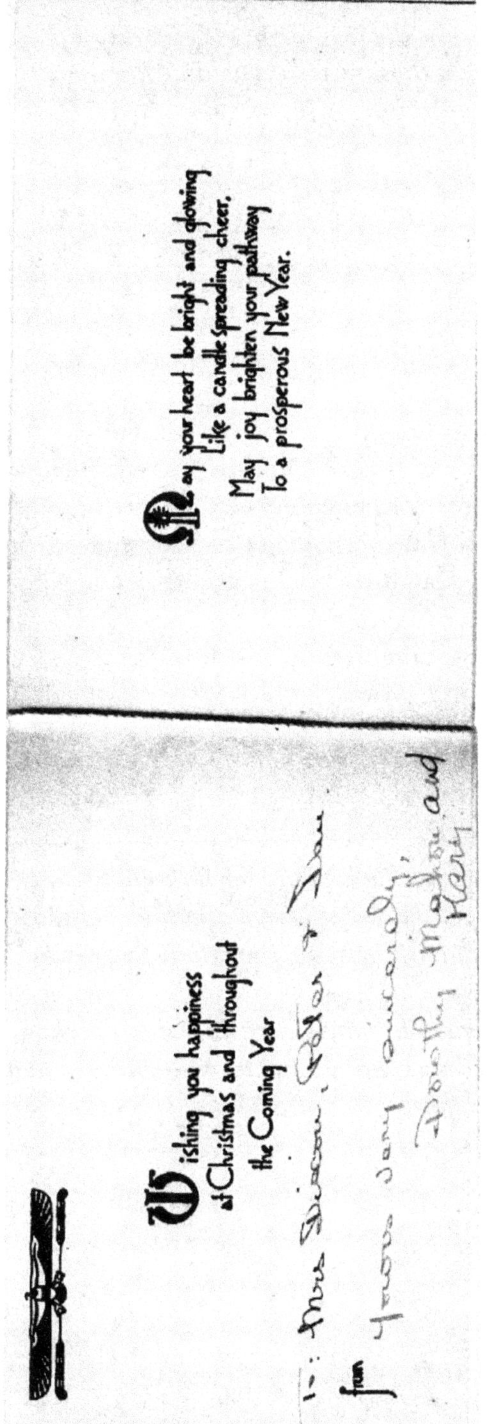

Interior of Christmas Card.

This letter was written soon after Roma got the first telegraph re Terry's plane going down. (It is wise to understand that these two women only knew each other through their boys' childhood friendship).

written 29th September 1942,
21 Lorwood Rd,
Bayswater North Shore,
AUCKLAND.

Dear Mrs. Symons, *(clearly by the spelling of this surname it is obvious they were only acquaintances)*

I am terribly grieved and shocked to hear your sad news of Terry. Let us hope you will hear better news before long. I wired Don this morning. He will get a fearful shock. I expect you will hear from him yourself in a day or two. Is there anything I can do for you? Would you and Pete like to stay with us for a few days. Perhaps it might be easier for you, if you had new surroundings for a while.

My thoughts are with you during this time. I know just how you feel. I am not much good at putting my thoughts into words.

I remain Yours Very Sincerely

May Hewson.

(Now it is obvious from this letter that May, who had other boys who had gone to war and not come back and had most of the men in her household away in some capacity doing their duty / service, did indeed have an understanding of what it was like to have sacrificed a child to this war-time effort. She obviously had a lot to do with my Uncle Terry because of his great friendship with her son, Don. When I was growing up, I can remember my father thinking a great deal of Terry's friend Don, who often appeared at family gatherings —and was to me always a very kind, happy - jolly gentleman)

This next letter is written by Terry's best childhood friend, Don Hewson; they planned to join the Air Force together. They did, but Don failed because of a medical reason and was destined for Ground work in the RNZAF. They were the same age, and raised to be so much more responsible, accountable and indeed feeling when times were down.

Dear Roma,

Just at this moment I find myself thinking of Terry so much that I felt I must write to you. I have felt like doing so several times, but something really urged me to do it this time. It is a wonderful night tonight, still and quiet, one of those nights that makes one stop to think what life is all about, and then when I think of Terry, everything seems so futile and meaningless, that I begin to even doubt if there is a God and Eternal guidance. A person has really either TO Believe Wholeheartedly in God or not at all because why should Terry go and I remain? Does God want Terry? Then why should all the best fellows be taken away? I won't say I don't believe in God, but heaven knows I don't pretend to understand Him or His ways. Perhaps this is really a tribute to the finest and best friend I ever had and ever will have. I'd have liked to have spoken to you when I was up in Auckland, but I think I was scared to. When I read what Terry wrote of me in one of his last letters I almost broke down - God knows I could have wished for nothing better. I'd have given my right arm for those words he wrote. If my life has grown better, my morals cleaner, and my thoughts purer since I've known Terry, then I attribute them wholly to him. He was the finest fellow, Clean and decent and pure. Something seems to have been hacked away from our lives now, doesn't it? For a while all I could think was why? why? why? But I received no answer and that is what makes it so hard. Because he was my best friend and only confidant I've ever had, I used to dream of his coming back and making plans of what we should do and SO sorry Roma, to go on like this, but I've felt I had to write to you for a long time and that is why I have written in pencil because I suddenly had the impulse. So if God has really taken Terry to Himself, then I pray that He will compensate you by letting you know in some way, so that you will be happier in yourself, spiritually, perhaps by knowing that "One does not die; Nor is one left alone", and this life is just a phase as we are taught and when it runs its course, then we shall meet those who left us a little earlier. You have been wonderfully brave Roma, p'raps I know better than most people because I know what Terry and you meant to each other.

Goodnight Roma,

Don

DREAMING OF THEE

This letter is from a Northland local friend of Terry's biological father, Cyril Dixon. I think it shows how they did things in those days, and remained all very civilised and indeed, enjoyed one another's special characters - I was told when I was growing up, what great joy Terry had brought to so many lives - because while my Grandmother was growing into herself as a teenager and single Mum, the rest of the township - indeed the district - that knew of how Terry came to be, enjoyed this very special child/young man.

sent 4th October 1942,
Noukopuni

Dear Roma,

I know it is useless trying to say how sorry we all are. You poor thing - How can you bear it - I should just want to shut myself up and just die. Somehow, I do not think Terry will ever be far away from you. Just as though he were in another room, unseen, unheard but always there. Later on when that awful sense of desolation has lessened a little, you will have his memory, the wonderful memory of all he has been to you, the things that he liked and the things you shared together to help you along ~ To be a guiding star, something that nothing can take from you - The letters he wrote, that perhaps have given you a greater understanding and appreciation of the fineness of Terry's character, which otherwise you may never have had an opportunity of realising.

Oh Roma, I do know these are only empty words and all that matters to you is the fact that Terry will not be coming home - I know the hard part will be when some simple thing, a flower, music or a certain scene, will just unexpectedly and unbearably remind you of him - But yet knowing you I somehow know you will carry on the fight.

As for Terry himself, seems now he has joined Duncan (Duncan) and all those other glorious boys that have gone before, no word of praise will ever be worthy of them - He will not be lonely.

If this letter seems over sentimental, it is because of what Terry has been to you and what life will mean without him - I know how I should feel in your place.

With Love from us all

- Lin

(The Fight that Lin refers in this letter is that for everyone in New Zealand, the "Fight for Freedom, God and Country - For Democracy, for their 'Mother nation's cause", permeated this Little Nation's pulse)

೮೦೧೩೮೦೧೩

This letter was written 5th November 1942. No doubt as a swift result of the National News Papers daily reports of who was on their 'Roll of Honour' or were believed lost :-

It was from the Dunedin Head Office of Office of Ross and Glendining, the company Terry had worked for before enlisting:

Dear Mrs. Simons,

We have learned with deep regret that your son, Pilot Officer T. A. Dixon, has been reported as believed killed, and the Directors wish to convey to you their sincere sympathy in the very sad time through which you are passing.

The latest advice from the authorities is "believed", and our wish is that there may yet be some word of your son's safety. The best we can hope for is that the report, not being conclusive, may yet be corrected.

Yours Sincerely,

I. SutherlandRoss

<u>CHAIRMAN OF DIRECTORS</u>

(This shows me how our little nation at the time no matter what state or size of the business and its people, had a drive to stay connected and united with one another in the belief that these young men were giving their lives for a better World and a better way)

This letter is written by a W.E. Parry who I understand worked for, or was the Minister of, Social Security.

Dear Mrs. Simons,

It has been my practice since New Zealand men began to play an important part with the Fighting Services overseas to watch newspaper cables for references to them and their work and, in addition, The Roll of Honour.

Naturally, many of the names appearing in the Roll are of men belonging to the Auckland district and a good number of these I personally know, or I am acquainted with their people.

The Roll of Honour appearing in the press today, includes, I notice, the name of your son. I sincerely hope good news of him will be shortly received to relieve the anxiety you must be suffering. I hope, also, there is consolation for you in the knowledge your son served with the R.N.Z.A.F., whose brilliant deeds have won world-wide admiration.

Yours with every good wish,

I am,

Yours Sincerely,

W.E. Parry

ഌൠഌൠ

This letter simply addressed to my Gran, Mrs. Simons

13 Audrey Rd, Milford, NZ
Post stamp reads Nov '42, but the letter simply has at the top MILFORD (with no date)

Dear Mrs. Simons,

The Members of the Women's War Workers learn with Deep Regret of the loss of your Gallant Pilot Officer Son, and wish to extend to you their heartfelt sympathy and to tell you we all look upon Terence as one of our 'Boys' as we received such chatty letters from him, and feel for you during these sad and anxious days.

Yours very Sincerely,

A. Wallis – Hon Sec. M.W.W.W.

ഌൠഌൠ

This letter is from the Head of Seddon Memorial Technical College, Wellesley St, East Auckland, dated 1ˢᵗ October 1942,

(It is wise to note that at the time, my Uncle Pete was attending this educational institution while my father was attending Dilworth Boarding School.)

Dear Mrs. Simons,

I am so sorry to learn of your sad news concerning your son. I understand that there is some doubt as to whether the information shall hold. I can only express my sympathy to you and your family, and hope and pray that your son may yet return to you safe and well.

Yours Sincerely,

C.L. Molloy.

** The above letter was sent home with Pete … written on the envelope was addressed:-*

*Mrs. **R**. Simons   per favour Peter Simons*

(later on, my Gran had written on the envelope the name: "Happy Molloy" - this indicates to me that he was another person my Gran was closely acquainted with.)

ഇൗഅഇൗഅ

Dated 30 October 1942

W.A. 2 Pattulo N., 2780

W.A.A.F.

R.N.Z.A.F. Whenuapai, <u>WEST AUCKLAND</u>

My Dear Roma,

Yesterday, when I got word from Mother about your terrible sorrow, I just felt as if the End of Everything had come. Please accept my deepest sympathy and love for both yourself and Pete.

Terry & I were always so much together, and I loved him just as if he had been my brother, so I think that is why I felt it so much. Let's hope and pray that he will turn up, even if it is as a prisoner.

It certainly is a funny world, when you think that only a few days ago, we were so happy because he had been promoted, but it is just the way of this world!

I will be in for my two days leave next week, so will come in to see you. Am going home tomorrow just for the day to see Mother as she seems so terribly broken up.

Well, Roma, this is very short but I just feel I can't write anymore, I know you will understand how I feel.

Once again, I want you to know how Sad I feel for your loss as Terry was so loved by all.

Give my love to Peter and Dem.

Fondest love and Sympathy

Nganae.

Nganae is Roma's sister's child, and as such a cousin and one of Terry's friends growing up, for then these families in the small towns and surrounding districts kept very well informed of one another's "doings" - again they stayed very closely connected. Many times, her name is spelled in Terry's letters as Nganie, which may simply be that he was not sure himself of the actual spelling, and spelled it as he said it).

ಬಿಎ⊗ಬಿಎ⊗

The next letter is very difficult to transcribe given the scrawly nature of the old style of handwriting. But as my Gran kept it also with her letters and treasures of those times, I am attempting to transcribe.
Addressed from 4 Napiri Ave, Takapuna, Dated 25 October 1942

Dear Mrs. Simons,

I want to tell you how sorry I am to hear the news that Terry is missing. I was so pleased to read of his promotion and even cut the piece out of the local news to pass on to John – These hard times – I have to say I haven't been able to write since having the Measles – my system was sorry – I want to send you my sympathy in these anxious times you are going through now. I was also sorry to hear of your other loss (Duncan – Duncan) – John is in England now. So, my anxiety really starts missing; of course, there is still hope. You must have been so proud of him doing so very well.

Yours Truely and Sincerely,
Nia Beattie.

ಬಿಎ⊗ಬಿಎ⊗

This next letter was written by Terry's Commanding Officer's Mother from the Middle East. It will unfold in the letter that this was the Commanding Officer in the Middle East with whom Terry was better acquainted than the one who wrote after Terry went missing on his final transfer trip back to England, to take up his new and special commission.

Dated December 2nd 1942

The letterhead is from

SHOLBEY HOUSE
RINGWOOD, HANTS.
CANADA
Tel: Ringwood 285

Dear Mrs. Simons,

May a stranger offer you sincere and deep sympathy in the anxiety you are going through at the report that your son was missing in an aircraft accident on September 14th 1942.

My son was in the same Aircraft, and Sgt T. Dixon served under him in the 37th Squadron – Middle East Forces from March until August when my son, the Wing Commander R.O.M. Graham D.F.C. relinquished his command.

My husband and I are praying and hoping that our son escaped with his companions before the final crash, though we are told there is very little hope. Miracles do happen all the time in this war.

At the moment we have staying with us, a New Zealander who two years ago was shot down over Tunisia. Imprisoned, but he has been released. He is in touch with all those who were with him and have been released – He too, was a friend of your son's and stayed with us before going out on his unlucky journey.

If there is any news you would like to know, if I could possibly find out for you, please let me know.

Sincerely Yours,

Edith Graham.

(This shows me that the Mothers, Wives, Sisters and Brothers of these boys in all the Dominions loved and respected and cherished one another's boys while they were so very far from their Natural Birth families. They treated them as their own and it created a warmth and love which one would hope the nations would never forget.)

This letter is again from Terry's Paternal side of his family, in other words, although Terry had met his father before he went to war, (he said, out of curiosity), he took my father, Dem, with him for the meeting and my father, years later, said there seemed to be no love between them and rather a strained endeavour, it seemed, but he felt that Terry was, after the meeting, at ease and very strong in his identity.

It is dated November 1st, 1942
C/- The Railways
WAIUKU

Dear Mrs. Simons,

I am writing to tell you that I am very sorry to hear that Terry is missing and I sincerely hope that he will turn up. Do not give up hope. I only met Terry once in Auckland. I was with Cyril and I must say, I thought he was a fine boy and certainly a great credit to you. Cyril has gone overseas. He went away at such short notice. I did not see him before he went away. I am in the next ballot myself. I understand the railway is appealing for me, but of course, that does not say I shall not have to go. If you happen to hear anything of Terry, would you please let me know. I wrote to Wellington some time ago for his address but have had no reply. Pilot Officer Joycie's sister from Hamilton lives next door to us – I shall now close with my best wishes.

I remain,

Yours Sincerely,

Les Dixon.

Cyril, of whom Les speaks in the above letter, was Terry's actual Birth Father, and like my Gran, was a very young naive teenager when they discovered their innocent fumblings as teenagers had led to Terry's conception. I can only imagine in many ways, they both paid a high social price – but it is a credit to the families that they kept things civil and open for Terry's sake, as when he felt the need to make contact.

I understand from my Father's later inquiries that Terry's father did indeed return from the War and although a little broken, as many of these boys and men were, once they returned, he did go on to remarry and have a new family post-WW2.

જી⊂રૈ⊱⊃⊂૨

This next letter was written to Gran by my father's Aunty Jean, one of Grandad Kawenata's sisters – It is just a note really, sent after the news of Terry's loss. It shows no date or post stamp, and on the outside of this note in my Gran's handwriting is written the address:

43 Alberta Rd,
Port Chevalier,
AUCKLAND WEST

Dear Roma,

Words can not express how deeply I feel for you. Dear old Terry, he had a special place in my heart – God bless him.

I would like to come and see you sometime later on. If you would let me know what day would suit you.

God bless and comfort you, my Dear.

All my love, Jean.

ഓരുഓരു

This letter arrived with a post stamp from New Zealand;- It was sent to my Grandmothers place of work with the WAAFs ~

It was dated 2nd of October 1942,

Dear Mrs. Simons,

The Officers, N.C.O.'s and cadets of No. 19 Squadron extend to you our heartfelt sympathy in your great sorrow.

We feel that through you we have all lost a personel friend.

Yours Very Sincerely,

(The signature is difficult to work out, but it looks like G. Williamson)
After looking up details of our New Zealand Air Force history of the Squadrons, I find I cannot find 19 Squadron detailed in this leaflet, therefore I can only assume it was a ground Air Training Corps division that was referred to?

ഓരുഓരു

A.—1a.]

DOMINION OF NEW ZEALAND.

AIR FORCE HEADQUARTERS,
WELLINGTON C.1.

In your reply
15/AIR.
please quote this number.

13th October, 1942.

Mrs. R.E.L. Simons,
Auckland Wing, A.T.C.
AUCKLAND.

Dear Mrs. Simons,

It is with deep regret that I have heard of the loss of your son
on active service.   On behalf of myself and members of the staff I wish
to express our deep-felt sympathies with you in your sad bereavement.

R. A. Nicholls

COMMANDANT : AIR TRAINING CORPS.
Wing Commander,

On His Majesty's Service.

IF NOT CLAIMED WITHIN 10 DAYS
PLEASE RETURN TO
AIR DEPARTMENT PRIVATE BAG WELLINGTON

This was sent from Te Awamutu on   ***October 14th 1942,***

Dear Roma,

We were indeed sorry to learn that you have had such sad news of your dear lad. Both Aunty Norma and Nganae are very grieved and upset, they were so fond of him too. It seems to me that if one has anyone in the Air Force, they have Said "Good Bye" to them, several dear lads that I was very fond of have been lost. They were all so fine and so young. I am also aware you have just so lately lost your dear Brother too, and we send you our sincere sympathy in this time of sorrow and great sadness.

Yours Affectionately,

Aunty Amy.

(I am not sure which branch of the family Aunty Amy comes from, but it would seem as she mentions Nganae and Norma that she is connected to my Gaga's side of the family) .

஠ௐ஠ௐ

I have mentioned earlier that my father was given a placement at Dilworth Boarding School. This School was supposed to be a Christian boarding school for Boys only - These boys were supposedly from fatherless homes, but because my father did have a living father who I am soon to give you a little more detail on, I believe they chose my Father because of his highly competitive nature and desire to please - He said he was average, but he was actually quite a high achiever both academically and in sport and swimming - I think their selection process at the time and even when I put my son's name forward two generations on, Dilworth made its choices based on the student's possible successes and ability to conform and comply.

I understand why my father both hated and was made to be grateful for the so-called opportunities Dilworth afforded him, but really my Gran was able to get him on the list of applicants and into this so-called prestigious school (which my Uncle Pete always thought was better than the run-of-the-mill schooling in Auckland at the time), because Gran knew all the right people and her application fitted, not so much the financial requirements or guidelines, but had all the correct religious and social connections to allow this to happen.

Yes, she was a single Mother, and she was working very hard for the WAAF, but she had a husband whom she'd chosen to leave, and who indeed provided what finances were required for the raising of his sons.

Through no choice of my own, I too, became a single Mother – I had only a son and a daughter then, and I felt desperate to place my son in a good place where he would receive a positive male influence. My father suddenly became incredibly agitated when he learned of my application to have my son accepted at Dilworth. I will never forget his disclosure of the sexual abuse he had suffered as a young boy in this school's care during WW2. His words were, "No grandson of mine is going to suffer what I experienced. The good education was not worth the suffering."

I was ASTOUNDED and I think he was shocked that he had released a secret he had carried his whole life. He saw it as something all boys had to endure in such environments.

₧₨₧₨

The following letter was written by the Dilworth Head. I present the transcription, and the scan of the actual letter on the following page.

Dear Mrs. Simons,

I sent a message of sympathy to you by your son, but I feel I would like to write to you and tell you how very sorry I am to hear not only of your news, but of the possible confusion which the cables at present seem to have created.

These are very trying times for everybody and if the worst should be confirmed in the case of your son, you must try as so many brave mothers are trying, to console themselves with the thought that heavy as the price has been, it is your and your son's contribution to a noble cause. I still hope, however, that you may get better news.

I am,

Yours Sincerely,

Noel Gibrau

Dilworth School,
Auckland, S.E.3.

1st October, 1942.

Mrs. Simons,
13 Audrey St.,
TAKAPUNA.

Dear Mrs. Simons,

I sent a message of sympathy to you by your son, but I feel I would like to write to you and tell you how very sorry I am to hear not only of your news, but of the possible confusion which the cables at present seem to have created.

These are very trying times for everybody and if the worst should be confirmed in the case of your son, you must try as so many brave mothers are trying, to console themselves with the thought that heavy as the price has been, it is your and your son's contribution to a noble cause.

I still hope however, that you may get better news.

I am,

Yours sincerely,

DREAMING OF THEE

This letter is written by Ian Medwin's Mother. My Gran has written that this was the second letter Ian Medwin's mother had sent her after the news of Terry's loss.

23rd of May 1943,
40 Te Aroha Street, Claudelands,
HAMILTON.

Dear Mrs. Simons,

I was so pleased to receive your letter some time ago and should have answered it sooner, but I put it off from day to day and it just never got done. I expected to be in Auckland some three weeks ago and was going to call on you, then my plans were altered at the last minute, and I didn't go. I certainly will make a point of seeing you first chance, and if you come to Hamilton at any time, we will be very pleased to see you. Our boys were such friends, I feel that we should be friends too. Perhaps Ian told you that it was the merest fluke that he was not in Terry's plane on that fateful trip which cost Terry his life. I know it has caused you so such suffering. I am glad to hear you say that you will rise above it and carry on as your boy would have liked you to - I know Terry would be so proud of you too. It is a hard world and now there are many sad hearts in it, perhaps more today than ever before and still we must go forward with more determination than ever, although I know it is very hard. I didn't know that you are still at work as a WAAF and yet I do think I remember Terry had mentioned it in one of his Broadcasts, or am I mistaken? Or was it someone else? Ian is still in England instructing and he has now been promoted to Flight / Lieutenant and of course we are so very proud to know he has done so well.

Our elder son Edric who is F/O is in the Solomons and my daughter's husband has gone oversees too. He is in the Air Cre. So, we have NO boys at home, we are only four in the house at present.

We are Mr. Medwin, Edric's wife, our daughter Edna and myself, the boys have been away nearly two years now.

Seems so very much longer sometimes.

I will be very pleased to hear from you again- Do call any time you are in Hamilton. I am enclosing a wee book of beautiful verses which I hope you will find a comfort to you. May God Bless and Comfort you,

 Yours Sincerely

  Your Friend

   Rhoda Medwin

This next letter came as a bit of a shock to me, as it showed a part of my Grandfather Kawenata Simons that was quite contradictory to what I'd been told, growing up. I never knew him well, so this letter has given me some new insight into the man he was. This letter was sent to my Gran after Terry's plane was reported to have gone down off Gambia. The letterhead below, tells me a great deal about some of his position and commitments as a then well-considered and respected member of the local district farming community and indeed, businessmen's associations.

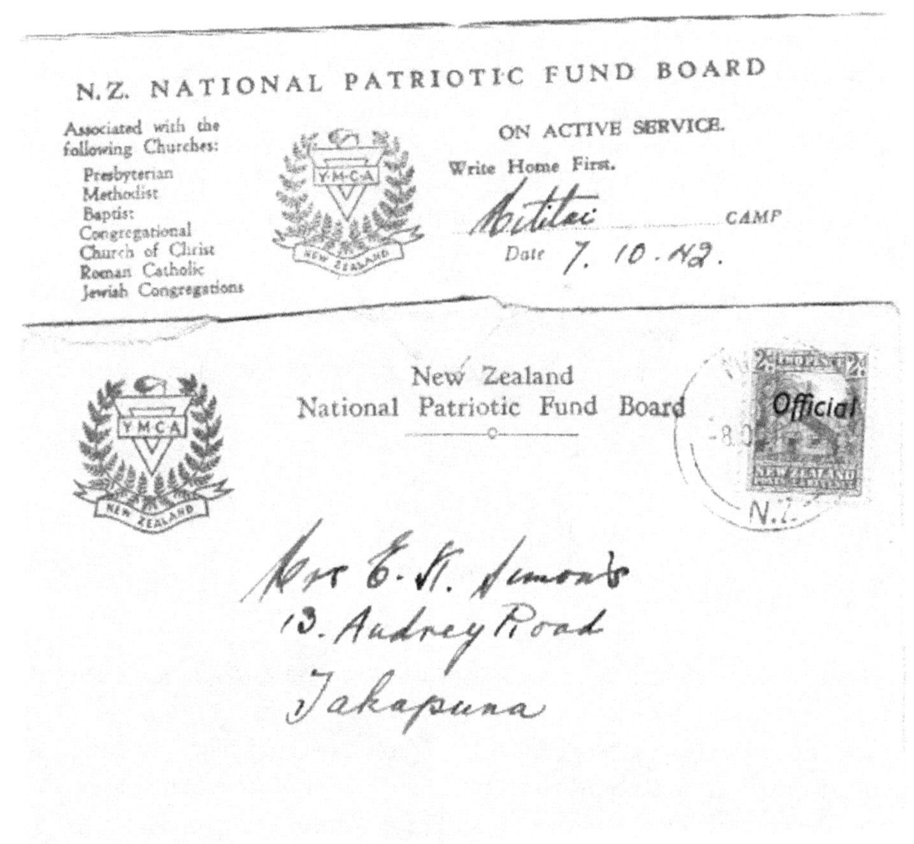

From this letterhead, one can also confirm what I knew to be true from my other Grannie "Cookie", who I will talk of much later on in this story that Grandad ran the local "Home Guard". He also rose through the ranks of the Freemasons over the years – I am not sure when this came about – post WW2 or earlier.
From Mr. E.K. Simons (Edward Kawenata) – written on NZ National Patriotic Fund Board Stationary marked on Active Service

DREAMING OF THEE

Dated 7th October 1942

Dear Roma,

This is the hardest letter I have ever set out to write. I somehow always expected Terry would be back, and when I read the account of his adventures in the Middle East, though surely, he would be let off, for a couple of months.

I can understand how the news must have shocked you. Please accept my Sincere Sympathy, and I will pray that the good fortune of his last crash may be repeated.

Gwen tells me Mrs. Marsden mentioned several survivors. Surely some of them would know the facts.

It may seem strange, but I have never been more upset in my life. It makes me also understand how tough it is on you, and the boys.

The fact that he has gained the greatest honour anyone can, in serving his country, doesn't seem to help very much, somehow.

Boys such as Terry are scarce, and you have every right to be proud of him and his career.

I have not yet heard if the Army has sent you my allotted 4/6d per day as yet.

It is no wonder there are so many muck-ups, when they don't seem to be able to attend the ordinary everyday matters.

Wishing you the very best of News and Luck

Cheerio, Kawe.

₱ℝ₱ℝ

Now, at this point, I find it necessary give a little more information about this man, Kawe.

As mentioned before, after Gran's first, very short marriage had ended, she married Edward Kawenata Simons (Kawe), and together, they had 2 sons close together, Desmond (Dem – my dad), and Peter (Pete). Terry was adopted into this marriage, and as far as my grandfather was concerned, he was a much-loved stepson.

Grandad Kawenata came from a family of siblings of which were 4 sisters and 6 brothers – my Grandad was the youngest boy. He was descendant of Maori and was led to feel a little ashamed. In the small town he grew up in, I can remember Cookie telling me she was not allowed to play after school with the Maori or the Yugoslav, so she often kicked off her expensive lace-up boots and paddled down by the river with the Maori children – my Grandfather was only ¼ caste or ½, my family is not sure. He may have been treated badly at school also, but he never let this get him down.

His wise mother encouraged Kawe because of his gentle loving nature, to become a man of the land – a farmer – I understand that she worked in the Maori land transfer office and was a Maori chieftainess of some high standing. Her own mother was a Maori princess. His sisters loved him very much and followed his fortunes during his life. As a result, they all befriended his wife and his 'Love', my Gran – I believe they gave her much respect no matter the situation between my grandfather and her…

In the above letter, Kawe mentions Gwen and Mrs. Marsden.

Mrs. Marsden was a very special lady, who had travelled to New Zealand post the first World War with her new husband and her two boys and Gwen, her daughter. They were terribly English and very fresh immigrants – They built a wonderful house on the Hill in this small town, where Mrs. Marsden, sadly, was to become a widow. She was good friends with my Gaga, through the two girls, Gwen and Roma, and later, after Roma was disgraced and had given up her marriage to the father of her firstborn, while all the dramas of my Gaga's broken marriage was staged as a great scandal in the small town, Mrs Marsden took both my Gran and Terry in. It was Mrs. Marsden, "Blessit" who taught Gran many of her motherly duties and skills. She was also a wonderful baker and a very creative and ambitious woman who could turn her hand to most tasks, and more, do them with deft and meticulous skill. It was this woman with whom Gran many years later went into business with, as has been mentioned before.

Gwen (known to me as Cookie) and Roma and Kawe grew up together in a very small town. They all came from very different cultural backgrounds, but at different times in their lives, they all fell in a very unusual web of love – as a result there are now blood ties through my grandfather's line to both families.

Roma actually wanted the bright lights of the city, once the hard times had hit on the farm, and she had already had time in the city doing her apprenticeship at the big Department Store Farmers, as a Brassiere. She was also very influenced by the so-called Gentleman (Colly) who took over as a Father-figure and in no doubt, took advantage of a very troubled and easily influenced young girl who had just had a child, and was left to raise him on her own.

Both Roma and Kawe were still very young when they married, not long after Roma's first marriage ended. For reasons only my grandfather and my grandmother really know and understand, they had a falling out, and so, not long after the births of their two sons, their marriage also came to an end.

In all, Kawe had four sons: Terry, whom he had adopted, my father Dem, and his brother Pete, and later, after his failed marriage to Gran, he went on to have another son with Gwen (Cookie), named Jimmy.

Kawenata went on to be the farmer his mother had encouraged him to be, and later in the War, he was considered an essential Service Provider by being on a small piece of prime productive farming land. This land was rich, alluvial, riverside land which he worked very hard to maintain and keep when the Depression hit between Wars. Just as many others had walked off the land, he had gone to work in Auckland, but kept up payments on the land he so loved and on which he believed he could create a great living for his family, which much later, proved to be the case.

I think my father was led to believe by some "bitter pill" that his Mother had not the funds to provide for him and that his birth father, my paternal Grandfather Edward Kawenata Simons, had not been the kind of husband in terms of providing for my Grandmother's choices – whatever the reasons, I am sure, like me, my father came up with more questions than answers from those times.

But this letter showed me that Kawenata had always maintained an interest in his boys, and indeed, had tried to provide for them in his own way.

On the far left, is Francis McArthur, and next to him, is his mother, Granny Morm. The young man standing 3rd from left is unknown; the woman centre back is Sidney (Gaga), and in front of Gaga is Roma (Gran), the bride. The man on the far right is unknown. Seated from left to right is Mavis (Roma's sister); Kawenata, Roma's groom (Granddad Simons) and on the far right is Mrs. Marsden (Blessit)

DREAMING OF THEE

Now, I have to give a little more information about Colemore Williams. As you've read, he was the person Terry often has referred to in his letters, called Colly – my Gran's Lover. Sadly, when my Gran was still an impressionable teen, but had become a young mother, she had been employed by this "Gentleman" or that is how the town considered him. He was of high standing in the community; a much older father-figure of a man – a dynamic businessman, who travelled for his very dynamic and prosperous business. This man had given my Gran what she was so desperately seeking from a father-figure, and he had befriended her through the local church events, as well as giving her a much-desired job. BUT THIS MAN was also a married man, the father of, I understand, 8 children. Yes, they had large families then, and I understand both his wife and he were from what was called "moneyed" parentage. My Gran saw him as influential, and being connected to people who knew people meant you stood for something in her eyes and mind. It has to be said that in those times, a woman could not even have a bank account without having a father or husband endorse this. Titles to home and land, unless you were from the Maori culture, were all considered "not for women of the times". Yes, despite allowing women to vote, certain segments of society were still very narrow-minded. This allowed the relationship to grow and continue so very long.

Colly also involved himself in Roma's family, especially her relationship with her growing son, Terry (my father says they seemed inseparable to him as a little boy – he described them as a threesome). Roma and Colly were most definitely lovers – my father remembers Colly's visits when he was also allowed home around Christmas time, and other school holidays, that this Mr. Colly (as he is named in the letters) would drive down from the Northland town to supposedly do business, but was integrated into my Gran and my father's and Uncle Pete's lives. The delight my father remembers is the gifts of silk stockings and perfume for Gran and chocolate fish for the young boys, Peter and Dem (My father). Dad said Colly always asked them to do a hand-stand to see who could stay up the longest and drop chocolate fish down their PJ's legs before bedtime. He remembers this and now realises that Colly stayed over – while they went off to bed with their chocolate fish. There are many little stories that others have shared with me over the years, about my Gran and indeed, my father and my other Granddad, his father and their war efforts and events of their lives.

The other character who I must mention, of course, is Colly's wife, Lil, who my Gran believed to be a very frail, weak woman. Terry too, had been led to believe the same stories.

I notice this letter has a postmark having been posted from Paihia in those times this was quite some journey as was Auckland from his home town of Dargaville. There is no date on the letter inside but the post stamp, faded, looks like November 1942
Headed "Waitangi, Tuesday".

My Dear WAAF,

Your two letters addressed to Drenshaw just received with enclosures of Herald cuttings and notification from Minister. How utterly impossible it seems that we are still living and breathing in a world without Terry. It can never be the same beautiful place is was, for every time a seashore is in sight, we'll say or think: "wouldn't Terry just love this?" Quite unconsciously, I have often thought when I have stayed up here, linked him with this beauteous attraction – his exuberant spirit. He was able to create a whole world of happiness for all around him and it is impossible to realise what his passing over means except that the future must be dark and very dreary for those he has left behind. Do you, his mother, sister, pal and greatest Sweetheart realise? He would send a message with his last breath, not to mourn him too grievously, yet in knowing your inability to do ought else, for he too, knew that he was your all and prised the Great love that you had for him. Not knowing that it were impossible to withhold from him who evoked it and so well deserved it. Dear Terry, God will surely ?? you and have you there to meet again those who love you better than life itself.

Signed
LOVE DADDY

This man's hand-writing is rather rounded, simply and upright, but artistic. He has written this little small note of pink stationary with a purple lead pencil. <u>His Name was Colemore Williams</u> and he was known as the town's prosperous Auctioneer – a man with many upper-class connections. I know it seems strange that as much as they were lovers, he signed off as "Daddy," but that's just how it was.

DREAMING OF THEE

At first, I had thought that this next letter was from Colemore's wife, Lil, from the scribble my father had put on the envelope, but once inside and seeing the contents, I now think it may have been either one of this man's encouragements by his daughter, who seemed to be caring for the Mother. In any case, it has been sent from

104340 New North Road
Mt. Albert, EAST AUCKLAND
7 November 1942

Dear Roma,

I was very sorry indeed to hear about Terry, and want to express on behalf of Mother and myself, our very deepest sympathy, and we hope that there is some small measure of comfort in the fact that he may possibly be a prisoner-of-war.

He was a very fine lad and was liked by all who met him and knew him.

No words of mine can possibly express what I feel for you in your sorrow.

Trusting that you are quite well.

Yours Sincerely,

    Joan Colmore-Williams.

।ಔ।ಔ

This wee letter is from Aunty Norma. Now, I am not sure just whose side of the family she is from, but I do remember my father talking of one of my grandfather's sisters living in Remuera, so this may be from one of his sisters.

66 Clonbern Rd,
REMUERA
29th September 1942

Dear Roma,

Just a line to say you have all the love and sympathy we can give you at this very trying time. We can only hope that our darling Laddie may turn up safely, even if he is a prisoner; you will get him back.

May God bless and comfort you and the Boys. Thank dear Peter for ringing us this morning.

Love from Aunty Nancy and your sad old Aunty Norma.

    P.S. Can I do anything for you?

।ಔ।ಔ

This next letter, I believe, is from my father's first teenage crush – a girl he met from Dio at a dance, I believe. As a senior, somehow, he used to escape the boarding hostel at night and ride over to be part of this family. The girl he shared his first kiss with.

184 Orakei Rd,
REMUERA
30 September 1942

Dear Mrs. Simons,

Just a line to send you and Peter our sympathy. Des told us last night that there is a chance of there being a mistake. I do so hope that be the case. Mary & I feel we know Terry, as Des has told us so much about him. Such a dear-sounding young man.

Several of our sons are reported missing too, and have turned up, so don't give up hope, such wonderful things can and do indeed happen.

Yours very sincerely
Durelle Robertson.

ഇൻഝൻൽ

The letter below has been sent from a work colleague of my Gran's at the time

R.N.Z.A.F. Depot
Private Bag
AUCKLAND C1
30 September 1942

Dear Roma,

I find it hard to put on paper how I have felt for you since I heard the sad news regarding Terry. It is a heavy blow and I know there is no heavier one you could even have been given. The talks you and I have had together regarding Terry have made me feel that I too, know him, and seem to have learnt and understand something of his loving personality.

I had hoped after reading of the good news regarding his exploits in the Eastern Campaign, and his due return to England, that Terry would not be back in the fighting again for a while to come, but the supreme sacrifice has been made by your boy. In giving his life for his country I feel that Terry's wish will be that you will carry on bravely – as you have always done in the past. You have been blessed with three very loveable sons who above everything else adore their mother, and I know that Terry's desire will be that you and his two brothers will get all the joy out of living that is now possible in this tipsy topsy turvey world of ours. Des and Pete will be a great comfort to you and will give you strength to fight on at all times. Please excuse the badly written note, Roma – I will come and see you when I am up and about again. I am feeling much better today.

Sincerely Yours,

Norm Davenport.

৪০০৪৪০০৪

This letter has a very clear post stamp on the envelope:

It reads: LONDON W.C. 1:45PM 5th October 1942
Inside it is written on letter heading paper which reads as follows:
NUFFIELD HOUSE
(Residential Club for Officers of H.M. and Allied Forces)

9 Halkin Street,
(Near Hyde Park Corner)
S.W. 1.
P/O I. G. Medwin
C/- N.Z. Base P.O.
35 Afar Street, Strand, LONDON

Phone:
SLOAN 1539 (Secretary's Office)
SLOAN 2117-8 (Members)

Dear Mrs. Simmons,

Although we have never REALLY met, I feel as though I know you very well – Terry was always speaking of you and I saw your photo above his bed in our camp/tent every day.

I don't know how to start to tell you how sad I fell about his going. Please accept my deepest sympathy in this time of trouble – I do wish I could be with you to try and help – I could perhaps say things much easier than I can write them.

Terry was my best friend and the only Navigator I have ever flown with. He may have told you that I have been his pilot throughout his tour of operations.

This trip home to England was the first time since I have known him, that he had flown without me.

We started out from Egypt in the same place, but halfway home, we became separated and Terry was to follow on in another plane two days after me.

A few days after arriving in England, I heard that his plane had gone down and I have been hoping against hope that some news would come through, but I have not heard anything heartening as yet.

Terry and I were both recommended for our commissions in Egypt and upon return to England, I found that we had both been commissioned as Pilot Officers since Last May.

I am telling you this because there is a difference of pay between the rank of Flight Sergeant and Pilot Officer, and you should be able to get this money by making enquiries at Air Ministry.

Terry had back pay as Flight Sergeant from 1st January 1942 to 27th May 1942 at 2/6 per day, due to him also back pay as Pilot Officer from May 27th 1942 to September 7th approximately.

Also, with his Pilot Officer's back pay you should collect Colonial pay for being in Egypt, at the rate of approx. 7/6d per day for the period dated from 27th May to 7th September 1942. I am sure, that if you made enquiries at R.N.Z.A.F. Head Quarters, you would get some satisfaction.

I am at present stationed in England as an instructor and hope to be here for at least 9 months. If there is anything I can do to help you, over this side of the world, please do not hesitate to ask – I shall be only too glad if I am able to help in any way. Once again, Mrs. Simons, please accept my heartfelt sympathy. I had always regarded Terry as my special responsibility and had vowed to do my best to bring him through, but He 'God' who is above us all, has decided otherwise.

Someday there will be an explanation for all these worrying problems which today seem inexplainable.

Do call on me, if there is anything I can do for you.

Yours Sincerely,

Ian Medwin.

ಭರಣಭರಣ

I have read and re-read Ian's letter and have combed the documents written in all of My Gran's and Terry's Air Force files to try and make some sense of what exactly did happen - Why were Terry and his good friend and Pilot separated? I have read the flight details of how they flew from African country to country weaving their way across what was considered friendly skies in a sort of loop. I have pored over maps to try and work out why this flight path was taken. I have also wondered as my Gran and my Father did, just why Terry and some other important Air Force personnel were being transported across such dangerous territory in such an old slow and lumbering, very large and easily seen plane, as the Clare. I can only imagine how my father felt. He, like many, idolised his older brother and wanted to find a reason and someone to blame for how his mother and his little brother and he were feeling - Their Great Loss was most likely more hurtful to him, given the abuse he had grown to endure at Boarding school - When I was quite small, before he even knew of these letters, he told me he felt the Japanese had picked off the Clare. He so wanted to get into the War and avenge the Grief and loss of his Brother. There was no counselling, other than the church and his school authorities for a boy/young man who lived away from home. He was just supposed to step up to the Job of being the now very Responsible Eldest son and brother for Roma and Peter- This tragedy created a very unusual relationship with his mother that affected His marriage, his relationship with his father, and his relationship with both his daughters.

The effects of this family's Ultimate Sacrifice is still reverberating even now.

While reading all this information and seeking out more of their paperwork, poring over world maps and reading large amounts on our contributions during this time, as a small Dominion, I find more and more what a huge Lesson our little Nation sadly seems to have forgotten; some of the reason these men and families gave so very much and altered the course of all our lives forever more.

The strangest thing that still stands out to me, is this leg of Terry's journey back to England, when he was separated from Ian Medwin. He had been given orders to fly in a plane that was not even a Military service vehicle. I have some further information to share a little later on about this B.O.A.C. plane, the 'Clare'.

The following letter is dated the 24th February 1943, and still The War grinds on. (On the envelope in my father's writing is acknowledgement that this letter was from Ian Medwin's mother - Under this are the words that mean my Gran and Ian never did get to meet in person. That Ian Medwin died during operations on "D DAY").

40 Te Aroha Street,
Claudelands - HAMILTON

Dear Mrs. Simons,

I have so much wanted to write and extend to you our very deepest sympathy, in the loss of your dear brave son, Terry. It may sound strange, but I do feel that I have lost a real friend, for you see, Terry and I used to send messages to each other, and I learned to love him like another son. He and Ian were such close pals - poor Ian can't get over Terry's death. He still says he has lost his best friend in the R.A.F. plus the best Navigator who ever flew. To think he came out of that dreadful crash in the Desert only to lose his life while flying as a passenger, surely things are hard to understand sometimes. I feel so sad for you in your great trouble and I sincerely wish I could do something to help you bear your burden of sorrow in the loss of such a lovely and special boy. It is at these times we are so truely helpless.

I hope and pray that you will find comfort with the Dear Lord - who gave himself for us and who is always ready to help us.

Yours so Very Sincerely
Rhoda Medwin

ಬಂದ

DREAMING OF THEE

This letter was sent from Alf Drew. You will have seen and read Terry's connection to Alf Drew in his earlier letters.
It is dated 13th August 1943, and is simply headed ENGLAND,

Dear Mrs. Simons,

I sincerely trust you will forgive me for not having written this letter before now. I have hesitated because it is one letter I have never hoped I should write, and because I felt time would make it a little easier for us to talk about dear old Terry. I realise fully, how it all means to you, as you know Terry and I thought a tremendous amount of one another, we were always together and shared similar views on a great many things. Therefore, if I remind you of our great friendship, I feel sure you will fully understand how truely sorry I am and how very sincerely I have missed him. It seems such a long time now since we both started out together at Levin Air Training Camp. There both he and I agreed often that it would be so much better if we had no one at home to worry about us - yet rather often he/we sort out connections and family environments whenever we had leave. I suppose it rather a naieve and selfish view, you may think. but you must realise we both used to get a great thrill out of our flying careers. I had a letter from Bill Gibbes - you may remember him at Terry's Farewell party- Bill sadly is now a prisoner of war.

Enclosed I have sent you a book of Terry's which he loaned to me. I seem to have forgotten to return it before he was sent out to the Middle East, and I felt sure you would like to have this book Terry chose to buy while in Blighty. I still have the letter he wrote me from the Middle East telling me about his latest escapade and his silver boot. I met Ian Medwin (his Pilot and friend) in London on my last leave in December.

I am still in England and are becoming rather acclimatised after two years now. In a letter from Audrey some time ago, she said she had met you in Queen Street. I haven't the faintest idea of your address, so am writing to New Zealand House for it and hope they have it there.

In the meantime, I will say cheerio with best regards to Gaga - Grandmar and the Boys, Dem and Pete and lots of love for yourself.

Lots of Worlds of very good wishes.

Kindest Regards

Alf Drew.

CHAPTER TEN –
SO, WHAT ACTUALLY HAPPENED?

FLYING-BOAT LOST: The British Overseas Airways flying-boat Clare, formerly the Australia, has been lost on the course of a flight. Above, the Clare takes off.

PEOPLE PERISH

LOSS OF MAIL PLANE

(Recd. 5.35 p.m.)   LONDON, Sept. 19

British Overseas Airways Corporation announce that the Royal Mail aircraft Clare, on a passage from West Africa to the United Kingdom, was lost with 13 passengers and a crew of six on board. The loss was due to causes other than enemy action and these are the subject of investigation.

The flying-boat Clare was formerly named Australia and was intended for Australia-New Zealand service. The crew included Captain G. B. Munson and Mr. A. D. Jenkins was first officer.

UNA AIRMAN MISSING

OBSERVER OF BOMBER

Reported missing, believed killed on active service, Pilot-Officer Terence Albert Dixon is the eldest son of Mrs. R. Simons, of Audrey Road, Takapuna. Pilot-Officer Dixon, who is aged 20, was educated at Auckland Grammar School, leaving New Zealand last year for Canada, where he trained as an observer. He saw service in England and the Middle East and was the observer of a bomber, captained by Pilot-Officer I. G. Medwin, of Hamilton, which was shot down in flames last June when the Germans were advancing toward Mersa Matruh. The crew of the bomber, which had been engaged in low-level night bombing, came down in the middle of German troops. They had great difficulty in evading capture until they were finally picked up by British Army lorries engaged in mine-laying. At that time Pilot-Officer Dixon held the rank of flight-sergeant.

At the time of Terry's going down, Roma did all she could to find out exactly what happened. Many of her enquiries did not produce satisfactory answers. I think this is possibly because so much had to be kept secret at the time, that it was hard for her to find out the details.

Once I received these letters of Terry, and all the other documents and files, I did all I could to find out more, myself. In 2015, I received a letter in response to my enquiries, from the New Zealand Defence Force. This is what they told me:

> "According to EW Martyn's book, 'For Your Tomorrow', Terence was one of 13 passengers and six crew who died when the British Overseas Airways Corporation (BOAC) flying boat G-AFCZ (Named "Clare") crashed off the Senegalese coast. Eight of the passengers were returning to England on the completion of their tours with the 37 Squadron. Terence would have been one of these airmen returning to the UK, having completed an operational tour. The aircraft was in transit from Bathurst, Gambia to Britain and experienced engine difficulty and then possibly a fire. Both the engine problems and fire were reported by the pilot, so the accident was not the result of enemy action. The fate of the aircraft was not discovered until the 16th September when wreckage and six bodies were discovered in the water off the coast. The book notes that this flight was at the extreme operating limit of the aircraft type and that after this accident the type of plane was removed from this particular route."

The *Clare* was employed along with the *Clyde* as mail carriers, but as I have found out, these planes also carried some officials and one article even mentions a spymaster!

The *Clare* was a Short Sunderland S30. Sunderlands were the only long-range British aircraft which could reach the middle of the Atlantic for the first couple of years of the war. The *Clare* had been adapted to be refuelled while airborne.

At the time that Terry came down in the *Clare,* he had most of his precious possessions with him, as he was flying from Africa, having achieved his initial goal (to become a pilot), and been appointed Pilot Officer G/D P, on 27 May 1942 (Sqdn 37). He left Egypt for the UK on 4th September 1942. He disappeared over the Gambia on the 14th September 1942, according to scant and sketchy records.

SO, WHAT ACTUALLY HAPPENED?

When applying to the Poole Flying Boats Celebration (PFBC), for permission to use images of the Clare for this book, I learned the following: "Apparently, when an engine failed, it gave off a great amount of smoke, which would attract the attention of the aircrew, and the sad, immediate response would be to open the window or top hatchway to see what the situation was… and then it was likely sparks or a flare-up would ingress to be liable to cause the sudden and fatal explosion(s)."

The photo below was provided by the PFBC. In it, you will see on the left, is a small boat, the *Felicity*, owned by Gerald and David Davis, who had just 3 months prior, heroically saved the lives of many evacuees from Dunkirk!

I have dreamed of one day going to Gambia and flying or boating out to the

Clare with Gerald and David Davis in attendance in Felicity to the left

spot where the *Clare* is believed to have gone down… for Dad and for Gran.

After reading Ian Medwin's letter, I still could not understand why they got separated. He doesn't explain in his letter what the reasons were. And it seems this information will never be made public. It is ironic, that Terry went to Egypt, completed a full duty operation, was shot down, survived, walked back across enemy territory, and then to lose his life on a flight which would take him back to "Blighty" for a period of leave.

WFI/DPH   5/2/5833 IM.

CONFIDENTIAL

Mrs. R. Simons,   DESPATCHED   29th September 1942.
15 Audrey Road,
Takapuna,
AUCKLAND.

Dear Madam,

　　Further to the telegram which was sent to you by the Hon. the Minister of Defence concerning your son Flight Sergeant Terence Albert Dixon, I have to advise that the following details have been received from Air Ministry:

　　"Flight Sergeant Dixon was aboard the flying boat "Clare" on route to the United Kingdom from the Middle East.　A message was received from the aircraft on September 14th reporting engine trouble and a further S.O.S. was received stating that the aircraft was on fire, and an unsuccesful search was made by sea and air and later six bodies were recovered, but none of these were identified as Flight Sergeant Dixon, who has been classified as missing believed killed."

　　In view of the detailed information given it is requested that the above information be treated as confidential.

　　On behalf of the Air Board, I desire to express my deepest sympathy.　You will be advised immediately further information is received.

                                        Yours faithfully,

                                        P. C. WEENINK
                                        ACTING AIR SECRETARY.

C O P Y.

No. 5 Missing Research & Enquiry Unit,
A.P.O. S. 565,
Royal Air Force,
c/o B.T.A.

Ref.: 72159/GRAHAM.

21st June, 1948.

Air Ministry (S.14 Cas.),
2, Seville Street,
Knightsbridge,
London, S.W.1.

- - - - - - - - - - - - - - -

Copies to:
R.N.Z.A.F. Overseas H.Q.,
Halifax House,
51-55, The Strand,
London, W.C.2.

R.C.A.F. Overseas H.Q.,
11, Hill Street,
London, W.1.

- - - - - - - - - - - - - - -

	72159	W/CDR.	GRAHAM R.O.M.
	580863	W/O.	TURLEY A.
	655178	SGT.	GLANSFIELD. J.V.
	1059568	SGT.	KELLY W.
	J.5425	A/F/L.	MAGUIRE. J.P.
	NZ.404678	F/SGT.	DIXON T.
Bodies found { *	1014109	SGT.	HARDMAN G.B.
*	926353	F/SGT.	ALLBERRY. A.C.

P.O. Dept *

14. 9. 1942.

The above named personnel were being repatriated to the United Kingdom on 'Tour Expiry' as passengers in B.O.A.C. Aircraft 'CLARE', which force landed on the sea (position unknown) on 14th September, 1942.

2. An immediate search was carried out but no trace could be found of the airorfat or its occupants, though it is believed that the bodies of Sgt. Hardman and F/Sgt. Allberry were later recovered from the sea.

3. It would be greatly appreciated if any further information held by Air Ministry may be forwarded to this unit; alternatively Air Ministry's instructions on the closing of this case are requested.

(Sgd.) P. TENNISON,
for Squadron Leader, Commanding,
No. 5 M.R.E.U.,R.A.F.,B.T.A.

11 8 48

DREAMING OF THEE

This was sent to my Gran two years after I, Tere, her second granddaughter, was born and some nine years after the end of WW2.

11/E

22nd April, 1954.

Dear Mrs. Simons,

    I have just been advised that the name of your late son P/Officer T.A. Dixon will be commemorated on the Memorial to be erected at Malta by the Imperial War Graves Commission.

    This Department up till this moment had understood from the Commission that your son's name would be commemorated on the El Alamein Memorial.

    You may be aware of the position but I forward the advice to you just in case you have not previously been advised from some other official source.

    Yours faithfully,

Secretary for Internal Affairs

Mrs. R.E.L. Simons,
13 Audrey Road,
TAKAPUNA

Sadly, Malta is not a place my Gran or my father would or could ever hope to reach and even I, at the age of 67, and with a morbid fear of flying, will never see this memorial. I found it difficult to gather information on the Clare's last flight with Terry aboard from both RAF and RNZAF – seems around this area was a great deal of activity to do with movement of Italian prisoners of war, some 500 on a ship and torpedoing of shipping and the arrival of American planes to set up Island secret fuelling bases off Gambia. So, who knows where Terry was headed. He did not know and who knows why he was diverted, and the captain of his Squadron was not? Still too many questions.

DREAMING OF THEE

F/Sgt Dixon J. A.   N.Z. 404678

1 pr 3 boots   1 pr snowboots (1pr shoes inside).   1 pr shoes
2 pr. tennis shoes.   1 pullover   1 scarf.
1 balaclava.   8½ pr socks   1 kitbag
1 Empty writing case.   1 Diary   1 money belt.
1 scribbling block.   1 Common Prayer + Hymn book
2 new Testaments.   1 packet envelopes. 1 Trig. book.
1 Photograph Album   2 R.N.Z.A.F. badges 1 R/ badge.
2 Sgt. Chevrons   1 tin barley sugar (empty)
1 pkt. Chocolate cakes.   2 flying helmets (1 Helmet complete)
1 Carton Cigarettes   1 writing Pad 1 6" ruler.
1 tooth brush   2 pencils.   1 mascot brooch.
1 set Calipers   1 pr. swimming trunks   4 ties.
1 cigarette case 1 stamp case enclosed. 1 small tooth comb.
1 pr. flying gloves   2 prs mittens. 1 pr. woollen gloves
1 sport shirt   1 R.N.Z.A.F. sweater. 2 prs pyjamas
2 Shirts   6 Handkerchiefs   2 collars.
8 Vests   3 prs pants.   2 prs sports shorts (white

CHAPTER ELEVEN - DUNCAN MᶜARTHUR

I feel that I should give a little more detail on Duncan, Terry's uncle and inspiration, and what we know of his service. I am also endeavouring to show the strong relationship between my Gaga (Great Grandmother) and her son, born when she was 36 years old (which was thought to be quite old back then).

❧❧❧

Just a little bit about where the McArthur in Duncan Harold McArthur came from: Duncan's father was Francis Bannatyne Keddie MᶜArthur.

Francis was descended from the MᶜArthurs that came from ancient Dalriada clans of Scotland West Coast and Hebrides Islands. First recorded in (Argyle & Bute) Shire census.

The name comes from Celtic personal name Arthur which means 'noble'. Some went off to Ireland, and some emigrated to New Zealand, following the Great migration after Capt. Cook (1709-1769/1770). By 1838, British began buying land from the Maori. They often married into the Tribes/Whanau, even after the Treaty in 1840 (it is said not all the Ngapuhi agreed to the treaty or signed). It was a 6-month journey from Britain to New Zealand and on that boat came Jessie MacArthur on the Ship "Winterthur" in 1866.

Their motto and crest is held somewhere within the family.

Translation 'FIDE ET OPERA' - *"By Fidelity and work" - We so strive.*

Clan Arthur

Sidney's son, Duncan Harold McArthur was her youngest child and only son, born to her marriage to Francis B. K. McArthur. When they'd divorced, it was still considered quite a scandal, and so for convenience, and not to bring shame on her son, she filled out forms that her husband was already deceased. In truth, he died much later. These times, we must remember, were difficult and hard times for those women who did not have a provider and so this left my Gaga and her son, Duncan very strongly bonded. Young boys/men were raised to be and feel very responsible for their women (mothers, wives, daughters). In this strong bond, which the following letters and correspondence will highlight, we have to remember that Duncan was still just a teenager when he left his mother and his homeland and it is obvious from Terry's letters that both these young men, so far away from home, gravitated towards family environments to feel secure and gather comfort to brave up and carry on. They all did more than their duty in the End. But did the end really end up as it should have, in a moral sense? No one will ever know, but I am writing this story from the point of view of being a mother and trying to understand the strange and freaky similarities that arose some 4 generations on, in my own life as a single mother, not of my own choosing.

Before Duncan went to the Air Force, he worked on Gaga's then new husband, Mr. J.A. Wall's farm.

Duncan travelled great distances to both work and study in order to achieve his Pilot's commission and it is because of his mother's tenacity and connections that he was able to achieve this station.

As mentioned in Chapter Two, Duncan was inspired by his stepdad to enter the Air Force, and in 1939 he flew over to Britain in the first lot of NZ pilots.

While in England, Duncan met a woman named Peggy. From Terry's letters it appears that Duncan had fallen for her, and had according to her, got her pregnant. With much coercion from Peggy's mum, he married her, although he did not love her, or want to remain in this binding relationship. He, therefore, made sure to get on to one of the Middle East commissions. He was not interested in the child, and suspected that he was not truly the father, but in those days, it was hard to prove anything of the sort. Sadly, he never annulled the marriage, and as a result, when he was shot down and killed during his second commission flying over the Libyan Desert, Peggy was his *Next of Kin*, and received all his medals, pensions and pay, much to the agony of his mother. Peggy was never interested in giving Gaga an opportunity to get to know this supposed grandchild of hers, and refused to let her have any of the medals. In the end, the only keepsake of his duty as pilot in the R.A.F., was one of his two logbooks.

Later on, when I was a young woman myself, my father, who was keen to find this son of his Uncle in the U.S.A., wrote to Peggy to ask if he could have an address to come and visit this now Man, who was supposed to be family – I understand from my father that he was nice enough, but did not seem at all like any of our family, nor did he seem much interested in keeping up contact with his (supposed) father's family at all.

I feel this woman left another big hole and many more questions than answers to what often happens in times of war. Only recently, have we been able to determine, through DNA tests, that this child was indeed not Duncan's child at all, and it is sad that the medals he was awarded have been lost to us forever. I now understand why Duncan ran from Peggy and her insistent mother.

What follows, is the detail of his military service as found in his files.

RAF.36243 : Flight Lieutenant Duncan Harold McArthur, D.F.C.
Mother   :   Mrs. S. E. Wall of NORTH AUCKLAND
Widow   :   Mrs. P. BENDER of NEW YORK (remarried) one child

On leaving school, he was employed in farming by his step-father, Mr. J. A. Wall of Tai Tapu, Canterbury, and was so engaged on the 8th April 1938 when he applied for a Short Service Commission in the Royal Air Force. This application was successful, and on the 7th February 1939, Flight Lieutenant McArthur commenced his flying training at Wigram with the Canterbury Aero Club.

On May 25th, he passed the Pilot's "A" License test, and on the 14th June was granted a temporary commission in the rank of Acting Pilot Officer, in the R.N.Z.A.F. and posted to No.1 Flying Training School, Wigram where he continued his training on Vildebeeste, Gordon and Ayro Aircraft. On the 1st December Flight Lieutenant McArthur embarked on the "Tamaroa" for the United Kingdom to take up his appointment in the Royal Air Force.

On arrival on the 17th January 1940, Flight Lieutenant McArthur was granted a Short Service Commission in the Royal Air Force, in the rank of

Pilot Officer and posted to No.1 Depot, Uxbridge, Middlesex for a short course prior to proceeding on the 31st of the month to No. 63 Squadron, Benson, Oxfordshire. Here he trained on Battle aircraft, joining No. 52 Squadron, also at Benson on the 28th March. His next posting was on the 5th May, to No. 215 Squadron Honington, Suffolk, where he converted to Wellington bomber aircraft prior to commencing operational flying on the 15th of the month as a member of No.75 (NZ) Squadron, Feltwell, Norfolk.

I now include some of the letters written by Gaga and Duncan, to apply for training, and the replies. Please note that some of the letters are signed "Deirdre" which seems to be a name Gaga chose for herself, and by which even Terry knew her, and wrote of her in his letters. But as mentioned in Chapter Two, her formal name is Sidney, and so many of the later letters are signed with this name.

Tai Tapu
9th May 1938
The Air Secretary,
Bunny St,
Wellington

Dear Sir,

I trust that Mr. Bayley's reference is sufficient to prove my standard of education. The two years' work with him was really equal to three years' school work, for I stayed with him during my holidays, and studied long hours days and nights. I worked every month of the year, taking no school holidays at all. Re the Gilby College reference – That was just a refresher course, I kept up through the year.

I sincerely hope this will meet with your educational requirements, for I am desperately keen
to become an "Air Pilot".

I am,

Yours Respectfully,

Duncan McArthur.

CHRISTCHURCH,

NEW ZEALAND.

5th May, 1938.

        I understand that Duncan McArthur, as an applicant
for a post in the Royal New Zealand Air Force, requires
suitable detailed evidence as to his educational qualifications.
These I am happy to furnish to the best of my ability and my
personal experience of him.

        He first came to me for coaching for the University
Entrance Examination at the beginning of January 1935. He then
held his proficiency certificate, and had had two terms of post-
primary work at the Whangarei High School. He studied with me the
usual matriculation course continuously for the next two years, up
to December 1936. His subjects included English, French, Arithmetic,
Algebra, Geometry, History and Chemistry. By November 1936 he was,
in my opinion, competent to sit the examination with fair prospects
of success, but unfortunately, for family reasons, he was unable to
sit that year.

        McArthur impressed me as being highly intelligent. I
admired his perseverance in buckling down to arduous coaching
studies, when he was unable to avail himself of the easier method
of attendance at a secondary school. In the last two years he has
developed very rapidly, both physically and mentally, and he has a
maturity of judgement and sense of responsibility which is unusual
in a young man of his years.

        I can without the slightest hesitation recommend him for
any position that may be open to him. He has keenness and ambition,
and very high principles of honour and duty. These are the result
of a careful upbringing, with the most desirable home influences.
His late father was a successful dentist with a large practice in
Rotorua, and his step-father, Mr. J.A. Wall, is a former officer of
the Royal Air Force, and ex-pupil of the Imperial Service College,
Windsor.

                (Signed) H.G.W. BAGLEY   B.A.,Dip.Journ.

                        SUB-EDITOR,

                        "THE PRESS"

DUNCAN M^cARTHUR

AEU/BM

5/2/343

13th May, 1938.

Dear Sir:

I have to acknowledge receipt of your letter of the 9th instant enclosing an education certificate in support of your application for appointment to a short service commission in the Royal Air Force.

It is anticipated that the Selection Committee of the Royal N.Z. Air Force will be interviewing candidates in Wellington towards the end of the present month and a further reply will be addressed to you as soon as possible. It must be understood, however, that all expenses in connection with reporting for interview will be borne by yourself.

Yours faithfully,

AIR SECRETARY.

Mr. D. McArthur,
Post Office,
TAI TAPU.

Ref. No. 5/2/343

AIR DEPARTMENT,
Bunny Street,
WELLINGTON, C.1.

22nd August, 1938.

Dear Sir,

<u>Application for Appointment to Short Service
Commission, R.A.F. or R.N.Z.A.F.</u>

I have to advise that you have been provisionally selected for a short service commission. The date of sailing or of joining the Flying Training School will be communicated in due course, but it is not anticipated that this will be before   January   at the earliest and you should therefore not give up any employment on which you may be engaged.

The following papers forwarded by you are returned herewith: -

References (2)

Yours faithfully,

(Sgd.) T. A. Barrow
(P. C. W.)

<u>AIR SECRETARY</u>.

<u>Encls.</u>: 2

Mr. D.H. McArthur,
TAI TAPU,
<u>CHRISTCHURCH.</u>

DESPATCHED
1938/300 .... 2 ......encles .......H.B. Inits.
.... separate packs. 22/8/1938

DUNCAN McARTHUR

Tai Tapu,

Oct 28th.,1938.

Group Captain Isitt,

    Air Headquarters,

        Wellington.

Sir.

Regarding my acceptance for a"Short Service Commision" , I applied for the N.Z.R.A.F. Division with the intention of training at the F.T.S. Wigram if that were possible.

My reasons - Firstly- My flying experiences have been limited,and I wish for a thorough grounding before going home to England.

Secondly - I am very keen, and ambitious enough to wish to make a success of my training with the object of gaining a permanent Commission.

Should a vacancy occur at Wigram I should be very grateful to be nominated.

I am living within a few miles of the F.T.S. and could report there immediately if necessary.

If the selection rests with you may I hope for your favour in the matter.

I am,

    Sir,

      Yours obediently,

      Duncan McArthur.

From this syllabus, we can see that these pilots didn't just sit in the plane!

<u>Syllabus of Mathematics and Mechanics for preliminary
course of study by short service officers before
commencing course at the Flying Training Schools.</u>

Mensuration of the rectangle, parallelogram, triangle, circle, prism, pyramid, cylinder, cone and sphere. Area of an irregular figure. Use of formulae. Logarithms. Use of logarithmic tables.

Equations - simple, simultaneous and quadratic. Factors of algebraic expressions. Graphs of statistics. Graphs of linear and quadratic expressions. Graphical solution of equations.

The trigonometrical ratios. Solution of right angled triangles. Simple cases of solutions of triangles other than right angled. Graphical solutions of any triangle. Harmonic motion (brief outline only).

The vernier and micrometer screw gauge.

Moment of a force. Couples. Centre of gravity. Problems of equilibrium. Triangle of velocities, relative velocity, angular velocity. Parallelogram and triangle of forces. Mass. Density and specific gravity. Acceleration caused by a force. Work power and energy. Machines, friction and efficiency. Elasticity.

Two suitable text books which may be obtained through any bookseller, are: -

"Applied Mechanics," (Morley & Inchley)
(Longman 8/3d.)

"Mathematics for Engineers, Part I," (Rose)
(Chapman & Hall 17/-.)

DUNCAN M^cARTHUR

This letter from Gaga, dated **November 28th, 1938**, and her postal address was then a little place not far from Wigram, TAI TAPU, shows how much she wanted to be close to her son for as long as possible. *(Note that she signed this letter as Deirdre, and in Terry's letters he also refers to her as Deirdre, not Sidney – it seems this was a nickname she chose for herself. Later communications are signed Sidney).*

To: T. A. Burrow Esq., Air Secretary
WELLINGTON

Dear Sir,

My Son, Duncan McArthur has just received orders to sail to England by the "Tainui" on February 1st, and he is busy filling out the paperwork etc. currently.

Is it at all a possibility of his training at Wigram for the first 8 months at an end?

You see, Sir, I want so badly to be near him – to watch his progress, to encourage him, to be assured of his success in his new undertaking. He is my only son, and he is only 18 years old.

If there is no acknowledgement or alternative, then I shall smile when I bid him Goodbye in just two short months' time.

Sir, the world is in turmoil and I just suppose as do others, that war will come within the next few months!?

I do hope this does not sound disloyal – Duncan of course, himself is determined to go home to England and support King and Country.

I am so anxious also often to go home to England, but I know he would have been pleased to go first to Wigram.

Sir, Duncan does not know I am writing you on this matter. He is so keen to commence – I have been hoping someone would fall out at Wigram Training School and that would leave him a place – and that this would persuade you to allow Duncan his place to first train near home. Does this ever happen, Mr. Burrows? John Cooper has spoken to me and encouraged me to make certain that you will understand my longing to keep my boy near me for a little longer and that by writing you a private letter, this will in No way interfere with Duncan's chances and wishes to present himself on the line for the Mother Nation.

If he must go, then I shall try and be brave and trust to a Higher Power to bring my boy back safely to me in five years' time.

Sir, please forgive me for worrying you, won't you?

Yours Most Truly

Deirdre Wall.

229

And the reply:

30th November, 1938.

Dear Madam,

I appreciate the feeling which prompts you to write regarding the possibility of Duncan's being given his early training at Wigram.

Arrangements are being made for your wishes to be met and I have to-day written to Duncan advising him that his preliminary training will be undertaken in New Zealand. In a letter he wrote dated 17th November he indicated that he preferred his training to be undertaken in New Zealand and we are pleased to be able to meet the wishes of you both.

Yours faithfully,

T. A. BARROW,

AIR SECRETARY.

The next letter was handwritten by Duncan on 8th December 1938 from Tai Tapu, Mr John A. Wall's (Gaga's 2nd husband) WW1 Rehabilitation Farm, Near Wigram.
Addressed to T.A. Burrow Esq.. Air Secretary
Bunny Street,
Wellington.

Dear Sir,

I am in receipt of your letter of the 2nd December 1938.

I wish to thank you very much for making it possible for my training to commence in New Zealand. My mother also, is so Grateful to you for your interest in the matter.

I am,

Yours Obediently,

Duncan Harold McArthur

Stamped in Duncan's File as received 13/12/38

In both the above photos, Duncan is in the middle,
with Dem on the left and Pete on the right.

Duncan was one of the first pilots to go to England from NZ before the start of the Second World War. It was supposed to have been a "short commission" for the R.A.F., but as he was still there when war broke out, he stayed on to *do his duty* for the war effort.

SHORT SERVICE COMMISSIONS, ROYAL
AIR FORCE (NEW ZEALAND TRAINED).

The following twenty candidates, whose application forms are attached, have been provisionally selected for appointment to short service commissions in the Royal Air Force for training in New Zealand at the Auckland, Wanganui, Wellington, Canterbury and Otago Aero Clubs:-

Barnett, M. R. F.	Dunedin
Brabyn, O. R.	New Plymouth
Cameron, R. C. J.	Christchurch
Denton, F. H.	Greymouth
Duigan, J	Wellington
Gilmour, D. V.	Dunedin
Humphries, A. G. L.	Christchurch
Morton, J. E. G.	Christchurch
McArthur, D. H.	Tai Tapu
McFarlane, W. H.	Christchurch
McDermott, J	Wellington
McKay, R. M.	Christchurch
Newton, P. O. H.	Christchurch
Gutram, H. A	Dunedin
Parker, G. N.	Auckland
Pownall, C. A.	Wellington
Rolph-Smith, D. W.	Auckland
Raymond, W.	Wellington
Scott, R. C. W.	Wellington
Shorthouse, J. G.	Foxton

It is proposed with your consent to approve of the selections and the relative press notice is enclosed.

APPROVED.

F. J.

27/3/39

DUNCAN MᶜARTHUR

From the Feltwell, Norfolk base, as pilot of Wellington bomber aircraft,
Duncan took part in thirty-seven operational flights, the targets including
Minden, Kassel, Frankfurt, Hamburg (2) Kamen, Wessel, Hamm Keil (2), the
Marshalling Yards at Soest, an aerodrome in the Black Forest, Berlin, Leipzig,
and Gelsen Kirchen, all in Germany; Cambrai, St. Valery, Charleville, Salon,
Dunkirk, and Le Havre in France: the aerodromes in Schipol (3) and Walhaven
in Holland; and Nieuport, Roulers, Trelon, Antwerp (2) Brussels and Ostend (2)
in Belgium.

Form 688B.
J.M.

AIR FORCE MESSAGE.

Serial No. 94

TO: AIR HEADQUARTERS, WELLINGTON.

DATE: June 12th.

TIME OF RECEIPT: 0006   DESPATCH: 1230

FROM: N.Z.L.O. AIR MINISTRY.

SYSTEM: W/T   H

ORIGINATOR'S NUMBER AND DATE.

NZLO 94. June 10th.

Flying Officer Duncan Harold McArthur D.F.C. R.A.F. reported missing
air operations June 9th.
Now reported safe June 10th. His wife Mrs. D.H. Mcarthur Hill House
Methwold Norfolk has been informed by Air Ministry.

Following the raid on the oil works at Gelsen Kirchen, undertaken on the night of the 10th October 1940, the immediate award of the Distinguished Flying Cross to Flight Lieutenant McArthur was made, the citation covering the award reading as follows:-

"Pilot Officer McArthur was the captain, and Sergeant Mylod was the front gunner of the aircraft detailed to carry out an attack on a target in the Ruhr one night in October 1940. On the return flight and while still over enemy territory, Pilot Officer McArthur attacked an aircraft which he had observed giving recognition signals on being caught in the searchlights. When the searchlights were extinguished, he put his aircraft into a steep dive and Sergeant Mylod opened fire when within range and, by his excellent shooting and judgement, shot down the enemy aircraft in flames with only four short bursts. Pilot Officer McArthur has completed numerous major bombing operations during which he has shown a grim determination to carry out his instructions. Sergeant Mylod has taken part in several major bombing missions and has shown great determination, initiative and keenness."

FLYING CROSS AWARD

NEW ZEALAND PILOT

FORMERLY OF WHANGAREI

The Distinguished Flying Cross has been awarded to Pilot-Officer Duncan Harold McArthur, only son of Mrs. J. A. Wall, of Christchurch, according to advice received on Saturday by his sister, Mrs. R. E. L. Simons, of Penning Road, Milford.

PILOT-OFFICER D. H. McARTHUR

Pilot-Officer McArthur, who was 20 years of age in July, was educated at Parua Bay and the Whangarei District High School. Early in 1939 he was granted a short-service commission in the Royal Air Force, and after the requisite period of training he left for England in December last.

On October 23rd 1940, Flight Lieutenant McArthur was posted to No.20 Operational Training Unit, Lossiemouth, Scotland, for duties as an instructor. While at this unit, on the 17th January 1941, he was promoted to the rank of Flying Officer and one year later , his promotion to Flight Lieutenant was promulgated. Meanwhile, on the 22nd March 1941, he joined the Middle East Flight, Stradishall, Suffolk, and on the 6th April proceeded by air to Luga, Malta, prior to his posting on the 24th of the month to No. 37 Squadron, Shallufa, Egypt. With this squadron, he took part in further operations including a raid on the aerodrome at Derna. In early May, the Squadron moved to Shaibah in Iraq, and from this base as Pilot of Wellington aircraft, Flight Lieutenant McArthur participated in a further twelve operational flights bringing his total to 50. These comprised attacks on Iraqi troop concentrations in the Habbaniya area, the aerodromes at Bagdad, Rachid and Mosul; Tapolia in Greece and the Maleme aerodrome at Crete.

This is the aircraft that Duncan piloted when shot down.

On the 9th June 1941, Flight Lieutenant McArthur was the pilot of a Wellington bomber engaged in a bombing raid on the docks at Benghazi, and the Benini aerodrome, when owing to enemy action, the aircraft was badly damaged and force landed in a rough sea, Flight Lieutenant McArthur and other members of the crew, spending 31 hours in a dinghy. As a result of this, he spent three weeks in the 27th General Hospital, Egypt.

This survival earned Duncan a spot in the Late Arrivals club, of which the badge was a little Silver Winged Boot, just as Terry earned later, and wrote of.

On his recovery, on the 2nd August, he was posted on loan to Khartoum for duty with British Overseas Airways and piloted Lodestar aircraft to West Africa, the route being via El-Fasher, Geneina, Lamy and Kano.

In October he joined No.223 Squadron, Shandur, Egypt, flying Maryland aircraft, and carrying out several reconnaissance flights. On the 3rd March 1942 Flight Lieutenant McArthur proceeded to No. 108 Squadron also based in Egypt, and as pilot of Liberator, Lysander, and Wellington aircraft took part in supply dropping missions and Army co-operation flights to Ismailia.

On the night of the 3rd/4th May 1942, Flight Lieutenant McArthur was the pilot of a Liberator aircraft which took off on air-operations to attack the shipping in Tripoli Harbour and failed to return to base, all members of the crew being classified as missing. Owing to enemy action the aircraft crashed, and it was revealed later that two R.A.F. members of the crew had been captured by the Germans, and that one had died of wounds and been buried at Barce in Libya, the remaining four members of the crew, including Flight Lieutenant McArthur, being killed. In consequence, his death was officially presumed to have occurred on the 4th May 1942. No trace has been found of the grave of Flight Lieutenant McArthur, or his fellow members of the crew and it has been concluded that they have been effaced by sandstorms.

In total, Duncan flew 1036 hours and had 2 logbooks, of which Gaga only received one.

PILOT-OFFICER D. H. McARTHUR, D.F.C. (CHRISTCHURCH)

DUNCAN McARTHUR

This is a copy of a letter written to Gaga by one of Duncan's crew, who survived this crash, but got taken prisoner.

COPY OF LETTER FROM F/LT. P. CAMP FROM THE
GERMAN PRISON CAMP, STALAG LUFT. 111.

Dear Mrs. MacArthur,

          You must please forgive me if I
blunder in on your great sorrow.   By now you know
that your son Duncan has given his mighty all for his
King and Country.   Words cannot express my sympathy
or my own great sorrow at the loss of "Mac My Skipper"
and best friend.   It will be poor consolation for you
to know he died as he would have wished - fighting!
It happened in the early hours of 4th May after a
battle with a fighter.   Our kite caught fire and
there was no alternative but to "Bail Out."   I was
one but last to leave and the memory will live with me
to the end of my days of Mac still at the controls,
turning round and giving me the "Thumbs Up" sign as I
went out of the hatch.   Later, after I had been
captured, I stood beside his earthly remains and did
the only thing I could - I prayed for him.   He had
stayed at his post till last to give his crew a chance
of life.   "Greater love hath no man than he lay down
his life for a friend."   Now he rests in Lybia in
company with two others of his crew, in an airman's
grave, with a propeller blade as a headstone.

        Sincerely yours in sympathy and sorrow,
          (Signed) Philip J. Camp.

Reference:-
S.63955.

Standing Committee of Adjustment,
Royal Air Force,
Middle East.

8th May, 1942.

Dear   Mrs. Wall   ,

A Standing Committee of Adjustment has been set up at this Headquarters to deal with the effects in this country of all missing personnel amongst whom is F/L. D.H. McARTHUR who was so reported on 3/4.5.42.

We join you in the hope that he may, in fact, be safe and well.

Among his correspondence which has been forwarded to this Committee is a letter from which we have taken your address.

Further news when it is received will be sent to his next-of-kin. If you wish it to be sent to you also, or if there is anything else that we can do for you, we hope that you will let us know.

Yours sincerely,

Squadron Leader,
President.

Underneath is written, "I was his next of Kin when he left NZ," signed S.E. Wall.

The above letter, arriving just shortly after she must have received the first telegram reporting Duncan missing, must have been a double blow to Gaga. Not only had her son been shot down, and presumed killed, but now she had to deal with the fact that she no longer was his "next of kin", and some woman whom she'd never met, would be notified first if he was alive or dead. At this point, I wonder if it already occurred to her, that all his effects, and his war pay would go to this widow of Duncan's.

NEW ZEALAND POST OFFICE TELEGRAPHS.
(If prepaid in stamps, affix in this space.)

Date-stamp.

5/2/343

No.______

Code :______ Time :______ Words :______

Instructions :______ Charges :______
(For conditions of acceptance see over.)

ADDRESS.

Mrs. J.A. Wall,
C/o H.G. Bagley,
Press Office, Christchurch

FOR OFFICE USE ONLY.	
Sent______	Checked.
To______	
By______	
Ackgt.	

Deeply regret to learn that your son Flight Lieutenant
Duncan Harold McArthur D.F.C. has been reported missing
on operations. The Prime Minister desires me to convey to
you on behalf of the Government his deep sympathy with you
in your great anxiety.

F. JONES   MINISTER OF DEFENCE

Note.—The name and address of the sender if not to be telegraphed must be written on the back of the form.

URGENT   5/2/343

Mrs J. A. Wall,
C/o H. G. Bagley,
Press Office,
CHRISTCHURCH.

Regret to inform you that Air Ministry has now officially
presumed the death of your son, Flight Lieutenant Duncan
Harold McArthur D.F.C., to have occurred 3rd May, 1942.
The Prime Minister desires me to convey to you on behalf of
the Government his sincere regret.

F. Jones,
Minister of Defence.

Below is a summary of Duncan's service in the R.A.F.

<u>Record of Royal Air Force Service of</u>

<u>Duncan Harold McARTHUR, D.F.C. (36243)</u>

<u>Date and Place of Birth</u> :
15th July, 1920. Warkworth, New Zealand

<u>Previous Service</u> :
Nil

<u>Appointments</u> :

Granted a Short Service Commission for 5 years as Pilot Officer in the General Duties Branch, Royal Air Force	17. 1.40.
War substantive Flying Officer	17. 1.41.
War substantive Flight Lieutenant	17. 1.42.
Death Presumed	4. 5.42.

<u>Postings</u> :

No. 1 Depot	Supernumerary temporary Admin.	17. 1.40.
Station Benson	Operational training	31. 1.40.
No. 215 (N.Z.) Squadron	Flying duties	4. 5.40.
No. 75 (N.Z.) Squadron	Flying duties	11. 5.40.
No. 20 Operational Training Unit	Flying duties	22.10.40.
No. 3 Group Wing Flight	Flying duties	22. 3.41.
No. 267 Squadron Middle East	Spec (Flight Lieutenant)	18. 7.41.
No. 223 Squadron Middle East	Flying	25. 9.41.
No. 108 Squadron Middle East	Flying	3. 3.42.
Missing (F.B.)		3. 5.42.
Previously missing now missing believed Killed in Action Death Presumed		4. 5.42.

/ Education

Air Secretary,
Air Department,
Private Bag,
WELLINGTON, C.1.

5/2/343 A82.

Log Book(s).

I hereby acknowledge receipt of my late son's

SIGNATURE.... *G E Wall*

DATE....... *17ᵗʰ Nov 1948.*

This is the one item that Gaga received of Duncan's.

It represents the essence of Duncan's contribution during the war effort in terms of his time and in terms of his short life, and was all the closure my Gaga received back.

Following, are scans of 2 of the pages.

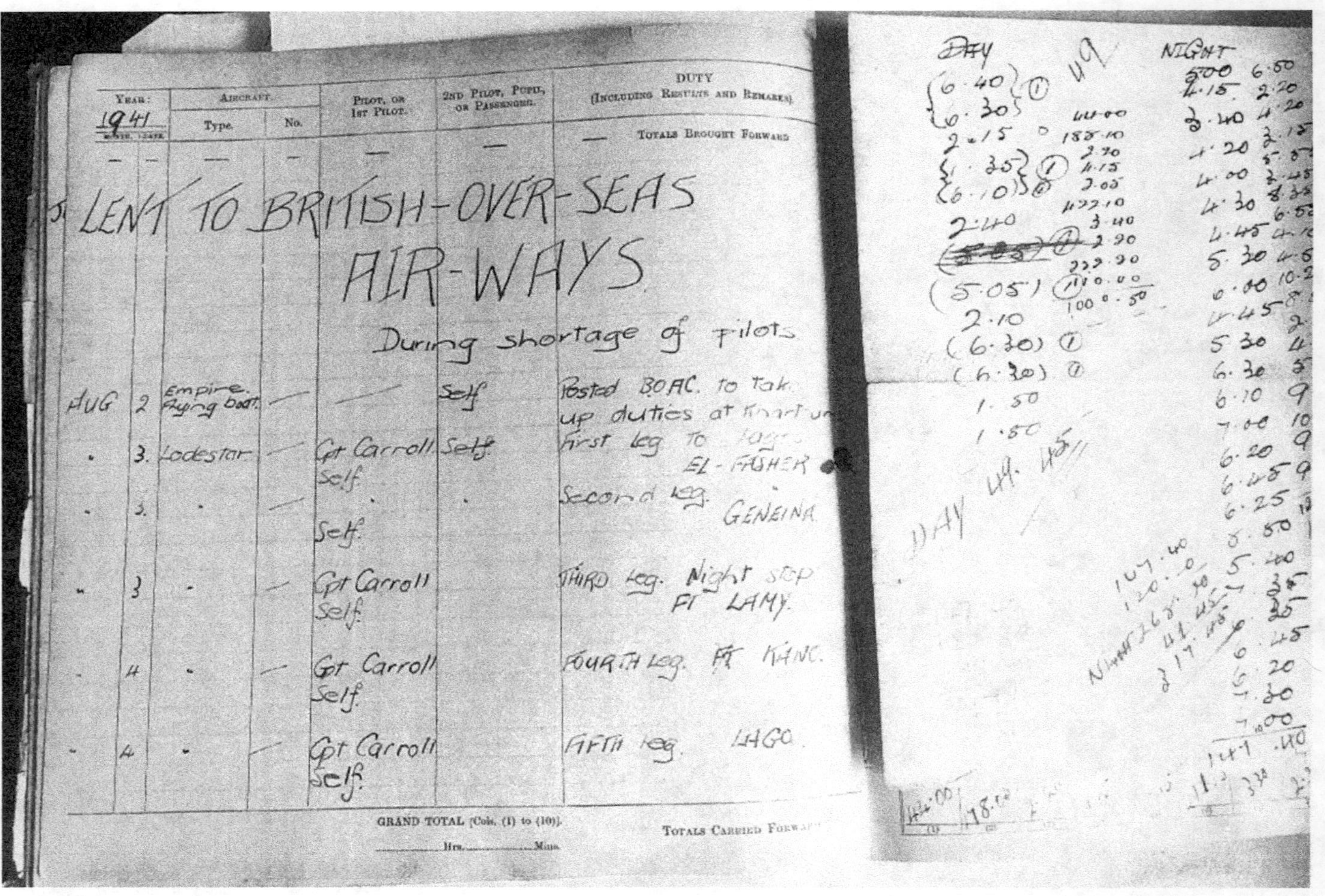
Year: 1941
Aircraft — Type — No.
Pilot, or 1st Pilot
2nd Pilot, Pupil, or Passenger
Duty (Including Results and Remarks)
Totals Brought Forward

LENT TO BRITISH-OVER-SEAS AIR-WAYS
During shortage of pilots

AUG 2 Empire Flying boat — — Self — Posted BOAC. to take up duties at Khartum First leg to targ... EL-FASHER
3. Lodestar — Cpt Carroll Self — Second leg. GENEINA
3. Self
3 — Cpt Carroll Self — Third leg. Night stop Ft LAMY.
4 — Cpt Carroll Self — Fourth leg. Ft KANC.
4 — Cpt Carroll Self — Fifth leg. LAGO.

GRAND TOTAL [Cols. (1) to (10)].
Hrs. Mins.
Totals Carried Forward

DAY   NIGHT

NO 20 'OTU LOSSIEMOUTH "B" FLIGHT

Year		Aircraft		Pilot, or 1st Pilot	2nd Pilot, Pupil, or Passenger	Duty (Including Results and Remarks)	Single-Engine Aircraft				Multi-Engine Aircraft				
Month	Date	Type	No.				Day Dual	Day Pilot	Night Dual	Night Pilot	Day Dual	Day 1st Pilot	Day 2nd Pilot	Night Dual	Night 1st Pilot
						Totals Brought Forward	44.00	172.45	2.30	1.45	1.15	57.45	2.25	2.30	71.50
OCT	23	WELLINGTON	L7775	SELF	NO 4 TC (P)	EX 2 ROUTE 4									
"		"	2527	"	"	"						3.00			
"	24	"	"	"	"	"						2.00			
"	24	"	9206	SELF	NO 4 TC (P)	X COUNTRY AS DETAILED						2.30			
"	25	"	2908	SELF	NO 4 TC (P)	EX 3 ROUTE W3.						2.30			
"	27	"	9206	"	"	"						1.00			
"	27	"	"	"	"	BOMBING						1.20			
"	28	"	2980	"	"	EX 4 ROUTE 4						2.30			
"	28	"	2884	SELF	"	ROUTE 16									
"	29	"	2980	SELF	"	HIGH LEVEL BOMBING						3.00			
"	30	"	"	"	8FT 4 HMB.	EX 4 ROUTE 8.						2.15			
"	31	"	2578	"	"							2.30			
"	31	"	2548	"	"	X COUNTRY B – BUCHAN – B									

GRAND TOTAL (Cols. (1) to (10)) Hrs. ________ Mins. ________

TOTALS CARRIED FORWARD

This letter is written to the Ministry Re Duncan's affairs, post WW2 by Gaga from R.D. Okaihau on February 25th 1946.

Mrs. J.A. Wall, nee Mrs. McArthur, nee Herdson.
To the Honourable Mr. Jones – NZ Military Division for War Service Gratuity – assessments.

RE: THE GRATUITY

Dear Sir,

In reading your Leader's Speech and listening to Mr. Nash's speech on the radio I have plucked up courage to write, and ask you if you consider I am eligible for my deceased son's gratuity.

Enclosed you will find photographs and particulars of part of his R.A.F. Career.

A few months after reaching England, where he was very homesick and miserable, he met a dangerously attractive, unscrupulous English woman, older than himself and far more sophisticated if you understand my meaning. He was only 20 and she persuaded him to marry her.

She turned out was badly unfaithful and cruel, allowing him to go away on his night bombing operations, with the idea that she would be out with other men while he was risking his life.

Finally, after long waits for mail to and from home, he applied for Middle East Service in order to get away from her and the powerful family influence/pressure he felt under. He applied for the Middle East in order to get away from her, and it is there int eh Middle East that he entered a second round of operations after his first crash that he finally met his death. His death was the death of a hero, only three weeks to his "Leave", when he intended coming home to New Zealand to see me.

He died gloriously, keeping his blazing liberator in the air while most of his crew were able to parachute to the ground, and some of them were taken prisoner.

It was from one of his men who was imprisoned that I learnt all this information. I adored my only son and his being reported missing then reported deceased, nearly broke me. My heart is broken; a large piece of me is gone.

DUNCAN MᶜARTHUR

It seems his 'wife' has claimed everything – his deferred payments, short service commissions monies and all his belongings (around the range of some £500).

I did write for some little thing to hold in memory of him and to keep a connection to the supposed child, but she refused. I thought I might receive his Cross, after educating him and fitting him out for the Air Force and sending him away with a prayer in his heart and his powerful sense of duty to his King and Country (His Mother Country)

So, I prayed for his safe return.

I am now over 60 years old (he was born when I was aged 36).

Sir, I am still doing very hard work on the farm, which my boy, Duncan would have delighted in doing, had he been spared and come home.

I do understand the division of the gratuities is left to your discretion, and I pray that you will consider the claim he would want his mother to seek – I have enclosed some of his letters and ask you to consider this for the mother of my brave lad who gladly gave his life for his country. I am sorry to have to seek your assistance and for the need to go these lengths of shining some light on the matter of his very short union (marriage). I thought I should submit this to make your decision easier by giving you full particulars. I do thank you for explaining the matter so fully in both the Newspaper and the radio.

Yours Truly
Sidney Elvira Wall
Mother of Duncan Harold McArthur
No: 36243 – Ft. Lt. P/officer

```
Copy.                                              (Form N.Z.-397.)
            Army Headquarters                      (Banded in Reams)
               New Zealand Military Forces    In you reply  8212
                  Wellington C.1.             Please quote this number.
                  May 15th 1946.

      Mr. S.E.Wall
         R.D.Okaihau
            Northland.

                  War Service Gratuity.
                  The late No.8212-Homann G.S.S.

Dear Madam,

            In reference to your application for the War Service
Gratuity payable in respect of the above named deceased,I have been
directed to inform you that it has been decided that the Gratuity
shall be divided equally between you and Mr F.E.Homann,father of the
deceased,i.e.£100 each. Letters (2)returned herewith.

                                       Yours faithfully,
                                          F.B.D -
                                          Army Secretary.
```

Army Headquarters,
  New Zealand Military Forces,
    Wellington C. 1,

[Form N.Z.—
(Handed in Rean

IN YOUR REPLY

8212

please quote this number.

18th June, 1946.

Dear Madam,

 With reference to your application for the War Service Gratuity of the late 8212 G.S.S. Homann, would you please state definitely the month and year he came to live with you.

 In your letter to the Director of Base Records, of the 16th March last, you stated that you have a considerable number of letters from the deceased, and I should be glad if you would forward me say, half-a-dozen of these letters for my perusal. The dates of these letters should be spread as far as possible.

 An early reply would oblige.

  Yours faithfully,

ARMY SECRETARY.

Mrs. S. E. Wall,
R. D. Okaihau,
NORTHLAND,
AUCKLAND PROVINCE.

R.D.Okaiha,U,   *Northland.*
July 29th.,/46.

Th' Hon.Mr Parry,
    L.iister for Internal Affairs,
        W E L L I N G T O N.

Dear Mr Parry,
            The above attached copy of a letter from the Army Sec.
has created for me a most embarrassing situation.
                            When I received it
we were reaping the result of a six months drought - it seemed like
an answer to a prayer.
                I showed it to two business people - they both
said that on the strength of such a letter,which was a promise
from the Government,they would willingly advance me the whole £100.
However I accepted haff,and got a measure of relief,promising to
return the advance as soon as I received my Gratuity Bank Book.
I knew only too well how glad my boy would have been to be of help
to me at such a time.
                Over a month later,to my horror and constern-
-ation,I received the second letter - I sent the further particulars
six weeks ago,but have heard nothing further.
                            Now I am placed in a
desperate situation.
                What do you advise me to do?
There was my own boy"Duncan Harold McArthur"Flt Lt at whose gallant
death I received a letter of sympathy from you. He commenced his
Air Force training at Wigram when there were rumours of war,and was one
of the first pilots to go overseas. He won his D.F.C. over Germany
and France,and lost his life just before his long leave was due,in
volunteering to take a crew minelaying in the Mediterranean.
When he was very homesick he made a war marriage in England,and
repented of it - his wife collected his Short Service Commission
and back pay money(about £500) and married an American **and** went to
live in his country.
                Dont you think I,his own mother who brought him
up,and educated him for the Airforce, then lost him,am entitled to
a Compassionate Gratuity?
                Re G.S.S.Homann - He talked of me to his
O.C. and his Padre when he lay wounded,and when he passed awaythey
wrote beautiful letters of symathy to me - those letters are now in
the hands of the Army Secretary in Wellington.
                            It is only in my extreme
desperation,that I am worrying you Mr Parry - knowing you,I hope
you will speak to your Collegue Mr Jones on my behalf.-There seems to
be no-one else who can help me.
                To me,and to others too, that letter was
a legal promise from the Government,I have the honour of supporting.
Was I mistaken?

                        Yours sincerely,
                        Sidney Elvira Wall.

                            S.E.Wall.

Mrs. S.H.Wall,
R.D. OKAIHAU,
NORTHLAND.

Ref: 5/2/343.

13th August, 1946.

Dear Madam,

Your letter of 29th July 1946, has been referred to me by the Hon. the Minister of Internal Affairs, and I have to advise you as follows:-

The late NZ.8212 Homann, C.S.M.

The payment of the abovementioned deceased serviceman's War Service Gratuity has been deferred pending the result of the investigation of certain information which has been received, and which may have an effect on the decision regarding the gratuity payment. You will be advised in due course of the decision in the matter.

NZ.36843 the late Duncan Harold McARTHUR.

Your application for the War Service Gratuity payable in respect of the above mentioned deceased serviceman has been received, but it will not be considered until such time as an application has been received from the widow. It is the general practice to pay the Gratuity to the widow unless she has been guilty of infidelity or misconduct during the time she was married.

As by your communication to me on 25th February 1946, you apparently have some letters containing information regarding your daughter-in-law's conduct during the time she was married to your son, I shall be pleased if you will forward them to Air Department, so that they may be perused and taken into consideration when the decision as to the Gratuity payment is made.

Yours faithfully,

(Sgd.) F. JONES

MINISTER OF DEFENCE.

DUNCAN M^cARTHUR

Dated 30th April 1947 (2 yrs post-WW2)

From R.D. Okaihau

Dear Mr. Parry,

Thank you again for your prompt reply. Yes, I have heard from the Social Security Department. It would seem I am not eligible for the 10/-. In fact, not eligible for any assistance whatsoever.

You can imagine my disappointment, Can't you? Is there no way in which you might help me?

My daughter Mavis is very ill in Suva (where her husband was posted during the War to assist in the Pacific). Would it be possible under the circumstances, to grant me a return Air fair (*sic*) to Suva? You see, Sir, I did not avail myself of the New Zealand free trip. I would have done so, had I not been kept waiting all those long months for the War Gratuity decisions. Doesn't the Government owe me anything? I would be so very grateful if you had the power to assist me, Mr. Parry.

This is one of my only two daughters left after the War effort. No doubt, I shall borrow the money and get to Suva somehow. If I manage to get the money somehow, and you cannot help me with the fare, could you expedite the passport regulations for me as soon as is possible.

Thank you for your ever unfailing kindness and courtesy/ I am sure you have done your best for my remaining family.

I have tried also to get berths in the Matau, but cannot get anything until next September. The seats in the planes that are available are such high prices. I look forward to hearing from you soon.

Yours Sincerely

    S.E. Wall (Mrs)

        Mother of Duncan Harold McArthur.

DREAMING OF THEE

5/3/87 - P.R.S.

28th Sept., 1948

Mrs. S.E. Wall, (M)   Mrs. P. Beadser, (re-married widow)
R.D. Okaihau,   24 Sth. Walnut St.,
NORTH AUCKLAND.   West Hempstead,
                        Long Island - NEW YORK

Dear Mrs. Wall,

Further to my previous correspondence concerning your son, Flight Lieutenant Duncan Harold McArthur, D.F.C., I have to advise that information now received from Air Ministry states that in spite of extensive searches carried out in the area in which your son's plane crashed, no trace whatsoever can be found of the graves of your son or the remaining three members of his crew.

Acting Group Captain F.M.V. May, who died as a result of injuries received when he baled out, is now buried in the Benghazi Military Cemetery.

Air Ministry are therefore reluctantly compelled to assume that the severe sandstorms experienced in this area have effaced all traces of the graves of your son and his crew members.

Arrangements are being made to inscribe the names of all airmen who have no known grave on a suitable memorial, and immediately the form of this memorial and its location has been decided, you will be further advised.

Yours faithfully,

AIR SECRETARY

Some letters missing in between.

DUNCAN M^cARTHUR

In reply, please quote:
R.G. 2/8/5848.

Registrar-General's Office,
P.O.Box 23, Government Buildings,
Wellington, C. 1.

15th October, 1948.

MEMORANDUM for:-

The Air Secretary,
Public Relations Section,
Air Department,
WELLINGTON C.1.

Re: RAF 36243 - F/L. Duncan Harold McArthur -DFC.

I have to acknowledge receipt of your memorandum of the 5th February, advising the place of burial of the above named serviceman, and have to advise that as yet I do not appear to have received a death card R.G. 147 relating to his death. Will you kindly forward one at your earliest convenience.

Deputy Registrar-General.

R.E. Okaihau
26th February 1950.

Dear Mr. Watts,

I thank you for your letter dated 20th February. Also, for your kindly and lucid explanation.

Re the net income mentioned of £302. That could not have been and was definitely wrong. During those two drought years, we had to borrow money from the Government to carry on.

Although I believe Mr. Tom Barrows did all he could for me, the Department did not see eye to eye with me, so the matter ended. Re my pilot son. He was a very home-sick boy in England at first, and against his brother pilot's advice, he married a beautiful English girl who was out for all she could get. He was only 19 and was very soon disillusioned. A war marriage. After that, I was not next of kin. He persuaded the Air Ministry to move him to the Middle East, and from there wrote me very cheerfully letters of the time he would be home again, managing the farm as before.

I listened in to a speech by Mr. JONES re these foolish war marriages – He was prepared, so he said, to divide any money left between the mother who had reared and educated her son, and given him to her Country, and the new wife.

My boy, Flt Lt Duncan Harold McArthur D.F.C., and I am very of that distinction, went straight from the farm which he ran for his stepfather and I, very efficiently, to Wigram – where he passed out as a first-rate pilot in 1939.

So, you see although I educated Duncan – even sending him to night school prior to his entry into Wigram and fitted him out for the Royal Air Force – I was not considered at all. I never took a penny allotment. So, everything went to a strange girl who did not even give him happiness.

He was longing to come home and relieve me of the work I was doing in his absence.

I am telling you all this to prove how hopeless it would be for me to apply for an award in respect of my beloved son's death, although I know he would have been horrified to see the work his 65-year-old mother was doing, and would have to continue doing, because a grateful Government makes all these decisions.

We can leave this Rehabilitation farm, and after your letter, no doubt I shall then be able to qualify for an age benefit. If you do not mind, when this occurs, I shall then write you again, after which I can deal through the usual channels. You will understand though that I am averse to the old red tape business, if there is no chance for me. It only means fresh disappointment.

I want to know if it would be any use applying for something due to my son not returning to carry on the farm work – even though he was lent to the British Government. No-one has ever been able to tell me this.

Thanking you again, Mr Watts, and wishing you all the success in your new and rather unenviable undertaking,

I am,

Yours truly,

Sidney Elvira Wall.

DUNCAN M^cARTHUR

AND REHABILITATION.

6th   April, 1950.

Mrs. S.E.Wall,
R.D.Okaihau,
NORTHLAND.

Dear Mrs.Wall,

     Mr.Watts has referred your letter of the 26th February
to me for consideration.

     The Air Secretary has advised me that there are no
monies which could be paid to you in respect of your son's service
in the Royal Air Force.

     I am sorry that there is also no provision for
assistance to you under the Rehabilitation Act.

     Yours faithfully,

MINISTER OF DEFENCE & REHABILITATION.

There are some letters missing here, but what we have, gives one a fair idea of the struggles Gaga continued to have. As you can see, Gaga tried to get just something from the government that she felt was her due. Sadly, although she continued to try over the years, she was not granted anything, and Duncan's "war-bride" got it all.

CHAPTER TWELVE – WHERE SHE GOES, WE GO

When Britain declared it was at war with Germany, on 3 September 1939, New Zealand was quick to follow suit. Her Prime Minister at the time, Michael Joseph Savage, made a memorable speech that echoed the feelings of most New Zealanders at the time.

> "Both with gratitude for the past and confidence in the future, we range ourselves without fear beside Britain. **Where she goes, we go**. Where she stands, we stand. We are only a small and young nation, but we are one and all a band of brothers and we march forward with union of hearts and wills to a common destiny."

I wanted you, the reader, to see just what a national contribution the people of New Zealand committed to the War effort. The many mentions of Parcels and letters sent to both Terry and Duncan - not just by his family, but by Volunteer groups - were a wonderful way of keeping up the men's morale and must have been a huge undertaking - most of it was shipped and took long periods of time, hence women working out for themselves ways to bake that kept food from going off in the long transit. The big flying boats were used for moving mostly the News Reels and important documents for the Military.

Hundreds of thousands of parcels a year were packed and despatched for prisoners of war, and for servicemen overseas; recreation huts in the camps and clubs in London, Cairo, Alexandria, Bari, and Rome, were staffed largely by members of the Women's Army Auxiliary Corps (W.A.A.C.); mobile canteens took tinned fruit, biscuits, cigarettes, and chocolate almost up to the front line; mobile cinemas and concert parties entertained the troops in their leisure time.

The National Patriotic Fund Board collected millions of Pounds for comforts and amenities for the Forces overseas and in New Zealand. Newspapers and current periodicals were sent overseas regularly, and libraries were set up in base camps, hostels and convalescent camps. Sports gear was provided for men overseas, and hundreds of musical instruments were supplied also.

The work of the National Patriotic Fund Board, however, was made possible only by the willing assistance of hundreds of voluntary workers in New Zealand, who packed parcels for prisoners of war and men serving overseas, staffed clubs for servicemen and women, and carried on all the other varied activities which contributed so greatly to the welfare of our forces.

Women played a vital part in the preparations against invasion, and in the war effort as a whole. When war broke out the Women's War Service Auxiliary was established to coordinate the work of the many women's organisations which were anxious to undertake war services.

As the demand for man-power grew, women replaced men in the Home Forces, thus freeing men for service overseas. Terry mentioned the high numbers of Kiwi men being drafted for subscription and how short his little country would be of manpower once they were all over there.

In January, 1941, the Air Force established the first women's auxiliary unit. It was then that my Gran joined up.

Many WAAFs performed highly technical and specialized duties, and as my Gran found out, the rules for women and working their way up the ranks were quite different to the boys' commission and pay rewards.

In all of these occupations, most of them strenuous, technical, and difficult, the women of New Zealand gave magnificent service - this is why I found it pretty upsetting when I read through my Gran's service records and documents. Apparently someone from high up did not like that fact she wished to work so hard for a higher commission and felt this was a jolly bother advising her superior leader to either discourage her or get rid of her - His words "There are plenty of other keen typist, drivers, clerks waiting for positions." This disgusts me reading this arrogance now, considering how she insisted in getting on with it even after her brother and son were killed just months apart.

Women also replaced men on the Farms, as did Sidney, My Gaga. In October 1944, there were more than 2,000 members of the Women's Land Service employed in all branches of Farm work.

While labour was needed for war Industry, men were needed just as urgently for the Forces. So, while the young fit men went into Services, older men came out of retirement back to their old trades and women, whose husbands, sons, or brothers were in the Forces, also learned new tasks in the munition factories.

Our Plants which assembled motor-cars in peacetime assembled munitions during the war; firms making jewellery made instruments for the Air Force; radio factories made military radio sets; toymakers business switched over to making ammunition carriers.

The efforts in New Zealand were per head of population far and away in excess of our duty.

The Story of New Zealand's defence construction is spectacular. Camps were built to accommodate 170,000 men; over a hundred aerodromes were constructed; hospitals providing more beds than all the public hospitals in New Zealand, were erected. Munitions factories, warehouses, wharves, magazines, gun emplacements, and operational centres were constructed throughout the country.

New Zealand was fortunate in some respects. In the years preceding the war the public Works Department had imported large quantities of mechanical equipment, and had carried out many extensive engineering projects. The necessary equipment was here, and skilled and experienced operatives were available. Work on erecting military camps had already begun when war came, enough aerodromes had been completed in the interim to meet the immediate needs of the Air Force, and batteries of six-inch guns were being installed around the coasts.

One of the first tasks was to build new camps for the Army. Of these, Waiouru and Papakura were the largest. More than a thousand men worked twelve-hour days to build a block of twenty-five acres of dormitories, mess-rooms, cook-houses, offices, and recreation rooms, complete with electric light and hot and cold showers. To house the huge quantities of stores and equipment that arrived in New Zealand, five million square feet of warehouses and stores were built. These buildings were designed so that they would be suitable for peace-time use also.

Over 382,000,000. feet of timber well over the total amount produced in New Zealand in a year - was used in defence construction, this timber would have built 37,000 houses.

The job of milling this timber was an achievement in itself, and it was done at a time when there were fewer men available to do it. Hundreds had joined the Forestry Units and other branches of the Forces. It meant harder work and longer hours for the men who were left at home.

In Nadi, Fiji, they built an airstrip capable enough for the Flying Fortresses to use. An aerodrome construction unit started work in the last week of November and a 5,000-foot airstrip of stabilized shingle was completed by New Year's Eve, 1942. Just a fortnight before the date set by the United States authorities.

Hospitals for the troops were built with similar speed. The Hospital in Cornwall Park Auckland would accommodate 1,500 men and was completed in three and a half months, The Hobson Park hospital, containing 1,000 beds was built in a month. Altogether, hospital accommodation for 9,400 patients was provided.

Feeding the Forces is also something New Zealand can be very proud of.

The only way to get enough meat, butter and cheese and other milk products for the Allied troops was to decrease either the amounts sent to Britain or the quantity consumed here at home.

Butter and meat rationing, were introduced towards the end of 1943, and this sacrifice fell mainly upon the New Zealand people.

My father remembers the rationing as a time of larger helpings at Dilworth - seems they had previously been served less than the Government thought they should be receiving as a helping.

This provided in full the food for all the Pacific forces – Yes, they were all fed from Little New Zealand. Vegetable production also was doubled, and their output of canneries was expanded eighteen times over. It was in vegetables that the most striking results were obtained. Before the war, New Zealand was able to export vegetables only in exceptional years, and as the war advanced and the demands on manpower and service increased, usually production would fall, but New Zealand with the pressure of the American Troops demanded exceptional measures. Not just summer increased the yields but demands specified qualities of different vegetables to be available all year long.

To meet these needs State Vegetable farms were established. Originally these farms were to supply the New Zealand troops with their fresh vegetables; they now also supplied the United States troops as well, and later American forces in the Pacific. Production efforts were considered magnificent.

Providing fresh canned and dehydrated vegetables and fruit was another additional wartime task that New Zealand assumed and carried out to the utmost success.

To enable the greatest possible amount of food to be sent to Mother England end the United States Forces, rationing of butter and meat was introduced. Ninety percent of New Zealand's cheese, three-quarters of its butter, and nearly half its meat went offshore to Britain. The United States Forces, by 1945, were receiving one-fifth of New Zealand's meat, 8 percent of its butter, and 7 percent of its cheese.

Almost alone among the food-producing nations, Little New Zealand increased her output of foodstuffs during the second world war. Partly this was due to scientific organization and co-operation between the State and the farming community; largely it was the result of sheer effort and great sacrifice of the New Zealand people. The farmers along with other members of the community, had had to contend with serious difficulties with the labour shortages and the war time lack of equipment and on top of this, they had a number of unfavourable seasons weather-wise.

In October 1941 before the second Libyan Campaign had begun, before even Japan had entered the war, the New Zealand parliament passed the New Zealand Rehabilitation Act, thus laying the foundations of the organization which, by 1946, had already assisted one hundred and fifty thousand sailors, soldiers, and airmen in their return to civil life.

My two uncles were not as lucky as the rest and never returned to their homeland, not even in a box. My other Grandfather and his brother did return, and I saw what could be achieved through their eyes and lives - but to our family there was always this gaping hole of loss and grief.

Our post-war system of rehousing and rehabilitation was watched and considered as top grade worldwide. The system aroused great interest in other countries, and drew high praise from overseas officials who came here to study our then system.

It was considered that "New Zealand is a return soldier's Utopia", this was the statement of the New South Wales returned soldiers' league who visited New Zealand in 1944 to study how our rehabilitation system was working. He wanted our scheme to be adopted in its entirety in their country as well.

So, in short, every person, Man, Woman and Child felt the full effects of the WW2, even though it was considered to be far from our shores. We now know it was often closer than even officials realised.

At the start of this War in the records it is said:

> "It was clear that the citizens of a democracy could discipline themselves to wage and win a war. The Farmers set out to produce more no matter the conditions of the land or the size or quality of workers available; every available piece of land no matter how productive, was expected to produce. The hardest critics were the workers themselves no matter what age they were, they worked to support their governments need for more and more. Businesspeople cheerfully accepted the price controls, and workers' organizations agreed to wage ceilings and willingly accepted all the obligations and limitations involved in national service and the National interests."

The Government noted that the people resolutely did their utmost, of facing difficult decisions with a fighting spirit. Lieutenant-General Sir Bernard Freyberg, V.C. speaking of New Zealand's part in the war, said:

> 'If I had to say what quality in them I most admired, I would say, Their

Wisdom, tenacity, and failure to get tempted to put self first, or rattled in a crisis. These qualities were typified by two decisions made by New Zealand. When New Zealand came into the war zone in 1942, and for the first time in history New Zealand shores were threatened, they still decided to keep and maintain their expeditionary Force in the Middle East. Later, when the Japanese drove south and east, and stretched out towards Guadalcanal, they took their only equipped and tried Force in New Zealand, and moved it to Fiji to hold it as an outpost. These were brave decisions, and history proved them wise and the policy right.'

The people who were skilled and in need in Fiji, were the likes of Gaga's daughter Mavis' husband – a double degreed Gentleman who served well in the best way he could to rebuild the Pacific – New Zealanders living in Fiji post-war were often struck down with illness. For Mavis it was from stress and childbirth that made her so ill and naturally, Gaga, her mother, wanted so very much to get to her, hence her plea to the Minister responsible for passports and internal affairs of the time, as shown in the previous chapter, p. 248.

We had it tough here in the colonies. New Zealand and our ANZAC brothers and sisters from Australia and the Pacific were a vital part of the British Empire, later to become the Commonwealth. Many of the men and women of New Zealand were indeed from Britain, Scotland, Wales, Ireland and as my DNA now states, part of Nova Scotia and the Iberian Peninsula, also the tiny 1% of Maori shows how strongly attached to this little nation of MIGHT we became (entwined into one). What we produced and provided to Britain was a HUGE contribution.

્ૐ્ૐ

I have extracted these pieces from our War-time history (WW2) to show New Zealand in a different light than we see her today. One hopes we are forever growing towards a better and more positive partnership with the other race and culture our ancestors chose to join in Aotearoa. The information given in this chapter was extracted from a small booklet, *War Record*, which has no copyright information, but was printed by the NZ Government in 1946.

A little more information about the Royal New Zealand Air Force (R.N.Z.A.F.).

WHERE SHE GOES, WE GO

In June 1923, the formation of the New Zealand Permanent Air force was authorised, backing by the Territorial Air Force for our reserve personnel. In one of these early training courses, Duncan rose through his ranks - One of the early flying schools had sadly gone out of business, but the airfield and equipment of the Canterbury Aviation company were purchased to become the air force's first base, which was renamed WIGRAM. In 1935, a combined airfield and seaplane base was established. The Territorial was reorganised in 1930 to have four squadrons. By 1933 we had only nine officers and forty-four other ranks of aircraft. Only three Grebe fighters and a Fairey III that were regarded as operational.

In 1934, Royal Ascent was given for the NZFC to be renamed ~ The Royal New Zealand Air Force, but it was not until 1937 that it became a separate service.

Expansion of the R.N.Z.A.F. BEGAN IN 1937. They constructed two new airfields and made the purchase of Thirty Wellingtons to provide long-range reconnaissance and bombing force to deal with enemy surface ships. In the event, all remained in Britain and were manned by our New Zealand pilots as number 75 Squadron R.A.F.

Soon after, other pilots were trained and then sent to the UK for experience with more modern aircraft and tactics with the R.A.F. squadrons.

As the War in Europe approached, plans were made for a major R.N.Z.A.F. training programme to supply pilots, radio operators and navigators to both R.A.F. AND R.N.Z.A.F units. Various obsolete aircraft and some Oxfords, were provided from the UK and Middle East while a production line of Tiger Moths was laid down at the de Havilland Factory of Rongotai.

At the time, New Zealand committed to offer up 880 fully trained pilots a year and later increased this to 2000, but only on condition that N.Z. had their own commanding officers and their own squadrons, and this is why there was even a separate Maori battalion, as the Maori were happy to offer their support, as long as they had their own squadron, and their own Officers.

To protect our own coastline, a small mixture of Vildebeests and Baffins undertook patrols and were supplemented by the occasional Tasman Empire Airways flying boats. In addition to the defence of the homeland, the R.N.Z.A.F also had the responsibility for Fiji.

In other words, New Zealand Airmen and women did a little more than "their bit", wouldn't you say?

CHAPTER THIRTEEN
– WE MOVE ON

After it was announced that the Second World War was at an end, and all the excitement had settled down, the average New Zealander had to adjust to still more stresses and difficulties. Given that most families had been touched by this huge World-wide conflict, the influx of their men returning, the War Bride issues; the men who had come back in dribs and drabs with injuries and illnesses, never to be the same for them or their families again, still the fighting spirit to go on with what they had and help one another, especially our Pacific Neighbours, continued.

My Gran's two remaining sons, my father Dem and his younger brother Pete, were coming into manhood and realised their need to help their mother through her massive loss and again change of life from Air Force WAAF to housewife.

My Gaga who had lost her only Son, Duncan, although she had remarried, she was now getting on in years and still doing the work on the farm with her new husband. They had not only had poor weather conditions to work with, but they also had to deal with shortage. They had petrol restrictions, they needed to apply for every tool or tyre that needed to come from overseas with special government approval before the overseas funds were allowed to be used. The way of life was crippling if one had little resources or savings.

It seems to me with every death, was a telling of some part of this small nation's history and with this my now small family's story.

My own mother, was a woman who was also affected by this war. Her father, my Grandfather Garvie was a first Expeditionary Force volunteer responder, became a medic, and was sent to Egypt for 3 years (in what he experienced as a living hell - not the adventure of a lifetime he'd expected). He did not need to enlist, but chose to do so. At the end of the 3 years in Egypt, he was sent home very ill – an illness (dysentery or malaria) that plagued him and his young family for the rest of his life and theirs.

He was already a father of 3 - my mother being the eldest child – and only 7 at the time. Although, he returned, he came home very sick and considerably changed. His country had changed too, and he was forced to sell the family home in order to manage. My mother never forgave him for selling her home. She was also very harsh when it came to her own mother, who was indeed left at home to raise 3 very young and spirited children alone for 3-4 years. For those who were wounded both physically and emotionally, their loved ones were still living in very difficult times - Times of huge sacrifice, blackouts, loss, grief, confusion and… would it ever end?

For many years since WW2, my father, Dem has pored over his brother's letters home to his mother, and also to his much-loved Uncle Duncan's Flight Logbook. Just before my father started to realise his memory was fading, he decided to attempt to share and pass on just what the War effort and the sacrifices meant to him, his brother and indeed how he raised his family post-WW2. He chose to contact a Newspaper journalist in April 2007, to see if he could share his Uncle's story or a little of it in the local double-page spread of the coming ANZAC services and remembrance issue, and what came out of this reporter's interview with my father, is presented on the following page.

I read a poem the other day which my father had written at his Boarding School Dilworth and I see from reading this little poem just how *dark* life seemed to him (of course no one was ever told of his own personal sacrifice and distress from the abuse he had to keep secret for all those years). This and many other events must have eaten away at their very existence. So, with the loss of our family's two boys - the grief that nothing of theirs came home and nothing of their last resting place is known or found - was even more distressing.

My Gran and Gaga's sons percolated into my father's psyche, creating massive internal rage, fear, anxiety and confusion, which later manifested in tough times as depression - They were obliged to *Shut up* and *Shut those feelings away* and be grateful to be alive - to carry on not knowing how to deal with the silent rage and fear, the Big Secrets, which would eventually weaken the spirit and those around them.

Letters bring the memories to life

By Saskia Konynenburg

Flight Lieutenant Duncan MacArthur was among the first 17 servicemen from New Zealand to be sent overseas during World War Two and one of many killed in action — but his memory lives on for a proud nephew.

This Northland hero, educated at Maungatapere Primary School and later Whangarei Boys' High, was a pilot during the war and his escapades read like a movie script.

Flight Lieutenant MacArthur described in a letter the excitement of one mission for which he was awarded the Distinguished Flying Cross: "We had a lot of fun zooming around, shooting everything up we could see. The Jerries let off everything they could at us, including rifles, but just to puzzle them a bit we flew behind trees and any sort of cover that we could."

Flight Lieutenant MacArthur's nephew, Desmond Simons of Onerahi, said his uncle's daredevil antics did get him in trouble.

"When he was training in Christchurch people complained about my uncle because he liked to dip and fly really low. He was daring and that bravery was what was needed to fight in the war," he said.

Flight Lieutenant MacArthur joined the RNZAF before the outbreak of war in 1939 and was one of the first servicemen sent abroad. He went to England, from where he flew Wellington bombers over Germany, later transferring to the Middle East.

He was killed in 1942 when his plane was shot down over Tobruk in Libya.

□ Every year around Anzac Day, Onerahi's Des Simons pulls out the photos of family members killed in World War Two — and the heart-rending letter saying his pilot uncle had died while saving his crew.
— PICTURE / Michael Cunningham

Mr Simons, who also lost his brother during the war, described how his mother was deeply saddened by the news.

"He was my mother's only brother and she was devastated when he died. When my mother also lost her son she was griefstricken, but very proud that they had died fighting. I went for my medical to join the services and she hauled me out and banned me from joining. I never forgave her for that — but she had lost her son and brother, so I do understand."

At this poignant time of year, Mr Simons finds his thoughts returning to his lost family members. "On Anzac Day I usually listen to the radio service and read the letters my brother wrote home during the war. I look at the photos and remember them both," he said.

"It is such an important time and I hope that the children of today can realise the value of Anzac Day and understand what these men went through."

To a grieving MOTHER

This letter was sent to Duncan's mother from Flight Lieutenant P Camp from the German prisoner of war camp Stalag Luft III:

Dear Mrs MacArthur,

You must please forgive me if I blunder in on your great sorrow. By now you know that your son Duncan has given his mighty all for his King and Country. Words cannot express my sympathy or my own great sorrow at the loss of 'Mac My Skipper' and best friend. It will be poor consolation for you to know he died as he would wish — fighting! It happened in the early hours of 4th May after a battle with a fighter. Our kite caught fire and there was no alternative but to 'Bail Out'. I was one but last to leave and the memory will live with me to the end of my days of Mac still at the controls, turning round and giving me the 'Thumbs Up' sign as I went out of the hatch.

Later, after I had been captured, I stood beside his earthly remains and did the only thing I could — I prayed for him. He had stayed at his post till last to give his crew a chance of life.

"Greater love hath no man than he lay down his life for a friend." Now he rests in Libya in company with two others of his crew, in an airman's grave, with a propeller blade as a headstone.

Sincerely yours in sympathy and sorrow,

— Philip J. Camp

DREAMING OF THEE

During the War with no parental support, my father developed a mistrust; a resilience that was foreign to my mother and it drove a wedge between them.

My father did not know of the issues his grandmother (Gaga) – Duncan's mother – had endured during the wartime… how could he? He was a young boy living his own misery at the Boarding School he loved to hate, but on so many occasions was told by his mother was a luxury and gift in times of war to be granted a place in such a school – the school she led him to believe was difficult to get a place in; however, he had achieved this place because of his academic prowess and he was told it gave him a well and rounded education and offered him a good future. In those times, there was a real old-boys network of "you scratch my back, and I'll scratch yours," if you came from a certain class or from certain educational institutes. I think my father was conned and mislead and it caused him to become something of a martyr. The code of secrecy and dominance was also at work; hence it was years before he blurted out in rage, "all boys are abused at some point in their lives and they must shut up and carry on."

So much has changed in how we think and react to such events now.

It seems to me it was so easy for one of my parents to blame anyone and everyone while the other, kept all the pain and grief bundled up in sorrow and secrets.

In the end, not long after my Gran had passed away, my mother, who had always threatened to leave my father, finally saw him realise what her own mother had told my dad many years before: that there would never be any pleasing her or indeed could he ever hope to do all for any woman – they needed to be strong and achieve their own dreams. They parted, and he had to let go.

I am proud to have come from such strength, and such wisdom, it is indeed that which is driving me now to have this war-time story put to paper.

A few years ago, after my Gran had passed away, my father and I were discussing why he was handing this small case of Gran's treasures to me, and he simply said, "You are Terry's Namesake." I pressed a little more for the why's of only sharing this information with me now, and he said Gran had asked him to burn the letters, but he'd not done so, and instead, started reading the letters for himself, and after that, every year at the time of the ANZAC commemorations, he would again take out the letters and pore over them. So, it would seem to me, he longed to understand my Gran and her relationship with her eldest boy and come to terms with why he'd been sent to, as he called it, "the prison" Dilworth, how he'd been accepted there. He seemed to have a love-hate relationship with Dilworth.

WE MOVE ON

Thankfully, the two families of my two sets of Grandparents remaining post-war, whom I grew up knowing, were happy to show love to me. As a group of Grandparents, I could not have asked for better. They all taught me worthwhile values and most of all, how to forgive others and myself. When I have gone through difficult times, people have asked what sustained me. I can honestly say, it was the love of my Grandmar & Granddad Garvie, My Grandad Simons, Uncle Cliff and my very influential Granny Cookie (Blessit's Daughter) who had even collated and gifted me with a scrap-book from during the War times, and furnished me with stories of my Gran and Grandad from when they were all teenagers and my Grandad courted my Gran. Living in the small town they all came from, for all of her 97 years, she was able to tell me many things no one else knew. I will always be forever truly grateful to all my elders for their generous lessons passed on from their lives, growing up in this little nation of ours with a very diminishing family, who also made a very exciting contribution to my future and my children's future in the gifts they shared with me, which I am able to share with my children and grandchildren. Family was so very important in this time and sadly, post-WW2 has fallen (in my view) into decay.

ॐ൧ॐ൧

A friend asked me recently why writing this book was so important to me, and my answer is:

> "Looking forward is so much better than looking back
> but in order to move forward with some understanding
> of where I have been and what I have achieved is important also -
> Important to learn lessons from our past...
> deal with the grief, pain, etc and move forward informed."

WE MUST NEVER FORGET THE GREAT SACRIFICE THAT HAS BEEN MADE IN THE NAME OF OUR DEMOCRACY

ALSO, this may inspire people to stand up for themselves. We must always watch and care for one another and stay connected. That is what makes us human.

Sir Bernard Freyberg, V.C., speaking of New Zealand's part in the war said,
"If I had to say what quality in them I most admired, I would say their wisdom, tenacity, and failure to get rattled in a crisis."

Well I would say My Gran and My Gagga and my two Uncles and yes, also my Father and Mother and their families, all showed these characteristics, but as young minds affected by this War and their circumstances within the Nature of their early lives, the war changed who they would grow up to be.

In recent years for Anzac Day, I decided to make my experience a celebration of those who have gone from our family, rather than make it a distressing time. I cannot help my father who does it so hard around this time, but I can make a difference in how I deal with the sadness of Anzac Month, 25 April each year. I have so much to be happy and grateful for, because I have 2 children. My eldest, a son, was born on the 21st of April, so for me April is always a month full of Hope, Love and Joy. But touched with my father's Great distress in April, I find that now, I can celebrate life and Family and connectedness.

The following words of a song I found and indeed was able to perform at my local folk club, was written by a New Zealand teacher, in 1998 from Dunedin. He wrote this song, but it resonated with me and I found sharing this song and the powerful lyrics and rhythm is so beautiful - I am grateful that Vic McDonald allowed me to insert the words in my book and share with you now. Vic has given me permission to arrange and perform this beautiful piece of Music – and I have only altered the wording slightly to include all the New Zealand Warriors from both the WW1 and WW2 conflicts.

WE MOVE ON

SONG FOR ANZAC – IN MEMORIAM
Written by Vic MacDonald 1998

Fires burned in Europe; our young men gathered round
They emptied out our cities and our farms, and country towns.
And we knew that they were better men,
we knew they'd serve us well.
We chose our Best and Finest boys to die for us IN HELL.

Chorus:
And the men from Naseby saw the Angel of Mons
The boys from Mosgiel bled into the Somme
"We'll fight for home and freedom" was their cry
As they sailed away to battle, and to die.
Another generation, Another Bloody War
The sons of the survivors came from Oamaru, Gore and more.
They fought across the ocean – on land and air and sea,
They fought with muscle, blood and bone
TO KEEP OUR COUNTRY FREE

Now as you go from town to town in this lovely empty land
Proudly in the heart of town, A Soldier's Statue stands.
Memorial in granite stone – that tears against the sky
Around its base the names of sons and brothers who have died.
Chorus (repeat)

There is no unknown soldiers, these are not forgotten men
But cousins, uncles, neighbours who will never laugh again.
But they'll not be forgotten, for the price they had to pay
For their children's children's children
will still march on ANZAC Day
No, they'll not be forgotten, for the price they had to pay
For their children's children's children
will still march on ANZAC Day

So now, in holding and reading these well-read and much treasured letters some 80 years on - I still find I am heartsore and often will weep for the lost family members and those who loved them so much and had to let go of the hope, of ever seeing either of them again.

I feel now that I have indeed had a relationship with them and have gained a better understanding of both My Gran and Gaga and indeed my father - I have tried to understand how they all managed to get by during those war-torn years. So, out of the well leafed pages and the envelopes sent home, even the censor has stamped and peered into their words of love, I am opening up the layers of just who these young men were and what stuff they were made of, their personalities sing out loud from these thin pages written home with such sincere devotion by Terry to his mother and family and indeed his hopes for a safe nation.

I am forever grateful for the decision my father made to keep these letters and pass them on - It is time now to share their contents - Time to learn the useless efforts of war claimed more than these young men's lives - We were robbed of their talents, wisdoms, and generous spirits - We were robbed of their Genetic influence - We were robbed — Let's hope those in power soon realise - What matters to a Nation when it is all summed up, is the People of this little land Aotearoa - He Tangata He Tangata He Tangata (*It is the people, it is the people, it is the people*)

Terry and Duncan gave the ULTIMATE SACRIFICE –
they died so that we may live free.

On Father's day, September 2nd 2018, I collected my Dad for a drive and afternoon tea - He shared more memories of his time when Terry and Duncan went off to fight for "Freedom" and "democracy" - He remembers really getting lectured about a sense of duty every time he suggested being able to come home: No wonder he now suffers from depression, anything that reminds him of Dilworth is a cause for all those memories to come flooding back of the War and how it affected him and his whole outlook on life :- He was able to find for me a poem he had written in the fourth form just one month after Terry was considered missing.

WE MOVE ON

Below is the Poem my father wrote and won a prize for and the other Poem written by a 5th former who also won a prize that year 1941-42.

Poem by Desmond George Simons - student number:-549 won a prize for this Poem written in his 4th form year, just one month after Terry was reported to have been first missing, then believed to be Deceased.

THE WANDERER
A mournful wind stirs in the dripping leaves
Ghostly eyes reflect a glowing night,
Shadows loom up and vanish ~ and all grieve
The Wanderer in the night.
Nothing but a continual drip is heard,
Nothing is seen ahead but gloomy shades,
The kindly moonbeams by the shadows blurr'd
With dim light fill the glades.
Dreariness overcomes his heart so spent,
Past deeds haunt his weary soul distressed,
As over his smouldering fire he sits, head bent,
Seeking that longed-for rest.
The last glowing cinder grows dim and fades,
As he turns, to seek dry leaves
and a land of dreams,
Till awak'd at morn among the leafy glades
And welcomed by sunbeams.

Yes, it is a pretty gloomy piece of poetry, but it helps to understand how he feels about what he felt was confinement and abuse at Dilworth, particularly after an Uncle and Brother were killed. No counselling, and not much time to go home and be with his Mother and brother, he put his energy into his efforts to achieve prizes and please his mother's very competitive personality.

The following is a Poem written also in 1941 by a Dilworth 5th Form boy :-
His name R.E. Alexander - 480 .

SACRIFICE
How many of us in these easy days
Would venture far from sheltered ways,
To set our course for uncharted bays,
Or to risk our lives in doubtful frays
Against an unknown foe?
How many of us would come to live
in an unknown land, far from the hive
Of civilized cities, and would strive
with all our strength, from the day we arrive
To Help this country grow?
How many of us are prepared to fight
For an ideal we have in sight
Which leads to a land with no law of right.
The only one being the law of might,
With many a wrong to show?

This last little note was sent in a card from the daughter of one of Terry's best girls in New Zealand. Rae was one of the girls mentioned in his letters home to his mother because Rae was actually a second cousin. Rae lived a wonderful life, but never forgot Terry - presumably because they were each other's very early loves - Rae went on to join the WAAF's Post-war. She married and had two daughters, one of them was Priscilla who wrote the following to my father after he had written to them with sympathy when Rae passed away around October 2013.

dated :- 26th October 2013, and the letter reads:

Dear Des,

Thank you for your thoughtful message on Rae's passing. Her memories of Whangarei and Auckland were very strong till the end.

Last autumn my husband Nick and I took Rae to the Airforce Museum in the South Island of New Zealand. She moved with very determined speed, with the help of her walker to the Memorial Wall, where she found Terry's name. After an interesting visit, we went one more time back to his name before she would leave. I have enclosed the book we purchased for her from the Museum for you to keep.

Nick thought the picture of Rae was quite similar to one of our daughters (though she is blond) at a similar age to Rae. Thank you. I have now a photocopy of the page. Thank you once again and kind regards from

Cilla Taylor (Priscilla McMullen).

P.S. I have the signet ring - that I understand Terry sent Rae from Canada all those years ago.

CHAPTER FOURTEEN - CONCLUSION

The cost of this war and the loss of these lives can never be measured in money or medals, or any other measure known to man. It is far too BIG. The loss, the grief, still lives on in many of our families – these families are now scattered around the world. Their stories, all valuable reminders and lessons of the endurance of both the human spirit and hopefully, the Power of Love.

My father was a boy who felt that he, too, should have been able to go and fight: I am grateful to my Gran for preventing his enlistment in every agency that he tried, even going so far as to forge a government document by altering his age to try and enlist, after the grief and loss of his eldest brother. I think she had given more than enough of herself and of her small family to this terrible time between 1939 and 1945 here in NZ. The War was considered over on May Day 1945, when Germany surrendered, but it was only over in so far as no more men and women were to lose their lives fighting this war, later known as WW2.

Following my father passing on the mantel of protector, I have decided to share the gifts of my Uncle's letters and that it was time to tell their stories and indeed share with the readers a little of my journey :- I wrote a couple of years ago to the Defence Forces Records Department and also started to scour the internet to find any information I could, about what exactly happened to both Duncan and Terry. To a certain degree I understand now what did happen to Duncan, BUT where Terry is concerned I only have a few pieces of data from his records and some Internet searching has allowed me to stumble over the B.O.A.C. records of the event, but again, more questions than answers - Where is the plane, can it now be searched for? There were very important people on this plane along with very secret despatched mail and war information. Why did my Gran get forced to give up seeking her son's true final hours???

I too, am forever *Dreaming of Thee*, Terry – the mysterious, forever-young Uncle, who, until I had read your letters, was just an image in a frame. I hope that you, the Reader, have enjoyed his story.

ABOUT THE AUTHOR

Tere Davies is the Niece of Terry Dixon, and the great-niece of Duncan Mc Arthur. She is the second daughter born to Desmond Simons at Te Kopuru, Northwest of Dargaville. Tere currently lives in Orewa, Auckland, New Zealand, has two adult children and three grandchildren.